THE POLITICS OF RAISING STATE AND LOCAL REVENUE

THE POLITICS OF RAISING STATE AND LOCAL REVENUE

Richard D. Bingham

Brett W. Hawkins

F. Ted Hebert

PRAEGER

PRAEGER SPECIAL STUDIES • PRAEGER SCIENTIFIC

204382

Library of Congress Cataloging in Publication Data

Bingham, Richard D
   The politics of raising State and local revenue.

   Includes bibliographical references.
   1. Revenue—United States—States. 2. Local
finance—United States. 3. Intergovernmental fiscal
relations—United States. I. Hawkins, Brett W., joint
author. II. Hebert, F. Ted, joint author. III. Title.
HJ2385.B56 1978   336'.02'73   78-8392

0-03-022306-7
0-03-041471-7 pbk

PRAEGER SPECIAL STUDIES
383 Madison Avenue, New York, N.Y., 10017, U.S.A.

Published in the United States of America in 1978
by Praeger Publishers,
A Division of Holt, Rinehart and Winston, CBS, Inc.

89 038 98765432

Preface

Few issues excite the political pulse more than those associated with taxation and the distribution of governmental revenues. They are, after all, central to the question "Who gets what when and how?" Attention to these issues needs little further justification; they are clearly central to the political process and are worthy of close study.

Unfortunately, no single book can deal with all the taxation and revenue issues facing policy makers. We were thus forced to be selective in choosing the issues we examined in detail. We selected those that are of current interest and, we hope, those that will be of interest for the next few years. While we would hope that some of these issues could be easily resolved, few will be. Most will be at the center of political struggles for some years to come—perhaps decades.

We owe our appreciation to several individuals involved in this work at various stages. Charles B. Williams worked closely with us during the project's formative period. We are indebted to T. R. Carr, Roby Robertson, Kraig Rodenbeck, and Robert M. Stein for their contributions to Chapters 6 and 7. Mary P. LeBlanc did extensive editorial work on the manuscript, and we are most grateful to her. We also appreciate the typing assistance we received from Jill Marchetti, Linda Olson, Zona Selensky, Mimi Michels, and Susan Rondeau.

Contents

LIST OF TABLES

LIST OF FIGURES

The Politics of Raising
State and Local Revenue

1
Revenue Policies:
An Introduction

"That will be $12.87, *plus tax.*"

A statement like the above is so familiar to Americans that they often give little thought to the sales tax or to its importance as a source of government revenue. But let there be a serious effort made to change the sales tax rate; let there be a clearly defined issue—then the sales tax will draw public attention. More important, it will draw the attention of policy makers, who must resolve the issue presented.

Reference to such a "clearly defined issue" can be deceptive. Policy makers, faced with a proposal to increase the general sales tax from 3 percent to 4 percent, probably confront a large set of issues—raising such questions as the following: Is the sales tax equitable? Is an increased tax really necessary? Who, in the population, should bear the burden of increased taxes? What is public reaction to an increase likely to be? What impact will an increase have upon economic health and growth? Will there be additional administrative costs associated with the proposed increase—as there might be if food purchases are made exempt?

The list could be even longer, for "issues" are all those points of dispute that policy makers face. A list of such points could be prepared for each of the revenue options available, and the options themselves are many: taxes (income tax, sales tax, property tax, severance tax, and so on); intergovernmental revenue (block grants, project grants, general revenue sharing, and so on); charges (park fees, aircraft landing fees, tuition charges, and so on); and miscellaneous revenue (interest on bank deposits, lotteries, and so on). Succeeding chapters will consider some of the major revenue issues associated with these sources.

The fact that other government programs depend on revenue raising makes the topic of this book central to the larger political process. To appreciate this, look at Table 1.1, which shows spending of state and local governments. Expenditures are divided into major functional categories, and 1976 general expenditures are shown for each govern-

1

mental level.* Policy makers have made important decisions not only in choosing to fund the many programs each category reflects but also in assigning responsibility to state and local governments, respectively. But those decisions would have meant nothing had not the same policy makers or others decided upon mechanisms for raising money.

These critical money-raising decisions are among the most difficult that policy makers face, made especially so by the fact that they often require the imposition of compulsory contributions—taxes. Seeking to

TABLE 1.1: Direct General Expenditures by State and Local Government, by Function, 1976

| Function | Billions of Dollars[a] | | |
	Total[b]	State	Local
Local schools	67.7	.6	67.1
Higher education	24.3	19.7	4.6
Other education	5.2	5.2	—
Highways	23.9	14.9	9.0
Public welfare	31.4	20.2	11.2
Hospitals	15.7	7.7	8.0
Health	5.0	2.1	2.8
Police protection	9.5	1.4	8.1
Local fire protection	3.9	—	3.9
Sewerage	5.9	—	5.9
Other sanitation	2.3	—	2.3
Local parks and recreation	3.9	—	3.9
Natural resources	4.7	3.6	1.0
Housing and urban renewal	3.2	.3	2.9
Air transportation	1.5	.3	1.2
Corrections	3.8	2.4	1.4
Libraries	1.2	.1	1.2
Social insurance administration	1.6	1.6	—
Interest on debt	10.3	4.1	6.1
Administration and public buildings	12.2	4.1	8.2
Other	18.4	7.5	10.8
Total[b]	255.6	95.8	159.7

[a]Direct expenditures do not include intergovernmental transfers. Funds so transferred are counted only when spent by the receiving unit for its own purposes.

[b]Totals of numbers may not equal given totals, due to rounding.

Source: U.S. Bureau of the Census, Governmental Finances in 1975–1976 (Washington, D.C.: Government Printing Office, 1977).

---

*General expenditures consist of all expenditures except those for operation of government-owned liquor stores and utilities and those from insurance trust funds.

avoid obvious controversy, policy makers sometimes delay revenue decisions to the point that government services drastically deteriorate. At other times, they seek an "easy way," attempting to avoid publicity and public confrontation. (Use of service charges or very small increases in present taxes may serve this end.) Some state and local governments make the revenue decision process additionally complex by requiring unusual legislative majorities for tax increases—for example, a two-thirds vote of the legislature—or by requiring public referendums. (As an example of this latter practice, of the 22 states authorizing municipalities to levy a sales tax, eight require voter approval.)[1] Local policy makers frequently find their options restricted by the state constitution or by legislative statute, and even the state legislature may find that a constitutional amendment is necessary in order to tap certain revenue sources. Both state and local policy makers often find that they have broad discretion to spend public money but are highly limited in actions to secure it.

These legal restraints and many other issues are explored in the chapters that follow. But those explorations can be facilitated by first looking at state and local revenue policies themselves and at their historical development. The remainder of this chapter will provide that background.

AN HISTORICAL SKETCH

It is significant that the central political role of revenue raising can be traced to the beginnings of parliamentary democracy. Medieval English kings collected from the nobility a variety of dues, fines, and imposts. When the king went to war, he required the nobility to supply not only money but military personnel as well. Over a period of several centuries following the signing of the Magna Carta, and especially in the late thirteenth century, kings began assembling representatives from throughout the realm to secure their consent to increases in general taxes. These early parliaments were held irregularly, and the breadth of representation varied, but one of their major tasks was the raising of revenue.

By the time of American independence, the role of parliament was well established. Even in the colonies there were legislative bodies that played a role in financial matters. After the Revolutionary War, the newly independent colonies, struggling to remain unified, had to deal seriously with revenue matters. The Articles of Confederation placed revenue responsibility on the individual states. As colonies, and during the war, these states had been raising revenue. It was assumed that they would continue to do so—using primarily tariffs. Support for the central government would come from the states; the Congress did not have authority to tax.

This arrangement changed with adoption of the Constitution. States retained their ability to tax, but the federal government received authority to do so, too. In fact, the federal government received exclusive authority over the major revenue source—tariffs. States were forced to seek other sources. They increased their use of the property tax, previously used by local governments; they adopted excise taxes— that is, sales taxes on such goods as coffee, tea, and glass; they sold state-owned land; and they conducted public lotteries.[2]

Local governments needed little revenue during this early period. Instead, they relied on services provided by able-bodied citizens to clean streets, repair roads, and fight fires. What little revenue they did collect came principally from property taxes.

At the time of the Constitution's acceptance, there was one revenue issue that was, in a way, a spending issue as well. During the war, many state governments had met their resource needs by borrowing heavily. For most, the payment of principal and interest on this debt was still their major financial need. They were forced to collect taxes in order to recover from the effects of their earlier revenue policy— borrowing.

An important issue for the new federal government was whether it should aid the states by assuming their debts. Doing so would help some states more than others, since some had used taxes more extensively during the war and would now be penalized. Nevertheless, the decision was favorable, and federal money was spent to retire state debts, freeing state-raised revenue for other purposes.[3]

During the early decades of the nineteenth century, a variety of revenue sources were used by state and local governments: intermittent property taxes, taxes on banks, lotteries, sales of land, and even extensive borrowing. As the decades passed, borrowing provided funds for canals, roads, railroads, and other internal improvements. One interesting revenue source—not unlike modern-day revenue sharing— was a distribution of federal surplus money to the states in 1837. Due to rapidly rising imports, the tariff produced revenues far in excess of federal needs. Simultaneously, land speculation drove up prices and dramatically increased federal revenue from sales of public land. The federal surplus for 1835 was more than total federal expenditures for the year, despite retirement of all federal interest-bearing debt—for the first and only time in U.S. history.[4] One further way to spend the money was to distribute it to the states, so they might use it for roads and other internal improvements. But this suggestion raised a critical constitutional issue. It was contended that the Constitution did not authorize direct federal provision of facilities and programs of a domestic nature. Although considerable public land had been distributed to the states and some support had been provided for the militia and for road and canal construction, there had not yet been a large cash grant. In a bill, Henry Clay and others proposed that the surplus be so used, but President Andrew Jackson vetoed it, seeing it as requiring federal action that might be unconstitutional. To counter this argument of unconstitutionality, the bill that was finally enacted provided for distribution of funds to the states as loans, but payable only if called by the federal government. A total of $28 million was distributed, with the hope of more to come, but an economic panic halted any further "loans."[5]

During most of the nineteenth century, the principal form of federal aid to the states was in land rather than money. Portions of federally owned land were distributed to the states, especially for support of education. Some of this land was used directly for school purposes—that is, school buildings were constructed on it. Other portions produced revenue that the states devoted to schools. A number of states still receive income from these lands and still use it for public education.[6]

In the last half of the nineteenth century, both states and local governments relied heavily on the property tax. This presented policy makers with issues concerning tax administration, especially concerning assessment. Since the property tax is levied as some fraction of the value of property owned, there must be a procedure for establishing that value—the assessment procedure. This was primarily a local responsibility. Problems arose when states began using the property tax more extensively. These flowed from the existence of widely varying assessment levels. For example, the state might levy a 15 mill tax (a mill is 0.1 cent), to apply to all property in the state. But two nearly identical pieces of property located in different counties might be assessed at $700 and $350, respectively. The first property owner would pay the state $10.50, while the second would pay only $5.25. Assessments with discrepancies this great were common. State efforts to enforce assessment standards met with little success. In fact, this administrative problem continues to plague the property tax today.

As state revenue needs grew, the states began using new revenue sources. Among them were franchise taxes on railroads, liquor license taxes, and inheritance taxes. Although each produced problems of its own, the strain on the property tax was somewhat reduced.[7]

Local governments faced pressure to increase public services toward the end of the nineteenth century, due largely to the rapid growth of cities. For a time they borrowed heavily, even beyond reasonable limits. In the 1870s many defaulted on their debts, and the states took action to restrict future borrowing. They established debt limits and required referendums before bonds could be issued.[8]

These restrictions and others have helped define local revenue issues in later years. The sources of revenue that cities can tap are still limited by the states, and many city councils and school boards are today forced to consider the political and programmatic implications of proposing the use of borrowed funds and then being turned down by the public—if, indeed, borrowing is permitted at all.

For a period since the beginning of the twentieth century, the development of state and local revenue policies can be presented in tabular form. Thanks to creation of a permanent Census Bureau, data on revenue sources have been collected systematically and repetitively. Table 1.2 displays the sources upon which state governments have relied in selected years from 1902 to 1976. Changes during this period are far more dramatic than those of the previous century. Notice, for example, the demise of the property tax as a state revenue source. (It will be shown below that the property tax remains important for local governments.) In 1902, of state general revenue, 43.2 percent came from this one source.* By 1976 the property tax contribution had declined to 1.4 percent. What taxes replaced it? The answer depends on the year examined. A more important development to note is the dramatic decline in importance of all taxes, from 82.1 percent of general revenue to only 58.7 percent. Intergovernmental revenue, primarily aid from the federal government, now provides over one-fourth of state revenue. The other nontax sources—charges and miscellaneous revenue—have recently gained in importance after several decades of decline. This latter category includes a wide variety of fees and charges: tuition at universities, fees for state park use, toll charges, and hospital charges. Also included is the interest states collect on invested funds.

Although the property tax decline began before introduction of income and general sales taxes, these sources did help fill the gap. In 1976 they contributed 36.9 percent of total revenue. The selective sales tax (applied to such items as tobacco, alcohol, and gasoline) reached a peak of importance in 1942, just before the states began a large shift to the general sales tax.

Clearly, revenue policy making is a continuous process. While there is no requirement that revenue decisions be reconsidered regularly—as must many spending decisions—there is still ample opportu-

---

*General revenue consists of all revenue except that from government-owned liquor stores and utilities and that collected for insurance trust funds.

TABLE 1.2: Sources of State General Revenue, 1902–76 (percent of total general revenue)

	1976	1972	1962	1952	1942	1932	1922	1913	1902
Intergovernmental revenue	29.4	28.4	24.0	18.5	16.7	11.0	10.0	4.3	4.7
From federal government	27.6	27.2	22.8	17.3	15.6	9.2	7.9	1.6	1.6
From local government	1.8	1.2	1.2	1.2	1.1	1.9	2.2	2.7	3.2
Taxes	58.7	60.7	66.0	73.4	76.1	78.0	75.5	80.0	82.1
Individual income	14.1	13.2	8.8	6.8	4.9	3.1	3.4	—	—
Corporation income	4.8	4.5	4.2	6.2	5.2	3.3	4.6	—	—
General sales	18.0	17.9	16.4	16.6	12.3	0.3	—	—	—
Selective sales	13.2	15.8	22.2	25.1	30.9	29.7	10.7	14.6	14.7
Property	1.4	1.3	2.1	2.8	5.1	13.5	27.8	37.2	43.2
Other	7.2	8.1	12.3	14.9	17.6	28.2	29.0	28.2	24.2
Charges and miscellaneous revenue	11.9	10.9	10.9	8.1	7.2	11.0	14.4	15.7	13.2
Total*	100.0	100.0	100.0	100.0	100.0	100.0	99.9	100.0	100.0

*Totals of numbers may not equal given totals, due to rounding.

Source: U.S. Bureau of the Census, Historical Statistics on State and Local Government Finances, 1902–1953 (Washington, D.C.: Government Printing Office, 1955); U.S. Bureau of the Census, Census of Governments, 1972, vol. 6, no. 4 (Washington, D.C.: Government Printing Office, 1974); and U.S. Bureau of the Census, Governmental Finances in 1975–76 (Washington, D.C.: Government Printing Office, 1977).

nity to shape and reshape the revenue system. The most significant trend at present is the decline of taxes as important sources. State policy makers have found it possible to rely increasingly on other sources, although this does not mean they have avoided tax increases. Those increases have simply not been equal to the increase in total general revenue; other sources have grown faster. Further developments in this trend should be followed closely. A continuing decline in tax reliance and a drop below 50 percent of general revenue would mark a major event in state financial history.

Table 1.3 presents historical data on local revenues. It can be seen that local governments passed that 50 percent milestone between 1962 and 1972. The decline in their reliance on taxes has been under way throughout this century, but became precipitous after 1932. Aid from the other levels, especially from the states, has been the replacement source. By 1976 local governments received more in intergovernmental revenue than they collected in taxes.

Unlike the states, local governments have depended heavily upon a single tax for the tax revenue they did collect. Figuring percentages differently than in Table 1.3, and looking at tax revenue alone, we found that in 1902 the property tax supplied 88.6 percent of local tax revenue. By 1976 this had declined only slightly, to 81.2 percent. Although non-tax sources have overtaken taxes, the property tax remains the dominant tax.

In addition to resembling the states in the decline of tax source importance, local governments resemble the states in their growing dependence upon charges and miscellaneous revenues. For both levels, these sources declined during the middle twentieth century but have since recovered.

Comparing state and local revenue trends reveals that the states have gone much further in diversifying their revenue sources—especially their tax sources. The federal Advisory Commission on Intergovernmental Relations (ACIR) has presented such diversification as a worthy goal.[9] Calling for greater use of sales and income taxes as opposed to property taxes, it is recommending that local governments follow a course the states have followed—but without completely abandoning the property tax. What little diversification has occurred at the local level has been a turning away from the property tax, toward nontax sources. But, since state aid has been one of these sources, the entire state-local revenue system may have become relatively diverse. Table 1.4 presents 1976 figures for the combination. Property and sales taxes (general and selective taxes combined) each account for slightly more than 20 percent of total general revenue, while income taxes account for 12.4 percent. This is a much closer balance than is found at either the state or local level alone.

TABLE 1.3: Sources of Local General Revenue, 1902–76 (percent of total general revenue)

	1976	1972	1962	1952	1942	1932	1922	1913	1902
Intergovernmental revenue	42.8	37.7	30.4	31.1	25.8	14.3	8.3	5.9	6.6
From federal government	8.3	4.3	2.0	1.4	0.8	0.2	0.2	0.4	0.5
From state government	34.5	33.4	28.4	29.8	25.0	14.1	8.1	5.6	6.1
Taxes	41.5	47.3	54.7	55.8	64.9	75.1	79.4	79.9	82.4
Property	33.7	39.5	48.0	48.9	60.0	73.1	76.9	72.8	73.1
Sales	4.4	4.1	3.8	3.7	1.9	0.5	0.5	0.2	—
Income	1.9	2.1	0.8	0.5	0.4	—	—	—	—
Other taxes	1.5	1.5	2.1	2.8	2.7	1.6	2.0	6.9	9.4
Charges and miscellaneous revenue	15.7	15.0	14.9	13.0	9.3	10.6	12.3	14.2	11.0
Total*	100.0	100.0	100.0	99.9	100.0	100.0	100.0	100.0	100.0

*Totals of numbers may not equal given totals, due to rounding.

Source: U.S. Bureau of the Census, Historical Statistics on State and Local Government Finances, 1902–1953 (Washington, D.C.: Government Printing Office, 1955); U.S. Bureau of the Census, Census of Governments, 1972, vol. 6, no. 4 (Washington, D.C.: Government Printing Office, 1974); and U.S. Bureau of the Census, Governmental Finances in 1975–76 (Washington, D.C.: Government Printing Office, 1977).

*Totals of numbers may not equal given totals, due to rounding.

In the next chapter, there will be an examination of the revenue systems of specific states, to see if the pattern exhibited by these aggregate data holds for each state separately. Since the state and local systems are closely linked legally and politically, the individual state data presented in the next chapter will combine state and local revenues, much as they are presented in Table 1.4.

REVENUE POLICIES: JUST WHAT ARE THEY?

In the historical sketch just presented, revenue policies have been treated as though they are the policies governing sources of revenue—what percentage of state or local revenue comes from each source? In fact, that is only one of many ways to view revenue policy. To describe fully the revenue policy of Illinois, for example, one would want to say much more than simply that Illinois gets 66.3 percent of its general revenue from taxes, 13.8 percent from charges and miscellaneous collections, and 19.9 percent from intergovernmental sources. Additional questions would include the following: (1) Is most of the revenue collected by the state or by local governments? (2) How high are tax rates? (3) What is the tax base? (4) How high are taxes per capita? (5) Who pays the taxes—the rich or the poor?

The revenue issues that policy makers face bring up some or even all of these questions. To understand the arguments presented and to participate in the revenue policy process, one must understand what these questions mean and how the decision maker, lobbyist, or researcher might try to answer them. Much of the remainder of this book

TABLE 1.4:   Sources of State and Local General Revenue, 1976 (percent of total general revenue)

Source	Percent	
Intergovernmental revenue (federal)	21.7	
Taxes	61.2	
Individual income		9.6
Corporation income		2.8
General sales		12.5
Selective sales		8.9
Property		22.3
Other		5.2
Charges and miscellaneous revenue	17.1	
Total*	100.0	

*Totals of numbers may not equal given totals, due to rounding.

Source: U.S. Bureau of the Census, *Governmental Finances in 1975–76* (Washington, D.C.: Government Printing Office, 1977).

is devoted to aiding that understanding. The brief sections that follow provide an introduction.

Locus of Revenue Responsibility

Table 1.5 shows the distribution of revenue responsibility in 1976. For the nation as a whole, state governments collected 53.5 percent of total state-local general revenue (excluding intergovernmental aid), but an examination of the list of states reveals wide diversity. Policies have been anything but uniform. At the extreme are New Mexico and New Jersey. The former has almost 80 percent of its revenue collected by the state, while in the latter the state collects only 41 percent.

Such diversity may result from historical accident, conscious planning, or political incompetence. Regardless of the cause, the revenue systems do differ, and these differences have impacts on state residents. Certainly the ability of citizens to influence revenue policies will be affected by the locus of responsibility.

A look at the distribution in Table 1.5 reveals two especially interesting features. It shows that the median level of state responsibility is 57.6 percent. But, 11 of the 16 southern states (using the Bureau of the Census definition of "southern") have responsibilities above that median level. In fact, the median level for the southern states is 64.6 percent. The revenue policy-making processes in these states have resulted in policies that differ markedly from the nation as a whole in the locus of responsibility. The other point of interest is the level of responsibility assumed by the newer states. Four of the five admitted during the twentieth century are above the median. Their positions are New Mexico—1; Alaska—2; Hawaii—3; Oklahoma—16; and Arizona—26.

Table 1.5 shows only the state-local division of responsibility. A more detailed description of a state's revenue policies would require the division of local responsibilities among various governmental entities. The significance of recent shifts at this level is discussed in Chapter 2.

Tax Rates

This chapter began with a phrase that has been made familiar by the general sales tax. Because it is usually collected openly and charged directly to the consumer, most people in sales tax states are somewhat familiar with the notion of rate (2 percent, 3 percent, 5 percent, and so on), a charge of so many cents for each dollar paid at the retail level, or for each dollar of gross income received by those selling goods and services. For other taxes, though, rates can be far more confusing and the taxes themselves hidden. Many income tax states provide a scale of rates, applying a lower rate to lower-income taxpayers. (The justifica-

TABLE 1.5: General Revenue from Own Sources: State and Local, 1976 (percent of total own source revenue)

	State	Local		State	Local
Alabama	64.3	35.7	Montana	50.8	49.2
Alaska	78.4	21.6	Nebraska	45.6	54.4
Arizona	57.2	42.8	Nevada	49.4	50.6
Arkansas	65.0	35.0	New Hampshire	43.9	56.1
California	48.1	51.9	New Jersey	41.2	58.8
Colorado	50.7	49.3	New Mexico	78.5	21.5
Connecticut	53.5	46.5	New York	46.0	54.0
Delaware	75.4	24.6	North Carolina	66.1	33.9
Florida	50.5	49.5	North Dakota	67.0	33.0
Georgia	51.4	48.6	Ohio	48.7	51.3
Hawaii	77.5	22.5	Oklahoma	63.8	36.2
Idaho	60.9	39.1	Oregon	50.4	49.6
Illinois	52.6	47.4	Pennsylvania	59.2	40.8
Indiana	58.1	41.9	Rhode Island	63.1	36.9
Iowa	54.8	45.2	South Carolina	67.6	32.4
Kansas	52.9	47.1	South Dakota	50.2	49.8
Kentucky	69.1	30.9	Tennessee	54.2	45.8
Louisiana	67.5	32.5	Texas	54.0	46.0
Maine	72.2	27.8	Utah	61.7	38.3
Maryland	55.7	44.3	Vermont	61.4	38.6
Massachusetts	51.8	48.2	Virginia	58.8	41.2
Michigan	51.6	48.4	Washington	61.2	38.8
Minnesota	61.5	38.5	West Virginia	71.2	28.8
Mississippi	65.3	34.7	Wisconsin	61.1	38.9
Missouri	48.3	51.7	Wyoming	53.5	46.5
U.S. Mean	53.5	46.5	Median	57.6	42.4

Source: U.S. Bureau of the Census, *Governmental Finances in 1975–76* (Washington, D.C.: Government Printing Office, 1977).

tion for this is discussed below.) For example, Missouri applies rates ranging from 1.5 percent of taxable net income if such income is $1,000 or less, up to 6 percent of taxable net income in excess of $9,000. Answering the question "What's the rate?" can be a lengthy, if not difficult, task.

Other taxes—gasoline, alcoholic beverage, severance (applied to minerals taken from the ground)—may have rates stated as flat amounts (8¢ per gallon of gasoline) or as percentages (12.5 percent of the value of oil severed). Individuals who enter the political struggles over revenue issues must devote careful attention to rates and to just how they are applied in a particular state or locality.

Tax Base

Questions concerning practical application of particular tax rates often focus on the base—the element against which the rate is applied. In the above examples, the bases mentioned were dollars spent at retail, net taxable income, gallons of gasoline, and dollar value of oil. Each of these, while seemingly precise, leaves many questions unanswered. Some states exempt sales of food from the sales tax base (as does Ohio), and this procedure results in a different tax policy than that in a state with an identical 4 percent rate, but with food included in the base (Alabama).

Similarly, knowledge that one city levies a 40 mill property tax rate, while another levies only 30 mills, is not sufficient to conclude that taxes are lower in the second city. First, legal assessment requirements may be different: Some states such as Oregon require assessment of 100 percent of true cash value, and others specify a percentage of true cash value (for example, Indiana at 33-1/3 percent). Second, assessment practices may vary, such that property values in one city are systematically higher or lower than legal requirements seem to specify: Wisconsin and South Carolina both require assessment at true value in money, but residential single-family property in Wisconsin is assessed at 46.7 percent of sales price and South Carolina at 4 percent of sales price.[10]

Either of these possibilities drastically alters the property tax base, affecting not only the property owners but also the ability of governments to raise revenue through the property tax.

When policy makers face the task of securing additional revenue and they determine that tax increases are necessary, the political struggles ensuing may center just as frequently on the definition of the base as on establishment of the rate. So descriptions of revenue policies demand attention to base as well as rate.

Per Capita Tax

One way to overcome the difficulties of comparing cities or states with widely varied tax rates and bases is to inquire about the impact of taxes on residents. Find out what the city's tax collections are and divide that figure by the number of inhabitants.[11] Table 1.6 show per capita property tax collections in 1976, with state and local collections combined. The total United States figure was $265.54 per capita, but there was a range from $57.37 in Alabama to $1,048.12 in Alaska. Similar figures can be presented for other taxes, as well as for intergovernmental receipts and for charges and miscellaneous collections. Alterna-

TABLE 1.6: Per Capita Property Tax Collections of State and Local Governments, 1976

State	Dollar per Capita	State	Dollar per Capita
Alabama	57.37	Missouri	194.87
Alaska	1,048.12	Montana	350.25
Arizona	282.18	Nebraska	318.78
Arkansas	101.20	Nevada	272.02
California	415.23	New Hampshire	347.91
Colorado	271.29	New Jersey	446.48
Connecticut	368.92	New Mexico	102.51
Delaware	130.12	New York	411.79
District of		North Carolina	130.19
Columbia	209.50	North Dakota	212.28
Florida	191.36	Ohio	223.65
Georgia	177.94	Oklahoma	123.84
Hawaii	173.52	Oregon	332.95
Idaho	190.12	Pennsylvania	175.62
Illinois	283.95	Rhode Island	294.14
Indiana	225.88	South Carolina	115.76
Iowa	227.60	South Dakota	288.08
Kansas	274.06	Tennessee	129.49
Kentucky	104.74	Texas	213.18
Louisiana	90.26	Utah	171.65
Maine	297.01	Vermont	307.88
Maryland	239.36	Virginia	172.63
Massachusetts	430.52	Washington	235.91
Michigan	324.22	West Virginia	105.96
Minnesota	254.20	Wisconsin	288.60
Mississippi	109.59	Wyoming	351.61
U.S. Mean	265.54	Median	235.90

Source: U.S. Bureau of the Census, *Governmental Finances in 1975–76* (Washington, D.C.: Government Printing Office, 1977).

tively, all of these can be combined to form total general state and local revenue from all sources. These latter figures range from $889.65 per capita in Arkansas to $3,349.04 per capita in Alaska, with the figure for all states combined being $1,193.41.

While interesting—and politically useful as an easily understood way to support claims that a state's taxes are markedly high or low—per capita figures can be very deceptive. In some cases, the taxes collected by a state or locality are not paid by its residents at all. The severance tax Louisiana charges on oil and gas—the bulk of which is sold in other, colder states—is largely paid by residents of those oil-consuming states. Cities with large regional shopping centers may collect sales taxes from shoppers living in many other cities. As a consequence of this difficulty of being certain just who pays the tax, per capita comparisons should be used with caution, giving consideration to the extent that taxes may be "exported."

Who Pays the Taxes?

Not only may some taxes be passed to others outside the state or city, but they may be passed to others in different income classes. Researchers and policy makers alike want to know just where the tax burden rests. They want to know whether it falls equitably on all individuals in the state or community or whether it rests more heavily on those in a particular category.

The concern most often expressed, and given much political attention, is the relative burden on persons in various income classes. Economists refer to this as concern for equity. Do all taxpayers share equitably in the burden?

Unfortunately, there is no way to answer that question to everyone's satisfaction. "Equity" implies a value judgment. Some argue that an equitable tax should obtain the same amount of money from each taxpayer. The poll tax, required for voting in some states until declared unconstitutional in 1966, was such a tax. Each individual, regardless of income, wealth, or any other characteristic, paid the same amount of tax. If uniformity is the accepted definition of equity, such a tax—if collected from everyone—would be equitable.

Others argue that an equitable tax should bear some relationship to ability to pay. They say that it would be proportional to wealth or to income. In years past, when most wealth was held as real estate, the property tax was seen as proportional to wealth. A flat rate income tax of 3 percent, applied to all income, would be proportional to income. A person with income of $5,000 would pay $150 in tax, while one with a $500,000 income would pay $15,000. This is often referred to as a proportional income tax and can be seen as equitable if one accepts the value judgment that payment in proportion to income is the desired feature.

Still other people contend that each dollar paid by the higher-income or wealthier individual is not as valuable to him or her as each dollar is to the lower-income person. They argue that equity demands an equal sacrifice, and this requires that a higher tax rate be applied against higher income, perhaps 3 percent or 15 percent or 70 percent. There is no way scientifically to determine sacrifice level, so there is no way to fix the rate precisely, except by relying on the collective judgment of policy makers and society. A tax that follows these recommendations is referred to as a progressive tax.

Even after an individual or group has decided upon a standard of equity, problems remain. Knowing just how much of a tax each individual (or class) will bear is a major difficulty. One reason for the twentieth-century popularity of the individual income tax is the assumption that it is difficult to pass along to someone else; the recipient of the income generally must pay the tax. Locating the burden is easier than for most other taxes. Not only can most other taxes be shifted, but economists have an extremely difficult time knowing to whom and to what extent they are shifted. Corporation income taxes may be born by the owners (stockholders) who receive lower dividends, or they may be passed to consumers who pay higher prices; property taxes on buildings may be absorbed by the owners or passed along to the renters. Economists have been only partially successful in describing just what does happen in such cases, since the location of the burden probably depends on the situation (for example, the degree of competition among firms or apartment owners) and on workings of the economy not precisely understood.[12]

CONCLUSION

This brief introduction to revenue policy, its history, and its substance forms a basis for succeeding chapters. The one immediately following explores the many constitutional and legal provisions, especially those at the federal and state levels, that structure the revenue policy-making process. Development of the elaborate system of federal aid that has become an integral part of both state and local revenue processes is also described.

Chapters 3 and 4 carry further this consideration of federal aid, first describing the character and structure of present aid provisions and then examining impacts that the aid has on state and local policies.

In the succeeding two chapters, attention turns to state and locally raised revenue. Tax sources are described in greater detail, and major current issues are examined. Central among these is concern over the property tax, which, in many states, has become both potentially excessive and inequitable. Several serious efforts have been undertaken to cope with the problems this situation presents, and these are examined in Chapter 6.

Although policy makers at both the state and local levels have some discretion in choosing revenue resources, it is likely that there are factors that encourage certain choices. Once those choices are made, they in turn probably influence other choices and actions. In Chapter 7 an effort is made to describe some of the factors that seem to influence revenue policy and to explore effects that policy has on expenditure decisions.

Since the securing of revenue involves government in obtaining money from the private sector, the link between revenue policy and economic policy is close. On the macroeconomic level, the federal government uses its taxing authority as a powerful economic tool. State and local governments frequently attempt to use their authority to influence microeconomic decisions, such as industrial plant location and population migration. Of course, the converse is also true. Revenue availability is very much influenced by economic developments. Chapter 8 explores these linkages.

The concluding chapter considers revenue policy making as a decision process. It also suggests areas in which further research would be profitable.

NOTES

1. See Advisory Commission on Intergovernmental Relations (ACIR), *Significant Features of Fiscal Federalism, 1976–77 Edition*, vol. 2 (Washington, D.C.: Government Printing Office, 1977), pp. 186–87.

2. Paul Studenski and Herman E. Kroos, *Financial History of the United States*, 2nd ed. (New York: McGraw-Hill, 1963), p. 57.

3. Ibid., pp. 51–53.

4. Ibid., p. 100.

5. Ibid., p. 102.

6. For an excellent summary of early federal-state relations see Daniel J. Elazar, "Federal-State Collaboration in the Nineteenth Century United States" in ed. Daniel J. Elazar et al. *Cooperation and Conflict: Readings in American Federalism* (Itasca, Ill.: F. E. Peacock Publishers, 1969), pp. 83–128.

7. Studenski and Kroos, op. cit., p. 193.

8. Ibid., p. 196.

9. Advisory Commission on Intergovernmental Relations, *Local Revenue Diversification* (Washington, D.C.: Government Printing Office, 1974).

10. ACIR, *Significant Features of Fiscal Federalism*, op. cit., p. 148.

11. A much more elaborate method of adjusting for such differences is applied in Advisory Commission on Intergovernmental Relations, *Measuring the Fiscal Capacity and Effort of State and Local Areas* (Washington, D.C.: Government Printing Office, 1971). See also John S. Akin, "Fiscal Capacity and the Estimation Method of the Advisory Commission on Intergovernmental Relations," *National Tax Journal* 26 (June 1973): 275–91; and Allen D. Manvel, "Tax Capacity Versus Tax Performance: A Comment," *National Tax Journal* 26 (June 1973): 293–94.

12. Two books on tax burden are especially helpful: Joseph A. Pechman and Benjamin A. Okner, *Who Bears the Tax Burden* (Washington, D.C.: Brookings Institution, 1974); and Donald Phares, *State-Local Tax Equity* (Lexington, Mass.: Lexington Books, 1973).

2
State and Local Revenues
Within the Federal System

A cursory glance at the tax systems and dominant revenue sources of the 50 states suggests that there are no restraints on state revenues. Policy is so varied that it almost defies description. The restraints placed on decision makers in state and local governments appear to be the result of the actions or inactions of the state governments themselves, not federal policy or the restrictions of the Constitution of the United States. Yet there are some significant restrictions placed on the states by the Constitution. Article I, Section 10, prohibits the states from laying imposts or duties on imports or exports, except as may be necessary for executing inspection laws. Many other restrictions are equally explicit. For example, restrictions on the states' taxing powers have been derived from Article IV, Section 2, prohibiting discrimination against nonresidents; and from the commerce clause, Article I, Section 8, prohibiting state taxes from burdening interstate commerce.[1]

Yet Congress has been quite liberal in its attitude toward state taxation powers. As a matter of policy, this has been of great practical importance to the states—especially in recent years. During the early years of the republic, federal policy relative to state taxation powers did not seriously affect state and local governments. This happy situation, however, is not characteristic of most of the twentieth century. The radical shift in taxing power brought about by the Sixteenth Amendment and the devastating effects of the Depression clearly pointed out the inadequacies of state and local fiscal powers. The states had long denied themselves and their local subdivisions flexibility in financial matters by imposing a host of constitutional and legal restrictions on their ability to tax and borrow.[2] The seriousness of this situation was clearly apparent in times of economic turbulence. During the years from 1930 through 1939, for example, there were over 4,700 defaults on debt issued by various units of local government, including 1,434 defaults by incorporated municipalities.[3]

In this chapter we will briefly examine the constraints placed upon state and local revenue systems by the United States Constitution. Since federal aid has become a major source of state and local revenues, we will also briefly examine the development of our present system of grants-in-aid. Additionally, we will discuss the difficulty in changing or amending state constitutions. Unquestionably, state constitutional and statutory restrictions on state and local revenue systems determine the revenue-raising tools available to administrators. The constitutional and statutory restrictions on revenue powers for nine selected states will therefore be examined in detail. Finally, we will look at the fiscal crisis in New York City and review a number of the ways states deal with their revenue constraints.

FEDERAL CONSTITUTIONAL RESTRICTIONS ON STATE AND LOCAL REVENUES

The U.S. Constitution places a wide variety of restrictions, both expressed and implied, on the revenue-raising powers of the states. Obviously, these restrictions apply equally in all states. States, for example, are limited in their ability to tax foreign commerce. Article I, Section 8, of the Constitution gives Congress the power to regulate foreign commerce. Imposts upon exports have been held to be a regulation of foreign commerce, and states have been restricted from such action.[4]

State taxation on interstate commerce is likewise limited. Any state tax that imposes a substantial burden on interstate commerce constitutes an attempt to regulate it and is forbidden.[5] Gross receipts taxes have also been invalidated when they were found to discriminate against firms engaged in interstate commerce.[6] Even when a state tax is imposed equally on internal and interstate commerce, if it places a substantial burden on interstate commerce it may be held invalid.[7] But this does not mean that firms engaged in interstate commerce are entirely exempt from state taxation. Such firms must pay an appropriate share of state taxes.[8] Likewise, there is no restriction on local governments in applying the property tax to property used in interstate commerce,[9] so long as it is applied without discrimination.

Article I, Section 10, restricts the states, without the consent of Congress, from laying imposts or duties on imports or exports except those necessary for executing inspection laws. The provision is thus absolute except for inspection fees. Inspection fees need not be based on an examination of quality but must be reasonably proportionate to the cost of inspection. Likewise, tax stamps are prohibited, as are taxes upon the occupation of the importer or on the article imported.[10]

Further restriction on state revenue sources are placed by Article IV, Section 1: "Full Faith and Credit shall be given in each State to the public Acts, Records, and judicial Proceedings of every other State." This section affects consideration of the tax claims of one state in the court of another state. The Supreme Court, however, has not yet settled the question of whether one state must enforce the revenue laws of another. Even when obligations are not within the bounds of the full faith and credit clause, one state cannot exempt property from taxation in another.[11]

Article IV, Section 2, provides that "The Citizens of each State shall be entitled to all Privileges and Immunities of citizens in the several States." Under the privileges and immunities clause, citizens of one state are protected from the discriminatory actions of another. Thus, in one case, this clause was invoked to prevent one state from charging a nonresidential commercial fishing license fee 100 times greater than the fee charged a resident.[12] Corporations, however, receive no such protection. While corporations are treated as individuals under the Fourteenth Amendment, they are not considered citizens under the privileges and immunities clause.

The due process clause of the Fourteenth Amendment also places definite limitations on the taxing powers of the states. There must be some connection between a taxpayer's in-state activity and an out-of-state sale before a tax may be imposed on the sale.[13] The due process clause does not, however, prohibit double taxation or retroactive taxation unless arbitrary or unreasonable.[14]

While this short summary only scratches the surface of the federal constitutional restrictions placed on the revenue potential of states, it serves to illustrate the complexity of the revenue issue in the federal system. Important restrictions stem from Article I, Sections 8 and 10; Article IV, Sections 1 and 2; and Amendment XIV. A more comprehensive review of federal constitutional restrictions may be found in the *State Tax Guide* published by the Commerce Clearing House.[15]

STATE CONSTITUTIONAL RESTRICTIONS

For the most part, American state constitutions are very different from the Constitution of the United States in length and language. While the federal Constitution is remarkable for its brevity and clarity of language, most state constitutions are "crowded with amendments, burdened with contradictions, and couched in cumbersome syntax."[16] In contrast to the constitutions of today, the early state constitutions were extremely brief—usually restricted to a few printed pages and confined to fundamental matters. Most were concerned with popular sovereignty—a recognition of the people as the source of political power. Seven states specifically adopted a bill of rights, while the remaining protected civil rights through reliance on common law and clauses in their constitutions guaranteeing specific rights. Early constitutions also gave some recognition to the principles of separation of powers and checks and balances. They segregated legislative, executive, and judicial powers, but the legislative branch was generally dominant. In most cases the governor was a mere figurehead—generally limited to a one-year term, chosen by the state legislature (except in New York and Massachusetts), and restricted in the use of the veto (allowed only in Massachusetts and South Carolina).[17]

State constitutions today vary widely in age. Seven states have adopted new constitutions since 1965, while nearly half of the states have adopted new constitutions since 1900. Several states, most notably those of the South, have had many constitutions. Louisiana adopted ten constitutions between 1812 and 1920; Virginia and Georgia have had eight, South Carolina seven, and Alabama and Florida six.[18]

State constitutions also vary widely in length and content. The Georgia constitution, notorious for its length, contains over 600,000 words—including 832 amendments. In contrast, four states have constitutions of fewer than 10,000 words (the approximate length of the Constitution of the United States, including amendments). Excessively lengthy constitutions often contain detailed restrictions on the use of revenue sources, limits on the amount of debt allowed the state and its subunits, and trivial earmarking provisions. (Even some of the shorter constitutions have restrictive fiscal provisions and trivial earmarking stipulations.)[19] Flexibility in financial matters is thus seriously restricted because constitutional amendments are required to change tax or debt limits and/or earmarking provisions—a slow and involved process.

All state constitutions have certain features. All now contain a bill of rights, provide the basic framework for the state government, establish systems of local government, and establish revenue systems for the states. Typically this includes authorization for the property tax, sales taxes, and/or a variety of other revenue sources.

GROWTH AND CHANGE

All state constitutions have provisions for growth and change—both informal and formal.[20] Informal change is accomplished through custom, usage, and interpretation. A custom may be as strong as law. One-fourth of the states, for example, have no constitutional requirement that constitutional conventions be called by the state legislature. Yet in the absence of legal directives, the legislatures of these states have historically assumed this power. Judicial interpretation also provides an informal method for growth and change. The courts of each state may be called upon to interpret clauses or sections of the constitution—at times permitting actions previously forbidden or prohibiting those permitted.

Formal changes to state constitutions are accomplished by amendment or revision, with amendment being more common. Amendment usually involves two steps—initiation and ratification. Initiation generally requires approval of the proposed amendment by constitutionally stipulated majorities of the legislative bodies. As is shown by Table 2.1, the majorities vary by state. Minnesota, for example, requires merely a simple majority of the voting members at just a single legislative session.

The constitutions of 14 states now allow the people to propose constitutional amendments through initiative. In these states (shown in Table 2.2) petitions are circulated until the required number of signatures are obtained and verified. The amendment is then considered initiated and is subject to ratification at the next general election.

Initiation may also be accomplished by convention. Conventions are often cumbersome and time consuming and have been used infrequently. Conventions were typically used only where they were the only method available. (Prior to 1964, the convention was the only method available to amend the constitution of New Hampshire.)

A constitutional amendment does not receive final approval until it is ratified in a manner prescribed by the constitution. As is shown in Table 2.1, ratification by the people is required in all states except Delaware. Again, states differ dramatically in the votes required for ratification. Thirty-seven states require only majority approval of the amendment by persons voting on it. Five states require not only a favorable majority of votes cast on the amendment but a majority of the total votes in the election. The state of New Hampshire is even more restrictive; it requires a two-thirds majority of those voting on the amendment.

When a state constitution requires extensive revision, revision is almost always accomplished by a constitutional convention. Normally, both the state legislature and the people are involved. While the convention is typically called by the legislature, whether constitutionally required or not, the people must first vote to approve the calling of the convention. Details of conventions vary from state to state, but, in general, they operate very much like a unicameral legislative body, adopting their own formal rules and procedures. Once the new constitution is drafted, it is presented to the voters for approval. Here again, the approving majority varies from state to state. The constitution of

TABLE 2.1: Methods of Amending State Constitutions

Initiation	*Ratification*	*States*
Constitutional initiative	(See Table 2.2)	Arizona, Arkansas, California, Colorado, Florida, Massachusetts, Michigan, Missouri, Nebraska, Nevada, North Dakota, Ohio, Oklahoma, Oregon
Majority of each house	Majority at election	Minnesota
Majority of each house two successive sessions	Majority on amendment	Hawaii[a]
Two-thirds of each house	Majority on amendment	Alaska, Hawaii[a], Maine, Mississippi
Three-fifths of each house	Majority on amendment	North Carolina
Majority of members elected	Majority on amendment	Arizona, Missouri, New Mexico, North Dakota, Oregon, South Dakota
	Majority at election	Arkansas, Oklahoma
Majority of members elected; two successive sessions	Majority on amendment	Indiana, Iowa, Massachusetts[b], Nevada, New Jersey[c], New York, Pennsylvania, Virginia, Wisconsin
	Three-fifths of votes on amendment	Rhode Island
Two-thirds of members elected	Majority on amendment	California, Colorado, Georgia, Idaho, Kansas, Louisiana, Michigan, Montana, Texas, Utah, Washington, West Virginia
	Majority at election	Illinois[d], Wyoming
	Majority on amendment plus approval of next assembly	South Carolina
Two-thirds of members elected; two successive sessions	No popular ratification	Delaware

(continued)

23

(TABLE 2.1, continued)

Initiation	Ratification	States
Three-fifths of members elected	Majority on amendment	Alabama, Florida, Kentucky, Maryland, Nebraska[e], New Jersey[c], Ohio
	Two-thirds of votes on amendment	New Hampshire
Other		Connecticut[f], Tennessee[g], Vermont[h]

[a] Either method may be used. Majority must equal or exceed 35 percent of total votes cast; if at special election, majority must equal or exceed 35 percent of registered voters.

[b] Initiation by legislative body sitting in joint session.

[c] Either method may be used.

[d] Or two-thirds of vote cast on amendment.

[e] Majority for ratification must equal or exceed 35 percent of total votes cast at election.

[f] Three-fourths majority of total membership of each house at two successive sessions. Ratification by majority voting on amendment.

[g] Majority of members elected; two-thirds of members elected at next session. Ratification by majority of votes cast for governor.

[h] Two-thirds majority in Senate, majority in House; majority of members elected at next session. Ratification by majority voting on amendments.

Source: Russell W. Maddox and Robert F. Fuquay, *State and Local Government*, 3d ed. (New York: Van Nostrand, 1975), pp. 48–49.

Minnesota, for example, requires that a new constitution be accepted by three-fifths of those voting in the election while New Hampshire and Rhode Island require two-thirds majorities. Almost half the state constitutions make no mention of the majority required for ratification—thus the matter is determined by the legislature or convention.

UNIFORMITY CLAUSES

One important constitutional limitation on the revenue-raising power of states and their subunits is the requirement that taxes be "uniform and equal." The constitutions of over 40 states have some sort of uniformity clause. Problems occur, however, in the interpretation of these clauses. Each state has adopted its own unique and distinct phraseology. Newhouse attempted to compare the phraseology and was able to divide the states into nine groups based upon the uniformity clauses in effect in 1959.[21] Table 2.3 shows these groupings. The first two types of uniformity clauses are identified by the use of the word

TABLE 2.2: Amendment by Constitutional Initiative

State	Signatures Required[a]	Conditions	Ratification
Arizona	15% votes cast for governor	—	Majority on amendment
Arkansas	10% votes cast for governor	5% of legal voters in each of 15 counties	Majority on amendment
California	8% votes cast for governor	—	Majority on amendment
Florida	8% votes cast for presidential electors	8% votes cast in one-half congressional districts	Majority on amendment
Colorado	8% votes cast for secretary of state	—	Majority on amendment
Massachusetts	3% votes cast for governor	—	Majority on amendment; must be 30% of votes cast[c]
Michigan	10% votes cast for governor	—	Majority on amendment
Missouri	8% votes cast for governor	8% in each of two-thirds of congressional districts[b]	Majority on amendment
Nebraska	10% votes cast for governor	5% of electors in each of two-fifths of counties	Majority on amendment; must be 35% of votes cast
Nevada	10% of registered voters	—	Majority on amendment[d]
North Dakota	20,000 signatures	—	Majority on amendment
Ohio	10% votes cast for governor	5% in each of one-half of counties	Majority on amendment
Oklahoma	15% of highest vote cast	—	Majority of votes cast
Oregon	10% votes cast for supreme court Justice	—	Majority on amendment

[a]In terms of votes cast at last general election except for Nevada and North Dakota.

[b]Legislature may reduce percentage required. Now set at 5 percent.

[c]Must be approved by one-fourth of all members of general court in joint session at two successive sessions before submission to popular vote.

[d]Ratification requires approval at two successive general elections.

Source: Russell W. Maddox and Robert F. Fuquay, *State and Local Government*, 3d ed. (New York: Van Nostrand, 1975), p. 52.

TABLE 2.3:   Classification of State Uniformity Clauses

Type 1:   Property shall be taxed according to its value.

Arkansas	Tennessee
Maine	

Type 2:   Property shall be taxed in proportion to its value.

Alabama	Illinois
California	Nebraska

Type 3:   The legislature may impose proportional and reasonable assessments, rates, and taxes upon all persons and estates within the state.

Massachusetts	New Hampshire

Type 4:   There shall be a uniform rule of taxation.

Michigan	Ohio
New Jersey	Wisconsin

Type 5:   Taxation shall be equal and uniform.

Mississippi	West Virginia
Texas	Wyoming

Type 6:   The legislature shall provide by law for a uniform and equal rate of assessment and taxation.

Florida	Nevada
Indiana	South Carolina
Kansas	Utah

Type 7:   Taxes shall be uniform upon the same class of subjects.

Colorado	Montana
Delaware	New Mexico
Georgia	Oklahoma
Idaho	Oregon
Louisiana	Pennsylvania
Minnesota	Virginia
Missouri	

Type 8:   Taxes shall be uniform upon the same class of property.

Arizona	North Dakota
Kentucky	South Dakota
Maryland	Washington
North Carolina	

Type 9:   There shall be a fair distribution of the expense of government.

Rhode Island	Vermont

Source: Wade J. Newhouse, Jr., *Constitutional Uniformity and Equality in State Taxation* (Ann Arbor: University of Michigan Law School, 1959), pp. 9–11.

"value." Type 3, while not identified by "value," is closely related to the first two. Types 4-6 are closely related because of the manner in which they use the terms "equal" and "uniform." Types 7 and 8 are identified by the concern for uniformity within classes, and Type 9 concerns a fair distribution of expenses. Thus the wide diversity in phraseology alone makes interstate comparisons difficult.

The problem goes further than mere phraseology, however. Like the commerce and equal protection clauses of the Constitution, the language is so general as to be meaningless without judicial interpretation. Since there are 50 state court systems, even if the wording in all of the state constitutions were exactly the same, there would undoubtedly be many different interpretations of it.

Another reason that generalization is difficult is the complexity of the uniform structures. Since many states supplement their uniformity clauses with other constitutional provisions, the entire state constitution must be examined rather than the uniformity clause alone.[22]

The uniformity clauses and their supplementary provisions have produced widespread confusion and litigation. The conflicting and overlapping uniformity structures within state constitutions often ignore many of the really important problems. In addition, those state constitutions containing only a basic uniformity clause provide insufficient policy guidelines. Newhouse suggests that state constitutions should spell out the degree of uniformity desired of all taxes. Uniformity clauses should specify universality, effective rates, and method of taxation. Many of the numerous court decisions in each state can be used to construct the phraseology of each state's uniformity clause. Clearly, there can be no national standard or model clause for state constitutions. Local policy factors, differing fiscal policy, and past history make each state unique.[23]

FEDERAL GRANT ASSISTANCE

In Chapter 1 we noted that federal grant assistance comprised over one-fifth of all state and local general revenue in 1976. Federal aid received has increased at an average annual rate of over 14 percent during the period from 1954 through 1976. More important for our purposes, however, is the growing relative importance of federal assistance to state and local governments. It is likely that by 1980 federal aid will provide nearly 30 percent of state and local general revenues. The significance of this figure is clearly understated, however, as it fails to include matching funds raised and expended by the state and local governments in order to secure the federal grants.[24]

Since federal aid has become one of the most important sources of state and local revenues, it is necessary briefly to review the legal history of federal grants and to document the significant trends in federal legislation.[25] The system of grants-in-aid in the United States can be traced back to early grants of federal land, usually to support public education. As mentioned in Chapter 1, land grants were the most common form of federal aid through the eighteenth and nineteenth centuries, with the federal government conferring approximately 15 percent of its land holdings on the states. The first attempt to provide lands to support public education was probably contained in the Land Ordinance of 1785 whereby one lot out of every township was reserved for the maintenance of public schools within the township. Other provisions for land grants for public education soon followed—in the Northwest Ordinance of 1787 and in the Enabling Act of 1803 admitting Ohio to the Union.

Although most federal land grants were devoted to support of education, early grants were not entirely restricted to this purpose. Significant financial assistance was provided to the states through the assumption of state debts in 1790 and through the distribution of the surplus in 1837. The federal government also supported development of regional transportation networks through land grants for railroads and canals in the early 1800s.

The federal role in grant-in-aid programs was substantially expanded in 1862 with the passage of the first Morrill Land Grant Act for Colleges of Agriculture and Mechanical Arts. The act gave 30,000 acres to each state for each senator and representative in Congress (as of the 1860 census). States not having public lands in their boundaries equal to their appropriated share were issued "land scrip" in lieu of acreage. The act also required that the moneys obtained from the sale of the land or scrip were to be invested and that the income derived from the investment was to be appropriated for at least one agricultural and mechanical college. The second Morrill act (1890) increased the endowment by appropriating the proceeds of the sale of 500,000 acres of public lands to the states and territories. The constitutionality of the Morrill acts was never questioned although the acts were interpreted by the Supreme Court in cases relating to a gift to Cornell University and to Wyoming's method of setting up a college of agriculture and mechanics.[26] The grants established under the Morrill acts are the prototype of many current grants—in effect, they were the first of the conditional grants.

As the land grant college system developed, the federal government recognized the need for an agricultural outreach program that would bring the knowledge of the agricultural colleges to the people. Consequently, the Smith-Lever Act of 1914 established the agricultural extension system, still existing today, of county agents and county home demonstration agents. The Smith-Lever Act was only the beginning however. In 1928 Congress passed the Capper-Ketcham Act initially authorizing an annual appropriation of $980,000, plus an appropriation of $500,000 starting one year after the $980,000 became available. Continuing support for agricultural education and extension was prevalent throughout the 1930s with the passage of the Bankhead-Jones Act of 1935, the Cooperative Farm Forestry Act of 1937, and the Additional Extension Act of 1939, to name a few.[27]

While the grants for agricultural education were important in establishing a federal system of grants-in-aid, their financial impact was small. The total of all grants prior to 1915, excluding those for the National Guard, amounted to less than $5 million in any one year. Shortly after adoption of the Sixteenth Amendment (ratified in 1913) Congress enacted several new grant programs that increased federal aid twentyfold—to approximately $100 million annually. This figure remained relatively constant from 1918 through 1930.

The Smith-Lever Act of 1914 accounted for a substantial portion of the $95 million increase; however, two other grant programs, the first Federal Aid Highway Act of 1916 and the Smith-Hughes Vocational Education Act of 1917, also contributed to the increase in no small way. The Highway Act of 1916 authorized the secretary of agriculture to cooperate with state highway departments in the construction of rural post roads. Participating states were required to establish a state highway department (or other agency given similar powers) as a requirement for federal aid. The act provided for the distribution of federal funds based upon the area, population, and rural delivery and star route mileage in each state relative to the total national mileage of such routes. For the most part, the states were quick to comply. By 1921 every state had a highway department, and 28 had made the necessary provisions for matching federal funds.

The highway program has been gradually expanded to cover functions well beyond the original act. Today federal aid to the states covers interstate highways, mail routes, school bus routes, farm-to-market roads, forest roads, and projects within urban areas, to name a few. The highway programs were unique, however, not in their expansion but in their administrative requirements. The highway grants were the first federal aid programs to be thoroughly supervised. States were required to have proposed projects examined in advance, were required to furnish detailed progress reports, and were subject to audits of expenditures.

Vocational education was the third major program of federal grants initiated during the World War I era. The statutory basis for federal aid for vocational education was established by the Smith-Hughes Act of 1917, and administration was similar to that of the highway program. A federal Board of Vocational Education had responsibility much like that of the Department of Agriculture for the highway grants. The programs themselves, again like the highway programs, were administered by state boards of vocational education with the funds channeled through the state treasuries.

While grant programs expanded during World War I and administrative requirements became more stringent, it was not until the 1930s that a real change in the nature of the programs occurred. The Roosevelt administration created a number of temporary programs designed to stimulate employment and to revive the economy. Programs administered by temporary agencies such as the Civil Works Administration, the Public Works Administration, and the Works Progress Administration soon gave way to more permanent programs, of which the social security program was by far the most important. The Social Security Act of 1935 provided that the federal government reimburse the states for a portion of the administrative and substantive costs for providing three types of programs: insurance programs (such as unemployment compensation), public assistance (such as old age assistance), and maternal and child welfare assistance.

The unemployment compensation program provides a good example of the change in the nature of federal assistance programs effected during the Roosevelt era. Under the program, participating states were required to tax employer payrolls, disburse money to unemployed workers, and provide for an administrative agency. In states participating in the plan, the state payroll tax canceled 90 percent of the national payroll tax. On the other hand, in nonparticipating states, the entire payroll tax went into the national treasury, although workers in these states were not eligible for unemployment benefits.

A series of court cases developed around the Roosevelt programs, culminating in judicial acceptance of the new system of grants. In reaching these decisions the Supreme Court virtually abandoned judicial restrictions on the spending powers of the federal government. In 1936, the Supreme Court had held the Agricultural Adjustment Act of 1933 unconstitutional, in that processing taxes were used to regulate and control farm production by coercing farmers into compliance.[28] In 1937, the court virtually reversed itself in declaring that the tax-offset device of unemployment compensation taxes did not unduly coerce the states merely because it provided them with a financial advantage if they cooperated.[29] Thus the court denied that strong inducements to the states were unduly coercive and asserted the right of the states to enter into agreements with the national government.

The Wagner-Steagall Act of 1937, another program of the Roosevelt era, added a further dimension to federal grant efforts—grants made directly from the federal government to local governments, bypassing the states. The act allowed the Federal Works Agency to make long-term loans to state and local housing authorities for up to 80 percent of the cost of low-rent housing. Loans, and later grants, could be channeled directly to local housing authorities once states had passed the required enabling legislation. Within four years of the act's passage, all but nine states had enacted the required enabling legislation, although a number of states restricted eligibility to one or two selected cities.

Grant-in-aid expenditures, as might have been expected, tapered off significantly during World War II. This trend was quickly reversed, however, with the cessation of hostilities, and there was a steep climb in the number of new enactments during the following decade. Major programs in this era were in the areas of public health, support for education, and in grants to urban and metropolitan areas. Two programs—the Hill-Burton Hospital and Medical Facilities Survey and Construction Program, and the Federal Airport Program—were among the more important enactments of the early postwar period. These two programs were significant contributors to the rise in grant spending from $900 million in 1946 to $2.4 billion in 1952.

Grants-in-aid for health purposes, although initiated early in our history, had little financial impact until recent years. One early act, however, the Sheppard-Towner Infant and Maternity Hygiene Act of 1921, was significant because its constitutionality was reviewed and upheld by the Supreme Court. The purpose of the act was to initiate programs to reduce the death rate of mothers and infants by making prenatal and postnatal medical care available to them. Two suits attacking the constitutionality of the act were considered by the Supreme Court. One was a taxpayer's suit and the other a challenge by the Commonwealth of Massachusetts. The Massachusetts suit sought to have the legislation overturned on the basis that the program served local, not national, needs and violated provisions of the Tenth Amendment. The court consolidated the cases in one decision—setting aside the taxpayer's protest on the grounds that his share of the taxes paid to support the funds granted under the legislation was so inconsequential that there was no reasonable basis for action—and dealt with the Massachusetts case by indicating that no state was required to accept the grant unless it chose to do so.[30]

The Hill-Burton Act, passed in 1946, provided federal funds to aid in the construction of hospital facilities. Under the law, the Public Health Service administered the program through state agencies, which were responsible for both planning and construction. By 1960, over 4,400 projects had been approved, with federal expenditures approaching $1.2 billion. The program was significant not only because of the new hospitals it helped to create but also because of the planning procedures and standards it created. The introduction of a continuing statewide health planning structure to develop plans for the distribution of health care facilities within the states was an important accomplishment of the program, as was the development of minimum design, construction, and equipment standards for hospitals and other health facilities. The Hill-Burton requirement that states establish regulations for the operation and maintenance of hospitals receiving federal aid resulted in widespread adoption of licensing laws. When the Hill-Burton Act was initiated, only 12 states had licensing laws affecting hospitals. By the early 1960s, largely as a result of the act, all states had adopted licensing laws and standards for nursing homes, and all but four had licensing laws for general hospitals.

As was clearly illustrated in Chapter 1, the late 1950s and 1960s were an era of tremendous growth of grants-in-aids in terms of both numbers of programs and dollar amounts. Programs were devised and initiated for almost every conceivable activity of government. Certain trends were evident including (1) large-scale growth, (2) excessive categorization and widespread proliferation, (3) direct federal-local relations, and (4) increased use of project grants.[31] The ACIR contends that the most striking of these trends has been widespread proliferation and excessive categorization.[32] This trend was clearly evident in the 1970 *Catalog of Federal Domestic Assistance*. The *Catalog*, a compendium of more than 1,040 pages, alphabetically listed 1,013 grant programs.[33] Many programs often served the same purpose. The most commonly cited example is the case of water and sewer grants—four separate programs under four separate agencies, all for the same purpose.

In an attempt to bring some order to federal grant programs President Richard Nixon, in 1969, announced his concept of "new federalism." He proposed a system of "revenue sharing" to rechannel power, funds, and authority to state and local governments. The thrust of the "new federalism" was to deemphasize the federal government's role in state and local programs and strengthen the role of state and local governments.[34] The "new federalism" concept was operationalized by the passage of the State and Local Fiscal Assistance Act of 1972, which provided $30.2 billion over five years to state and local governments. The purpose of the act was to provide funds with limited restrictions to state and local governments in an attempt to decentralize government, equalize fiscal conditions between wealthy and poor areas, stabilize or reduce the property tax, and alter the nation's tax system by placing greater reliance on income taxation.[35]

The Nixon administration also proposed several other measures designed to combine into block grants a number of the larger categorical grant-in-aid programs. Perhaps the best known of these is the compromise Community Development Block Grant Program (CDBG).[36] In creating the CDBG, Congress consolidated seven programs administered by the Department of Housing and Urban Development into a single package. While communities were required to submit applications, the act provided local "entitlement" funds based upon a need formula. Thus program decision-making responsibilities were transferred from federal to local officials. Local officials were given the opportunity to spend federal community development funds in accordance with locally set priorities (within the broad parameters of the legislation).[37]

Clearly the revenue systems of today's state and local governments are extremely complex. They have been complicated by the passage of the Sixteenth Amendment, the development and proliferation of categorical grant-in-aid programs, and more recently, the decentralization of the "new federalism." While the problems inherent in today's revenue systems are becoming increasingly clear, it is wrong to assume that all states' systems are similar—actually, they differ in many fundamental ways.

STATE RESTRICTIONS ON STATE AND LOCAL REVENUE SOURCES

This chapter documents recent trends in state and local revenues. Such an aggregate picture, however, may be misleading, as generalizations fail to capture the many differences between states. Generalizations often imply homogeneity. But in the case of state and local revenue, homogeneity does not exist. Table 2.4 shows the percent distribution of the various general revenue sources for the 50 states and the District of Columbia. Examining first the intergovernmental transfers from the federal government, we see that the state and local governments in Alaska derive almost one-third of their total revenue from

TABLE 2.4: State and Local Total General Revenue, by State, 1975 (total amount and percentage distribution by major source)

State	Total General Revenue (in millions)	Percentage Distribution								
		Federal Aid	Total	Tax Revenue						Charges & Miscellaneous Gen. Revenue
				Property	Individual Income	Corporation Income	General Sales	Selective Sales	Other	
United States	$228,194.9	20.6	62.0	22.6	9.4	2.9	12.8	9.1	5.3	17.4
Alabama	2,989.1	27.0	50.2	6.4	6.9	1.9	15.5	14.5	5.0	22.8
Alaska	806.5	32.1	36.8	9.4	10.8	2.1	2.7	4.4	7.4	31.2
Arizona	2,276.3	18.5	64.3	22.8	6.9	2.2	20.8	8.6	3.0	17.2
Arkansas	1,607.3	29.0	53.4	11.8	7.9	3.4	13.2	12.6	4.5	17.6
California	27,869.6	18.6	66.0	28.4	8.8	4.5	14.8	6.1	3.4	15.4
Colorado	2,813.8	21.3	56.8	19.3	10.0	2.1	15.3	6.4	3.7	21.9
Connecticut	3,130.1	18.8	68.9	34.8	0.4	4.5	13.6	11.5	4.1	12.3
Delaware	695.2	18.8	60.6	10.6	19.8	2.5	—	10.3	17.4	20.7
Dist. of Columbia	1,397.9	51.2	38.9	10.1	10.2	2.0	8.1	6.1	2.4	9.9
Florida	7,347.9	18.1	59.3	18.5	—	2.5	16.3	15.0	7.0	22.6
Georgia	4,616.8	24.7	54.2	17.3	8.1	2.6	13.3	10.5	2.4	21.1
Hawaii	1,241.5	23.5	59.4	10.5	13.6	2.5	23.1	7.4	2.3	17.1
Idaho	767.9	24.7	56.4	17.1	11.9	3.7	10.3	7.8	5.6	18.9
Illinois	12,001.8	18.2	67.8	26.1	9.5	2.6	15.1	9.9	4.6	14.0
Indiana	4,831.3	15.2	63.8	25.4	8.7	1.6	17.6	7.3	3.2	21.0
Iowa	2,940.6	19.6	62.2	25.7	12.2	2.1	9.7	6.9	5.6	18.2
Kansas	2,200.7	19.4	61.6	26.1	7.7	3.9	12.2	7.8	3.9	19.0
Kentucky	3,036.3	25.6	55.6	10.6	10.9	3.8	12.2	11.0	7.1	18.8
Louisiana	3,764.6	22.6	57.0	8.6	2.9	2.1	16.3	9.0	18.1	20.4
Maine	1,004.2	27.0	60.3	24.4	4.4	2.0	13.7	11.4	4.4	12.7
Maryland	4,693.7	19.1	63.5	18.6	21.0	2.0	8.4	9.7	3.8	17.4
Massachusetts	6,825.9	19.0	69.5	36.8	14.4	3.9	3.7	8.0	2.7	11.5

34

Michigan	10,339.3	20.5	60.4	25.8	9.6	2.2	11.4	7.0	4.4	19.1
Minnesota	4,870.4	19.7	60.8	18.6	16.6	4.0	7.9	8.8	4.9	19.5
Mississippi	2,009.4	28.7	52.1	11.4	4.6	1.7	19.3	10.5	4.6	19.3
Missouri	3,996.2	20.9	62.3	21.9	9.6	1.4	14.4	10.0	5.0	16.3
Montana	842.4	26.4	54.4	27.0	10.5	2.6	—	8.3	6.0	19.2
Nebraska	1,522.4	19.3	58.6	28.5	5.1	1.7	10.5	8.8	4.0	22.1
Nevada	763.3	17.8	59.7	19.7	—	—	13.5	18.0	8.5	22.4
New Hampshire	706.0	23.1	60.8	36.5	1.2	3.7	—	13.9	5.5	16.0
New Jersey	7,914.1	17.7	67.1	38.1	0.6	2.6	9.7	11.0	5.1	15.3
New Mexico	1,264.3	27.1	49.7	8.7	4.5	1.4	17.3	8.2	9.6	23.2
New York	27,891.8	17.9	66.6	24.0	16.1	3.5	12.5	7.3	3.2	15.5
North Carolina	4,599.9	26.4	57.5	13.9	12.0	3.6	11.7	11.8	4.5	16.0
North Dakota	751.5	21.4	51.8	16.2	8.6	2.7	12.6	6.3	5.4	26.7
Ohio	9,361.2	18.8	61.4	23.2	10.2	2.9	10.6	9.4	5.1	19.8
Oklahoma	2,456.8	25.5	53.2	12.9	6.6	1.7	10.2	10.5	11.3	21.4
Oregon	2,721.6	26.6	53.4	15.7	15.7	3.3	—	5.8	5.3	20.1
Pennsylvania	11,528.4	20.6	65.3	16.8	12.4	5.2	11.0	10.0	9.9	14.1
Rhode Island	961.4	24.0	62.2	26.0	8.3	3.8	10.8	10.1	3.2	13.8
South Carolina	2,321.2	24.1	54.1	12.2	9.1	3.6	14.5	11.4	3.3	21.8
South Dakota	688.9	27.8	53.8	26.4	—	0.3	13.5	8.9	4.7	18.4
Tennessee	3,408.7	24.6	55.4	14.3	0.5	3.7	18.8	10.6	7.5	20.1
Texas	10,609.9	20.7	59.4	22.1	—	—	14.1	11.8	11.4	19.9
Utah	1,144.8	26.9	53.3	16.0	9.2	1.6	17.0	6.4	3.1	19.8
Vermont	571.9	27.6	57.6	24.7	9.6	1.7	4.6	12.2	4.8	14.8
Virginia	4,615.2	21.6	60.6	16.9	11.9	2.5	10.5	12.9	5.9	17.8
Washington	4,138.5	21.4	57.9	19.7	—	—	22.7	10.5	5.0	20.7
West Virginia	1,691.1	29.9	56.8	10.8	7.0	1.1	21.3	11.3	5.3	13.3
Wisconsin	5,071.5	18.1	65.3	24.6	17.2	3.0	10.1	6.7	3.7	16.5
Wyoming	519.3	27.4	50.2	20.4	—	—	14.8	5.7	9.3	22.4

Source: Advisory Commission on Intergovernmental Relations, *Significant Features of Fiscal Federalism, 1976–77 Edition,* vol. 2 (Washington, D.C.: Government Printing Office, 1977), p. 30.

this source while those in Indiana receive only 15.2 percent of their revenues from it. In general, the southern and western states rely more heavily on federal funds than do northeastern or north central states.

Tax revenues are clearly the most important source of total state and local funds. Again, however, reliance on taxes varies widely among states and among regions of the country. As might be expected, states receiving relatively little assistance from the federal government rely on their own tax sources for large portions of their revenue. At the other extreme, taxes account for only 36.8 percent of Alaska's revenue. Alaska relies very heavily on charges and interest earnings as well as on federal aid. Regional distribution of reliance on taxes is negatively related to the reliance on federal aid. Southern and western states, with their aid advantage, place significantly less emphasis on taxes as a source of revenue than do northeastern and north central states.

Not only do revenue sources vary substantially between states but tax sources do also. Table 2.4 also shows the state-by-state distribution of state and local tax revenues. Substantial differences in reliance on specific taxes are apparent. The variation in reliance on the property tax is a case in point. Alabama relies on the property tax for only 6.4 percent of its total revenue while New Jersey derives 38.1 percent from this source. In general, the South is much less reliant on the property tax than is the rest of the country.

Southern states rely heavily on the general sales tax and a number of selective sales taxes. West Virginia, for example, derives 21.3 percent of its revenue from a general sales tax and 11.3 percent from selective taxes.

It is in income tax revenue, however, that the most interesting variations are seen. Most states rely on corporate income taxes for only a small part of their revenues. Only Pennsylvania, California, Connecticut, and Minnesota rely on the corporation income tax for more than 4 percent of state and local revenues. The individual income tax is much more important. Maryland derives over 20 percent of its revenues from this source. On the other hand, a number of states have no individual income taxes. Florida, Nevada, South Dakota, Texas, Washington, and Wyoming leave this source of revenue untapped.

States also vary widely in the restrictions they impose upon themselves with regard to borrowing. Table 2.5 shows the per capita amounts of state and local debt outstanding for the 50 states and the District of Columbia. Alaska leads all states, with over $3,600 of outstanding debt per capita, most of it long term. Idaho, at the other extreme, has only $313 of per capita debt outstanding, most of it used to finance the construction of local schools. Local school construction is the single most important use of debt funds, followed by the procure-

TABLE 2.5: Per Capita Debt of State and Local Governments, 1976

State	Debt Outstanding at End of Fiscal Year	
	Total	Long-term Only
U.S. average	1,118.46	1,030.98
Median state	947.23	920.09
Alabama	818.52	791.65
Alaska	3,618.23	3,456.45
Arizona	1,044.12	1,030.89
Arkansas	528.88	501.71
California	947.23	929.51
Colorado	810.56	790.56
Connecticut	1,601.32	1,401.15
Delaware	1,953.80	1,894.01
Dist. of Columbia	3,423.27	3,159.02
Florida	848.02	828.56
Georgia	808.82	783.04
Hawaii	1,848.10	1,810.13
Idaho	313.75	293.58
Illinois	931.05	821.15
Indiana	528.68	505.42
Iowa	458.08	447.16
Kansas	913.27	876.90
Kentucky	1,192.72	1,170.35
Louisiana	1,130.40	1,118.68
Maine	901.21	837.71
Maryland	1,404.93	1,364.25
Massachusetts	1,508.04	1,282.00
Michigan	963.05	920.10
Minnesota	1,206.51	1,143.68
Mississippi	746.58	726.41
Missouri	587.30	567.34
Montana	616.93	612.19
Nebraska	1,643.81	1,555.57
Nevada	1,103.02	1,097.52
New Hampshire	819.69	731.65
New Jersey	1,227.55	1,084.36
New Mexico	666.75	660.95
New York	2,545.75	2,084.91
North Carolina	467.87	433.59
North Dakota	548.83	541.24
Ohio	798.20	685.07
Oklahoma	830.33	807.55
Oregon	1,438.80	1,422.52
Pennsylvania	1,317.13	1,249.04
Rhode Island	1,083.97	952.59

(continued)

(TABLE 2.5, continued)

| | Debt Outstanding at End of Fiscal Year | |
State	Total	Long-term Only
South Carolina	761.03	746.04
South Dakota	327.19	322.27
Tennessee	961.76	922.88
Texas	968.70	951.59
Utah	532.29	531.88
Vermont	1,222.51	1,162.93
Virginia	779.82	731.16
Washington	1,663.26	1,637.43
West Virginia	968.36	938.87
Wisconsin	767.19	745.71
Wyoming	1,178.77	1,178.71

Source: U.S. Bureau of the Census, Governmental Finances, 1975–76 (Washington, D.C.: Government Printing Office, 1977), p. 66.

ment of assets for public utilities. Approximately 37 percent of all state and local debt is for these two purposes.

Most states restrict the borrowing powers of local governments. The Kentucky constitution, for example, limits the borrowing power of counties, municipalities, and school districts. The Minnesota constitution, on the other hand, imposes no such limits; all of its limits are by statute. Alaska places no limits whatsoever on subunit borrowing, while Idaho limits only municipalities (exception: county and school district debt incurred in any year cannot exceed revenue for that year without approval of two-thirds of the voters).

SELECTED TAX SYSTEMS

The purpose of this section is to examine briefly the tax systems and constitutional and statutory restrictions on revenue sources in nine selected states.[38] The states were selected because they illustrate how constitutional and statutory restraints on tax sources tend to skew the dependence on particular taxes. New Hampshire and New Jersey were selected because of their heavy reliance on the property tax. Mississippi and Alabama are discussed because they rely heavily on sales, use, and gross receipts taxes, while Alaska and Delaware are heavy income tax users. Two states, Colorado and Illinois, are discussed because their tax emphasis is very close to the national average. Finally, the tax structure for New York State is also examined because of the impact of state actions on the New York City financial crisis.

Not all state and local taxes will be examined in each case. Discussion is limited to the major state and local tax sources—the property tax, individual income tax, corporation income tax, and general sales tax. Percentages in Table 2.4 have been recalculated to show the contribution each source makes to total taxes (instead of total revenues). These are shown in Table 2.6.

Property Tax States

Both New Hampshire and New Jersey rely heavily on the local property tax for income. Of the nine selected states, only New Hampshire and New Jersey have no constitutional or statutory restrictions imposed on subunits relative to the property tax. Thus, subunits in these two states are free of many of the restraints on types of property covered and the rate limits imposed by many state constitutions.

Both states are forced to depend heavily on the property tax because they are extremely limited in the use they make of other traditional state and local taxes. Both states, for example, have long ignored a broad-based individual income tax, although New Jersey finally adopted such a tax in 1976. Even now the New Jersey tax is light—2 percent of taxable income up to $20,000 and 2.5 percent of taxable income over $20,000. New Jersey also imposes an income tax on New York and Pennsylvania residents working in the state and on New Jersey residents commuting to New York and Pennsylvania.

The New Hampshire personal income tax is also extremely limited. New Hampshire taxes income on interest and dividends only—at a rate of 4.25 percent. New Hampshire also imposes a 4 percent tax on the residents' income derived outside the state and on the New Hampshire-derived income of nonresidents.

As Table 2.6 indicates, New Hampshire derives no income from the general sales tax—no such tax is authorized either for the state or its local jurisdictions. New Jersey, on the other hand, adopted a general sales tax in 1966. Its dependence on the general sales tax now approaches the national average with a tax rate of 5 percent. In addition, New Jersey has several other forms of sales-type taxes: a compensating use tax, a retail gross receipts tax, and an unincorporated business tax. While gross sales taxes are not generally used by cities in New Jersey, the city of Trenton has a license tax based upon total annual gross receipts. Fees vary from $10 for less than $5,000 in gross sales to $750 for gross sales in excess of $1 million.

TABLE 2.6: Percent Distribution of State and Local Tax Revenue for Nine States, by Type of Tax, 1975

	Total	Property	General Sales	Individual Income	Other
Property tax					
New Hampshire	100	60.0	—	2.0	38.0
New Jersey	100	56.8	14.5	.9	27.9
Sales tax					
Alabama	100	12.7	30.9	13.7	42.6
Mississippi	100	21.9	37.0	8.8	32.2
Income tax					
Alaska	100	25.5	7.3	29.3	37.8
Delaware	100	17.5	—	32.7	49.8
Average distribution					
Colorado	100	34.0	26.9	17.6	21.5
Illinois	100	38.5	22.3	14.0	25.2
New York	100	36.0	18.8	24.1	21.0
U.S. average	100	36.5	20.6	15.2	27.9

Source: Advisory Commission on Intergovernmental Relations, *Significant Features of Fiscal Federalism, 1976–77 Edition*, vol. 2 (Washington, D.C.: Government Printing Office, 1977), p. 30.

Sales Tax States

Alabama and Mississippi are illustrative of states heavily dependent upon the general sales tax for a large portion of total state and local revenues. While 45 of the 50 states now have a general sales tax, Mississippi and Alabama were among the early adopters of this form of taxation, adopting the tax in 1932 and 1936, respectively. The sales tax rate in Alabama is 4 percent although certain items are exempt (for example, fertilizer, seeds, wood products for use as "chicken litter"). A few other items have lower tax rates (for example, automobiles and farm equipment are taxed at 1.5 percent). Both Alabama cities and counties may levy sales taxes, use taxes, or both. Taxes generally parallel the state sales and use taxes except for rate (usually 1 to 2 percent). In addition, a number of cities impose special taxes. Birmingham, for example, has a gross receipts tax on retailers, wholesalers, and manufacturers; and a number of municipalities have a tax on hotels, motels, or rooming houses.

The Mississippi state sales tax is currently set at a rate of 5 percent, having been increased from 3.5 to 5 percent in 1968. At the same time, authority for the local sales tax was repealed. Thus, Mississippi differs from Alabama in that its jurisdictions are not authorized to use the sales tax.

Both states have significantly lower property tax dependence than the national average, and, in contrast to New Hampshire and New Jersey, both place restrictions on use of the property tax. Alabama has both constitutional and statutory restrictions while Mississippi restricts use of the tax only by statute. Alabama and Mississippi both limit the millage rates for counties, municipalities, and school districts.

Individual income tax dependence in both states is only slightly below the national average. Mississippi takes personal income at a rate of 3 percent on the first $5,000 of taxable income and 4 percent on all taxable income in excess of $5,000. Alabama's rates range from 1.5 percent on the first $1,000 over exempted amounts up to 5 percent on amounts over $5,000. In addition, cities in Alabama are authorized to levy a local income tax up to a limit of 5 percent of net income. However, all cities in the state utilizing a local income tax have restricted the rate to 2 percent or less. For example, a 1 percent tax is imposed on the gross receipts of persons engaged in any trade, occupation, or profession in Birmingham. A 1 percent license (income) tax is imposed on individuals employed in Montgomery.

Income Tax States

The individual income tax is the dominant tax in both Alaska and Delaware. Both states also rely on the property tax for a significant portion of state and local revenues from own sources—although this reliance is substantially below the reliance for all states. Both Alaska and Delaware place statutory restrictions on the use of the property tax. Alaskan statutes restrict the millage on property taxes for cities, boroughs, and schools. Delaware, however, restricts the tax rate in only Sussex and Kent counties. There is no millage limit on the property tax rate imposed either by municipalities or school districts in the state.

Individual income taxes in both Alaska and Delaware are among the most progressive in the nation. Delaware adopted the income tax in 1917 and Alaska in 1949. Individual income tax rates in Alaska range from 3 percent on incomes under $2,000 to 14.5 percent on incomes over $200,000. In Delaware, rates range from 1.6 percent on incomes under $1,000 to 19.8 percent on incomes over $100,000. In addition, residents and nonresidents employed or working in the city of Wilmington are subject to a city income tax of 1.25 percent of all wages, salaries, commissions, and net profits.

Neither Alaska nor Delaware has statewide sales taxes. Alaska, however, is unique in that boroughs and cities in the state may levy and collect a sales tax not exceeding 3 percent on sales, rents, and/or services within their borders. Cities within boroughs that levy and collect sales and use taxes may also levy similar taxes on all sources taxed by the boroughs. If the borough does not levy a sales or use tax, municipalities in that borough may levy a tax at the rate provided for boroughs.

Typical States

In both Colorado and Illinois, the use of the property tax is restricted by statute. Counties in Colorado have specific millage limits while those for municipalities, school districts, and special districts require that the total levy shall not exceed 5 percent more than the aggregate for the previous year. Illinois, on the other hand, has specific millage limits on the property tax rate in counties, municipalities, townships, school districts, and special districts.

Colorado's individual income tax was passed in 1937, while Illinois's was passed in 1969. The Colorado personal income tax varies from 3 percent on the first $1,000 of net income to 8 percent on incomes over $10,000. Residents pay a 2 percent surtax on gross income in excess of $5,000 received as dividends and interest. The Illinois income tax is a proportional tax: a flat rate of 2.5 percent is imposed on net income of individuals, estates, and trusts.

Both Colorado and Illinois have used the general sales tax for many years—Colorado since 1935 and Illinois since 1933. A tax of 3 percent is imposed on the gross receipts from the retail sale of tangible personal property in Colorado. In addition, Colorado cities may impose sales and use taxes. In all localities, the total state, county, and city tax rate is limited to 7 percent. City sales taxes vary from 4 percent in Mount Crested Butte and Vail (two major tourist areas) to 1 percent in a host of cities. County sales taxes range from 0.5 percent to 2 percent.

Illinois imposes a retailers' occupation tax of 4 percent on tangible property sold. A use tax of 4 percent is also included. Counties and cities are authorized to levy sales and use taxes of 1 percent—and almost all have.

New York

The New York tax system is unique in several ways. New York has not adopted a system of segregating revenues for state and local purposes. The state assesses a wide variety of taxes that provide significant sources of income for the state and local governments. Also unique is the importance of the franchise tax, which accounts for more than 10 percent of state general revenues.

Local use of the property tax is restricted by the state constitution. Counties, municipalities, villages, and school districts all have constitutionally imposed millage limits.

Since 1919 New York has had an individual income tax. The rate varies from 2 percent on incomes under $1,000 to 15 percent on incomes over $25,000. In addition, a tax of 5.5 percent is imposed on the net income of any unincorporated business. New York City also has a personal income tax. The tax on city residents ranges from 0.7 of taxable income of less than $1,000 to $675 plus 4.3 percent of the excess over $25,000.

New York also makes extensive use of the sales tax. The state assesses a levy of 4 percent of receipts from retail sales on nonexempted goods. Cities and counties are also authorized to use the sales tax—most now range from 1 to 4 percent. State and local sales taxes in New York City presently total 8 percent.

Summary

Table 2.7 summarizes the brief descriptions of the major taxes in the nine states presented in the preceding paragraphs. The extreme differences are immediately apparent. The two states in which the property tax is most dominant have no constitutional or statutory restriction on use of the tax by local governments. Both states (before 1976) virtually ignored the individual income tax; New Hampshire still does. Nor does New Hampshire have a general sales tax, and in New Jersey the tax is relatively new.

The two states in which the general sales tax is dominant were early adopters of the tax and have an historic dependence on this source. While both have individual income taxes, both also restrict the use of the property tax. Neither of the income-tax-dominant states makes use of the general sales tax, and both have statutory restrictions on local use of the property tax.

Thus each of the six states that deviate widely from national averages in tax dependence has unusual constitutional or statutory provisions relative to revenue sources. Many potential sources of tax revenues are not authorized. Many potential sources, when authorized, are restricted. History also seems to account for part of the variation. Early adopters of a given tax tend to rely heavily on that tax rather than diversify into other tax sources. This brief examination of the constitutional and statutory restrictions affecting state dependence suggests that the major restrictions on state and local tax sources are imposed not by the federal government but by the states themselves. Once a state

TABLE 2.7: Dates of Passage and Summary of Constitutional and Statutory Restrictions of Major Tax Sources in Nine States

	Property Tax Restrictions	Individual Income Tax Authorized	General Sales Tax Authorized
Alabama	Constitutional and statutory	1933	1936
Mississippi	Statutory	1912	1932
New Hampshire	None	None[a]	None
New Jersey	None	None[b]	1966
Alaska	Statutory	1949	None[c]
Delaware	Statutory	1917	None
Colorado	Statutory	1937	1935
Illinois	Statutory	1969	1933
New York	Constitutional	1919	1965

[a] Restricted to stocks and bonds, commuters' tax.
[b] Prior to 1976 restricted to commuters' tax.
[c] Authorized for subunits only.
Source: Compiled by the authors.

adopts a particular tax, it seems to become dependent on it rather than diversify to other sources. This is not to say that states do not take advantage of unique features within the state that provide opportunities for additional revenues—they do. Mississippi has an oil and gas severance tax; Alaska has a mining license tax; Delaware has a well-developed corporate income tax; and New Hampshire now operates a state lottery. States do diversify but perhaps not to the extent that they could. State constitutional and statutory restrictions on revenue sources clearly impose serious restraints on state and local revenue policy.

CITY FISCAL EMERGENCIES

Unquestionably, many American cities are in a period of great financial stress. But what is the problem? If states and cities have the wide range of financial resources available to them suggested by the case studies, why are cities in trouble? Even before the recent crisis in New York City, the ACIR was concerned with the intergovernmental dimension of city financial problems.[39] It conducted a survey to locate cities having recent severe financial problems, especially those with financial emergencies. Thirteen cities, including New York city, were identified—eight were studied in depth. These included Hamtramck, Michigan; Darby, Pennsylvania; East Haven, Connecticut; Cleveland, Ohio; Somerville, Massachusetts; New Britain, Connecticut; Newark, New Jersey; and East St. Louis, Illinois. Each of the cities had an excess of expenditures over revenues, some persisting over a period of years. In all but one case the gap exceeded 5 percent. Six of the eight cities financed their deficit spending by issuing short-term debt. Cleveland resorted to internal borrowing, and Newark met its budget with the help of extensive state aid.

The case studies illustrated the important role the states play in both contributing to and alleviating cities' financial problems. Both Cleveland and East St. Louis were prohibited from helping themselves because of constitutional and statutory limits on tax rates. New Jersey contributed to Newark's problem by requiring the city to support state-mandated programs without providing funding. (New Jersey did eventually allocate resources to alleviate the emergency.) With the exception of New Jersey, the states failed to act to prevent serious financial problems from occurring in these cities.

What are the financial characteristics of cities facing financial difficulty? Most financial trouble begins when city expenditures exceed revenues. Persistent excesses of expenditures over revenues eventually lead to a fund deficit. General fund deficits are then accompanied by short-term borrowing. The burden of bonded debt also has a significant bearing on city financial health. In addition, underfunding of locally administered retirement systems is a major cause of city financial instability.[40]

Clearly nothing in the twentieth century, with the possible exception of the Depression, has had greater impact on intergovernmental fiscal relations than the near financial collapse of New York City. The city's financial problems reached crisis proportions on March 13 and 20, 1975, when it was unable to sell $537 million out of $912 million of short-term notes at tax-exempt rates of up to 8 percent. A ten-year history of financial problems led to this condition.

During the period between 1967 and 1975, the city accumulated a budget deficit of $2.6 billion. Though the city charter requires that the city write a balanced budget, a series of mayors have done so only in a technical sense. Throughout the period, expenditure/revenue imbalances were covered by short-term borrowing. Since the city never developed any surpluses during the period, it had no way to pay off its borrowing other than by floating new short-term notes. As the deficits grew, so did the amount of short-term notes outstanding until, by the end of 1975, short-term debt amounted to $5.2 billion. Thus, between 1967 and 1975, short-term debt increased at a compound annual rate of over 35 percent.[41]

Haider recently completed an insightful analysis of the causes of New York City's eventual "default" on its bonds.[42] He noted that during the decade 1966-75, New York City's expenditures rose at a rate almost three times the increase in the city's revenue from its own sources. Most of the difference was made up by intergovernmental revenues, with combined federal and state aid increasing from 32 percent of the city's budget in 1966 to 47 percent by 1973.

He found that city and state fiscal relationships were closely intertwined, with the election cycle being the most important variable in city-state budget negotiations. Haider noted that there is only one year in four in New York City when there is no federal, state, or city election. Since tax increases are generally perceived as a threat to elected officials, Haider hypothesized that tax increases would occur in the nonelection year. When he examined the election cycle since 1959, his hypothesis was confirmed. Tax increases generally occurred in the one-in-four off-years. There have been no major tax increases or impositions of new taxes by New York City in a citywide election year and none by the state in a statewide election year. All major revenue increases have been obtained in the odd-numbered fourth year of the cycle, except in 1965, when the state sales tax was imposed in a citywide election year. [43]

State-local fiscal relations are unique in another regard. In New York, the budget must be presented to the state legislature for passage of home rule provisions. Thus the state legislature, and the governor, were aware of the city's fiscal position. Actions taken by the state in 1971 clearly indicate that the state was aware of the "delicate" financial condition of New York City. The state largely accommodated a $400 million tax shortfall by freezing funds and postponing payments until the next year. The state amended the Local Finance Law to allow the city to overestimate revenues and to borrow against anticipated federal revenue-sharing funds. It created the New York City Stabilization Reserve Corporation to allow the city to borrow funds to repay past loans. "Thus the state agreed to permit the city to exceed its debt limitation, falsify revenue estimates and roll over its outstanding short-term debt."[44] The city charter requires that expenditure/revenue imbalance be covered by city council action to increase the property tax—yet this is impossible without state approval. Instead, a variety of "gimmicks" were used to "cure" the imbalance. For years the city borrowed up to 100 percent against revenues due from real estate taxes; the city counted as revenue in its last quarter revenue to be collected after the beginning of the next fiscal year, or sometimes pushed expenditures into the next fiscal year.

During the 1960s, New York City and New York State operated on two assumptions: First, that the federal government would eventually assume the cost of public welfare; and , second, that a growing economy would eventually allow both the city and state to increase revenues to the point where revenues would cover expenditures. As long as the city could continue to borrow, it could postpone disaster. National economic problems in the early 1970s, however, exacerbated the situation. A high rate of inflation, increased welfare costs, and declining revenues caused by the economic recession forced the city to increase its short-term borrowing. In one year, the amount of bond anticipation notes increased by 37 percent and revenue anticipation notes by 22 percent. New York City thus eventually accounted for 45 percent of all the short-term tax-exempt notes outstanding in the country. These events, along with the default of the New York State Urban Development Corporation (UDC) on $100 million in outstanding notes, finally dried up the market for New York City bonds.

The state was in only slightly better shape. The state had also been shut out of the money markets after unsuccessfully trying to sell bonds to aid the city. State debt had grown from $3.1 billion in 1961 to $13.4 billion in 1975. This fact, coupled with a series of poor economic indicators, made state debt a high risk. In addition, Governor Nelson Rockefeller (in the 1960s) devised a new system of financing capital programs that circumvented the constitutional requirement that full-credit borrowing receive voter approval. He created a system of public authorities and corporations (such as the New York State UDC), financing capital improvements by issuing "moral obligation bonds," which did not have the full faith and credit backing of the state. If investors were leery of city and state full-credit bonds, they were even more leery of debt with no legal obligation.

What happened in the city? Permanent default was averted when the state legislature created the Municipal Assistance Corporation (MAC) as an interim borrowing agent of the city; the federal government made $2.3 billion in short-term loans available to the city; the city payroll was reduced by 10 percent; a wage freeze was initiated; construction projects were halted; and pension fund contributions by city employees were increased.

More important from a political standpoint, however, was the creation of a board that fell just short of replacing Mayor Abraham Beame. The New York State Financial Emergency Act for the City of New York created the Emergency Financial Control Board to run the city's budget and approve all expenditures. The board is composed of the governor, the mayor, the state controller, and three other members appointed by the governor. Control of the budget has thus passed from elected city officials to the state. The state is now responsible for managing the fiscal affairs of New York City.

CIRCUMVENTING RESTRICTIONS

Why do states and cities find it necessary to circumvent their own legal restrictions? One important reason is the length of time required and difficulty in amending state constitutions. Since a portion of this chapter was concerned with New York City's fiscal crisis, it might be valuable to examine the constitution of New York (as of 1975) in this regard.[45] The process for amending the New York constitution is fairly typical of most states. Article XIX, Section 1, requires that proposed amendments to the constitution be submitted to the attorney-general, who must render an opinion on the proposed amendment with regard to its effect upon other provisions of the constitution. After the legislature receives the opinion, if the proposed amendment is agreed to by a majority of the members elected to each of the two houses, the amendment will be referred to the next regular legislative session convening after the succeeding general election of the members of the assembly. The proposed amendment must also be published for three months prior to consideration by the new legislature. If a majority of the members elected to each house approves the proposal, the legislature must submit the amendment to the voters for approval. If the majority of the voters approves, the amendment becomes a part of the constitution on the first day of January after such approval. The length of time such a process takes should be clear. In addition, the constitution requires that a majority of all members elected to each house must approve the amendment. Thus a member absent at the time of the vote, or a member abstaining, in effect casts a negative ballot.

The New York constitution limits the amount of revenue that can be raised by real estate taxes. Article VIII, Section 10, restricts the property taxes of cities of 125,000 population or more to only 2 percent of the assessed valuation (full value) over and above the amount required for debt payment. Thus the constitution places a strict limit on the property tax. The city of New York and the counties therein are further limited to a combined total of 2.5 percent.

Article VIII, Section 4, limits local indebtedness. New York City's debt limit is 10 percent of the value of the taxable real estate in the city.

Certain debts are excluded, however—debt for acquisition of railroad facilities, for example.

The obvious difficulty in amending the constitution plus the constitutional restriction placed on revenue sources exemplify the reasons cities and states resort to gimmicks to cover up revenue/expenditure imbalances. A "no-tax-increase" attitude among the citizens makes the task nearly impossible. Is it any wonder that New York's state and city officials sat around waiting for the federal government to assume the welfare burden?

How do states circumvent constitutional restrictions? In recent years states have resorted to circuit-breaker legislation to provide tax relief to low- and moderate-income homeowners and to changing the functional responsibilities of units of government to shift the costs of services.

Circuit-Breaker Legislation

Many states now have property tax relief programs for householders.[46] In 1965 only six states had programs to provide property tax relief to the elderly; today all 50 states and the District of Columbia have such programs. The most rapidly growing form of relief is "circuit-breaker" relief pioneered by Wisconsin in 1964.

As the name implies, circuit-breaker relief programs protect families from property tax "overload" just as an electric circuit breaker protects the home from current overload. When the property tax bill exceeds a set percentage of family income, the circuit breaker goes into effect and relief is granted to the taxpayer. Usually, although not always, the circuit-breaker program is a part of the state income tax program. When a taxpayer files a state income tax return, the state income tax administration examines the total reported income from all sources and computes the excess amount of property tax. The agency either credits the amount of relief against the state income tax due or, more frequently, issues the taxpayer a refund check.

There are a number of advantages of a circuit-breaker program over the more traditional homestead exemption. It can provide tax relief to those who need it most at a lower cost than homestead exemption; it can provide relief to both homeowners and renters; and it is less likely than the homestead exemption to encounter legal problems.

In most states, providing homestead exemption requires an amendment to the state constitution because of the constitutional uniformity clauses. Since circuit-breaker relief does not adjust taxable values or tax amounts, relief can be granted by statutory authority.

Changing Functional Responsibilites

Another significant trend in intergovernmental fiscal relations has been the recent tendency to reassign functional responsibilities.[47] Federal constitutional amendments, judicial interpretations, and an expanding system of grants to state and local governments have produced a substantial increase in federal involvement in what once were strictly state and local functions. Likewise, the dividing line between traditional state and local functions has been substantially altered or changed in recent years—largely through the adoption of constitutional home rule amendments. Thus, many local governments are authorized to exercise any power the legislature devolves except when forbidden by general law. In response to trends in urbanization, many states have enacted statutes transferring responsibility of functions from one local governmental unit to another or to the state. Economies of scale, a more even distribution of services, and a more equitable system of financing services are the major arguments in favor of an upward shift in functional responsibility.

Another reason has been the growing fiscal problems of cities. Many older cities have been experiencing serious financial problems due to a loss of population and tax base coupled with increasing demand for services. Thus, many municipalities have been only too happy to transfer functional responsibility for expensive services to the county, special districts, or the state. In 1968, after a strenuous lobbying effort by the Massachusetts League of Cities and Towns, the commonwealth assumed complete responsibility for public welfare.

However, only ten states have constitutional or statutory authority for the voluntary transfer of functional responsibility. Florida, New York, Ohio, Pennsylvania, and Vermont can transfer responsibility only with voter approval, while Alaska, California, Illinois, Michigan, and Virginia have no such requirement. Where city and county boundaries are not coterminous, voter approval is very difficult to obtain. Suburban taxpayers are not at all anxious to take up the costs of central-city-owned facilities or programs that tend to burden central-city residents.

The extension of constitutional home rule to counties has led to a higher level of assumption of functional responsibility among counties. The ACIR reports that a 1972 survey of counties in New York showed that charter counties provide an average of 35 different services while noncharter counties provide only 21.[48]

Many states have adopted statewide and regional authorities to assume responsibility for what were formerly state or local functions. New York, for example, has 42 such agencies. A number of other states are following this trend. Connecticut has five state-controlled authorities operating statewide, and Rhode Island nine. Other states utilizing this approach now include Minnesota, Maryland, Massachusetts, New Hampshire, Maine, and Florida.

In a recent survey of 3,319 municipalities, the ACIR found that 31 percent had transferred responsibility for one or more functions to another municipality, the county, special districts, or the state during the past ten years. Many of the transfers—hospitals, airports, ports, parks, libraries, and so on—were transfers from central cities to special districts to enlarge the tax base for their support. In other words, the transfer to a regional special district insured that suburban residents would pay for services that they also used.

The most common function transferred was law enforcement— making up 17 percent of the transfers. Other functions accounting for more than 5 percent of the transfers included public health (11 percent), sewage collection and treatment (10 percent), taxation and property assessment (9 percent), and social services (8 percent).

In terms of the future, the ACIR reports that municipalities favor county takeover of solid waste collection and disposal, law enforcement, and public health, while special districts are favored for transportation and sewage collection and treatment.

On the other hand, functional transfer is not always upward. Over 100 cities reported that they had assumed functions previously performed by the state government. Often these changes were mandated by state law. Many of the municipalities reported that state governments had mandated the performance of new functions that the municipalities had not previously performed.

The ACIR survey also found that a significant number of city managers, mayors, and other local officials believe that many other services should be assigned to counties and special districts. Services suggested for counties included public health, jails and detention homes, tax assessing and collection, election administration, public welfare, and all civil defense functions. Special districts were recommended for air, water, and noise pollution abatement; flood control; crime labs and police training; sewage disposal; solid waste disposal; and police and fire training.

SUMMARY AND CONCLUSIONS

In summary, there are clear indications that state and local revenue systems are changing rapidly. Intergovernmental transfers are becoming increasingly more important as sources of funds, especially intergovernmental transfers from the federal government. As federal aid increases, the property tax decreases in importance relative to other revenue sources. There has also been a clear trend for states to broaden the scope of their revenue sources. The rapid rise of the relative importance of state and local income taxes is indicative of the fact that more and more states are turning to heretofore untapped sources of revenue.

Yet some cities and states are still facing serious financial difficulties. Limitations placed on state and local revenue sources by the U.S. Constitution can hardly be faulted, however. While in many ways these restrictions are important, the brief summaries of the revenue systems of nine states presented in this chapter lead to the conclusion that adequate revenue sources are available to state and local governments to prevent the kinds of fiscal problems faced by New York State and New York City.

Although each state has many untapped or underutilized sources of revenue, the restrictive nature of many state constitutions makes it very difficult to use them. In most states the amendment process is long and cumbersome. Recent surveys show that, with few exceptions, citizens are not in favor of tax increases and are therefore unlikely to vote to liberalize the taxing powers of states and cities. The low-tax ethic pervasive in the country today and the feeling that state and local governments are not efficient spenders when compared to the federal government lead to an expectation of reduced growth for state and local governments.

Thus the major legislative response to fiscal emergencies has been to circumvent constitutional restrictions or alter the revenue/expenditure relationship. One way to circumvent restrictions on revenue is to rely increasingly on the use of deficit financing. State and local debt is increasing at a rate of over 9 percent a year with a growing emphasis on short-term debt.

Perhaps the best way to circumvent restrictions, however, is through the reassignment of functional responsibilities. Special districts now make up over 25 percent of all units of local government. Increasingly, areawide functions are being assigned to special districts to help alleviate the fiscal problems of central cities. In most states, special districts can be created without constitutional amendment; thus state legislatures may circumvent legal restrictions on municipal revenue sources by creating a new unit of government and transferring functional responsibilities and the accompanying expenditures to it. The revenue base is broadened by including suburbs in the new district, yet the city tax base is not necessarily reduced. The city may then devote the funds freed up by the functional transfer to other pressing needs.

We see no short-term changes in these trends on the horizon. Intergovernmental transfers will increase in importance, the reassignment of functional responsibility in an upward direction will continue, and states will slowly continue to broaden revenue sources. On the negative side, however, it is unlikely that the constitutional and statutory restraints on state and local revenue will be reduced. Local governments, especially cities, will continue to find diversification difficult— except by relying on even more intergovernmental aid. It is not likely that public attitudes will support major reforms, at least not in the next decade.

NOTES

1. W. Brooke Graves, *American Intergovernmental Relations: Their Origins, Historical Development, and Current Status* (New York: Charles Scribner's Sons, 1964), p. 438.

2. Richard H. Leach, *American Federalism* (New York: W. W. Norton and Co., 1970), pp. 196–97.

3. Charles L. Schultze et al., "Fiscal Problems of Cities," in *The Fiscal Crisis of American Cities*, ed. Roger E. Alcaty and David Mermelstein (New York: Random House, 1976), p. 216.

4. *Crew Levick Co.* v. *Pennsylvania*, 245 U.S. 292, 38 S. Ct. 126 (1917).

5. *Postal Telegraph Cable Co.* v. *Adams*, 155 U.S. 688, 15 S. Ct. 268 (1895).

6. *Maine* v. *Grand Trunk Ry. Co.*, 142 U.S. 217 (1891); *Wisconsin & M. Ry. Co.* v. *Powers*, 191 U.S. 379 (1903).

7. *Freeman* v. *Hewit*, 329 U.S. 249, 67 S. Ct. 274 (1946).

8. *Union Brokerage Co.* v. *Jensen et al.*, 322 U.S. 202, 64 S. Ct. 967 (1944); *Postal Telegraph-Cable Co.* v. *Richmond*, 249 U.S. 252, 259 (1919).

9. *Champlain Realty Co.* v. *Brattleboro*, 260 U.S. 366, 43 S. Ct. 146 (1922).

10. *Turner* v. *Maryland*, 107 U.S. 38, 2 S. Ct. 44 (1883); *Willcuts* v. *Bunn*, 282 U.S. 216, 51 St. Ct. 125, 128 (1931).

11. *Bonaparte* v. *Appeal Tax Court of Baltimore City*, 104 U.S. 592 (1882).

12. *Toomer et al.* v. *Witsell et al.*, 334 U.S. 385, 68 S. Ct. 1156 (1948).

13. *The American Oil Co.* v. *Neill*, 380 U.S. 451, 85 S. Ct. 1130 (1965).

14. *Cream of Wheat Co.* v. *Grand Forks*, 253 U.S. 325, 40 S. Ct. 558 (1920); *Welch* v. *Henry et al.*, 305 U.S. 134, 59 S. Ct. 121 (1938).

15. *State Tax Guide: All States* (New York: Commerce Clearing House, 1967; looseleaf updated through 1975), pp. 411–33.

16. G. Theodore Mitau, *State and Local Government: Politics and Processes* (New York: Charles Scribner's Sons, 1966), p. 9.

17. Russell W. Maddox and Robert F. Fuquay, *State and Local Government*, 3d ed. (New York: Van Nostrand, 1975), pp. 37–38.

18. Ibid., pp. 39–41.

19. See John A. Straayer, *American State and Local Government* (Columbus, Ohio: Merrill, 1973), pp. 52–55.

20. Maddox and Fuquay, op. cit., pp. 45–59.

21. Wade J. Newhouse, Jr., *Constitutional Uniformity and Equality in State Taxation* (Ann Arbor: University of Michigan Law School, 1959), pp. 11–600.

22. Ibid., pp. 3–4.

23. Ibid., pp. 767–70.

24. Robert M. Stein, "Federal Grant-In-Aid Programs: Equalization and the Application Process" (Ph.D. diss., University of Wisconsin-Milwaukee, 1977), pp. 1–3.

25. Much of the following material was taken from Graves, op. cit., pp. 478–573.

26. *Cornell University* v. *Fiske*, 136 U.S. 152 (1890); *Wyoming* v. *Irvine*, 206 U.S. 278 (1907).

27. For a brief description of these acts, and others, see Graves, op. cit., pp. 496–513.

28. *United States* v. *Butler*, 297 U.S. 1 (1936).

29. *Steward Machine Co.* v. *Davis*, 301 U.S. 548 (1937).

30. *Massachusetts* v. *Mellon* and *Frothingham* v. *Mellon*, 262 U.S. 447 (1923).

31. Richard D. Bingham, *Public Housing and Urban Renewal: An Analysis of Federal-Local Relations* (New York: Praeger Publishers, 1975), p. 2.

32. Advisory Commission on Intergovernmental Relations, *Fiscal Balance in the American Federal System*, vol. 1 (Washington, D.C.: Government Printing Office, 1967), p. 150.

33. U.S. Office of Economic Opportunity, *Catalog of Federal Domestic Assistance* (Washington, D.C.: Government Printing Office, 1970).

34. Leach, op. cit., pp. 16–17.

35. Richard P. Nathan, Allen D. Manvel, Susannah E. Calkins, *Monitoring Revenue Sharing* (Washington, D.C.: Brookings Institution, 1975), pp. 3–5.

36. Title I of the 1974 Housing and Community Development Act, P.L. 93-383.

37. Raymond A. Rosenfeld, "Implementation of the Community Development Block Grant Program: A Neighborhood Focus," paper presented at the Annual Meeting of the Southwestern Political Science Association, Dallas, March 30—April 2, 1977, pp. 3–6.

38. Unless otherwise noted, data for this section were taken from the *State Tax Guide: All States*, op. cit.

39. Advisory Commission on Intergovernmental Relations (ACIR), *City Financial Emergencies: The Intergovernmental Dimension* (Washington, D.C.: Government Printing Office, 1973).

40. Ibid., pp. 36–57.

41. Attiat F. Ott and Jang H. Yoo, *New York City's Financial Crisis: Can the Trend Be Reversed?* (Washington, D.C.: American Enterprise Institute for Public Policy Research, 1975), pp. 206.

42. Donald H. Haider, "Fiscal Scarcity: A New Urban Perspective," in *The New Urban Politics*, ed. Louis H. Masotti and Robert L. Lineberry (Cambridge, Mass.: Ballinger, 1976), pp. 171–215.

43. Ibid., p. 192.

44. Ibid., pp. 195–96.

45. Legislative Drafting Research Fund of Columbia University, *Constitutions of the United States National and State: New York* (Dobbs Ferry, N.Y.: Oceana Publications, 1975).

46. Advisory Commission on Intergovernmental Relations, *Property Tax Circuit Breakers: Current Status and Policy Issues* (Washington, D.C.: Government Printing Office, 1975).

47. Advisory Commission on Intergovernmental Relations, *Pragmatic Federalism: The Reassignment of Functional Responsibility* (Washington, D.C.: Government Printing Office, 1976).

48. Charles W. Jorgensen, *Survey of Functions at County Level: Fall 1972* (Albany: County Officers Association of the State of New York, 1972), reported in ACIR, *Pragmatic Federalism*, op. cit., p. 17.

3
Intergovernmental Revenue
from Washington

THE MIX OF FEDERAL AID

The purpose of this chapter is to cover the principal forms in which financial aid is received from Washington.[1] Federal aid has been growing rapidly. As a percent of total state and local general revenue, it has doubled in the last 20 years. In fiscal year 1977, federal aid to state and local governments increased by 22.6 percent over fiscal year 1976. This one-year increase, amounting to over $13 billion, was greater than the total amount of federal aid to state and local governments in 1966.[2]

Of course, there are ways of assisting state and local governments other than through intergovernmental payments. State and local governments benefit from federal old age and survivors' insurance because it reduces the need for public assistance. Also, where the economic policies of the national government have contributed to rising production and income, the result has been to enhance the state-local tax base.[3] In addition, the federal government could reduce its own taxes so that state and local governments might pick up the slack. To be successful, however, this move would require state and local governments to increase taxes, a proposal unlikely to be popular in this era of resistance to taxes. Alternatively, the federal government could wholly relinquish one or more of its taxes in hopes that they would be picked up by state or local governments. Again, however, state and local governments would find it difficult to take advantage of taxes vacated by the federal government because of opposition to tax increases, the legal restraints discussed in Chapter 2, and fear of placing themselves at a competitive disadvantage with other localities or states.[4]

Still more indirectly, the federal government might improve the revenue picture of local governments by assisting them in getting grants via federally funded regional planning bodies. There is recent evidence that regional planning assistance does indeed help localities secure federal grants requiring application. Federally funded regional planning bodies could target their assistance to localities with little skill in grantsmanship and thus improve these localities' capabilities to raise grant money.[5]

This chapter, however, focuses on the principal forms of intergovernmental aid: categorical grants, block grants, and general revenue sharing. Mention is also made of "countercyclical aid" and federal assumption of financial responsibility for previously state and local expenditures.

One way to organize federal aid in our thought is in terms of program discretion permitted recipient jurisdictions. "Categoricals" permit recipients to have very little program discretion. They require that federal funds be expended for specified purposes only and have quite specific planning, record-keeping, and reporting requirements as well. These "strings" are intended to insure that federal money will be spent for the purposes that the federal government intends. But strings make recipient governments unhappy.

Block grants permit a wider range of program discretion to recipient governments. The characteristics of block grants are as follows: (1) they authorize federal aid for a wide range of activities within a broad functional area; (2) they give recipient jurisdictions substantial program discretion; (3) they keep planning, reporting, and other requirements to a minimum, thus minimizing federal intrusion; (4) they award money on the basis of statutory formulas and thus provide a sense of fiscal certainty for recipients; and (5) eligibility provisions tend to favor general governments as against single- or special-purpose units.[6]

The least restrictive mechanism of federal assistance is general revenue sharing. It requires the federal government to share a percentage of its revenues with states and localities on a virtually no-strings basis.

Another necessary distinction is the difference between "project" grants and "formula" grants. Already mentioned as an attribute of block grants, distribution by formula makes use of a statutorily prescribed rule to determine which recipient governments get what amount of money. A project grant, in contrast, is awarded only on the basis of a federal agency approving a specific application from a state or local jurisdiction. Project grants are awarded to finance a particular operation that is defined in a narrow way in the application. An important point to keep in mind in distinguishing between formula and project grants is that the latter give allocational discretion to federal granting agencies. The way this discretion is exercised may cause conflict with state and local officials and their supporting interest groups.[7]

Project and formula-based categoricals are basic types. Formula-based categoricals may be further broken down into formula-project and formula-apportioned. Open-ended reimbursement grants are another type of categorical. In fiscal year 1975, there were 442 funded categorical grants for which state and local governments were eligible. (There were also over 145 nonfunded categorical grants.) Of the 442 funded grants, 296 were project grants requiring recipients to submit a specific application for each proposed project, with awards made by the administering federal agency on a competitive basis. Formula-project grants numbered 36 and specified a formula that determined the amount available to each successful applicant. There were 106 grants with funds allocated according to formula factors specified in legislation, or regulations promulgated by a federal agency. These constitute the formula-based group. The last type of categorical, open-ended reimbursement grants, requires the federal government to reimburse a specified portion of state-local program costs. Since all allowable expenditures are reimbursed, there is no direct competition for federal money among potential recipients; nor is there any need for an allocational formula. In 1975, this group included four major programs.[8]

We turn next to some of the pros and cons of the various mechanisms by which federal aid is allocated to state and local governments.

THE CATEGORICALS

Before 1966 nearly all federal aid to state and local governments was extended through categorical grants. That year the first block grant was created. Since 1966, major alterations have been made in the federal aid mix. In 1972, general revenue sharing was passed; in 1973 and 1974, three large block grants were enacted; and, in 1976, countercyclical assistance was authorized.[9]

Despite the growing congressional interest in other forms of assistance, categorical grants continue to occupy a predominant, although declining, position. In 1966 the categorical portion of the total federal aid package was 98 percent. By 1976, it was down to 79 percent,[10] and it is predicted to be 72 percent in 1977 and 1978.[11] The advent of general revenue sharing, block grants, and emergency measures suggests that the future role of categoricals in federal aid will be far different from their past role.

There are political reasons for the domination of categoricals in the federal aid system. The funding of project grant proposals has functioned as a kind of pork-barrel program; political motivations operate on administrators and congressmen alike. Congress is the architect of the categorical grant, which must be authorized and funded by Congress.[12] Categoricals reflect the preoccupation of individual congress-men with constituency interests and the comparatively narrow program focus that most congressmen have. Linked to these individual orientations is a subcommittee system that provides influence to nar-rowly focused, fluctuating coalitions that include program specialists and supportive groups. These factors have contributed to the narrower program emphasis reflected in categoricals.[13]

Besides narrower focus, another defining characteristic of categor-icals is federal control. These "strings" occasion much complaint. They are called needless, costly, and meddlesome. Typical of the control provisions associated with categoricals are the following: statements of permitted uses of funds (such as specifying by law how the funds are to be used or requiring the grantee to submit detailed plans of how the funds are to be used); expenditure constraints (such as that the money "supplement, not supplant" local funds); requirements that the grantee match the federal contribution with own-source funds; record-keeping and reporting requirements (for example, that grantees maintain ac-counting records of how they spent federal money); and requirements that nonaccounting data be supplied (such as reports on planned and actual resource use). Most categorical grant programs require the prep-aration of state or local plans as a condition of receiving aid, and most also require reports of program activities and accomplishments.[14] Still another requirement is "A-95 review" for project grants. Under a pro-gram set up by the Office of Management and Budget (OMB), local governments applying for a wide range of federally assisted projects must notify an authorized regional agency of their proposal. The re-gional agency reviews applications to ascertain conformity/noncon-formity to a regional comprehensive plan. However, the agency has only the power of comment. Regional bodies may not veto proposed projects.[15]

Narrow and restrictive though categoricals are, the extent of their restrictiveness can easily be exaggerated. Therefore, "federal interfer-ence" can easily be exaggerated. For one thing, formula-based categor-icals, as against project categoricals, assign no discretion to federal grant administrators in allocating the money, since who gets how much is fixed by statute. Similarly, open-ended categoricals assign a minimum of allocational discretion to federal administrators, since the rules that officials must use for allocation are fixed by Congress.[16] One important current program of an open-ended nature, Medicaid, is illustrative. Under Medicaid, the federal government pays 50 to 83 percent of state expenditures, depending upon the per capita income of the state. The states determine recipient eligibility and many of the services to be provided, and thus, in effect, they are permitted to define the program for themselves. The determination of need is made through their own legislative and administrative processes, and not by federal administrators or even through congressionally specified statistical measures.[17] Thus it is among project categoricals that the capacity of eligible recipients to play the federal grantsmanship game is a basic factor in getting an award. Therefore a big part of the criticism leveled against categoricals over the years applies only to project categoricals, and these are the fiscally less significant type. Formula-based categoricals are far more important in dollar terms than project categoricals. In 1974 project categoricals accounted for only about one-fourth of the total of federal intergovernmental aid, and about one-third of the dollar outlays within the categorical sector.[18] (On the other hand, project categoricals were about four-fifths of all types of grants in 1974, and this trend is reported to be continuing.)[19]

For other reasons as well, the term "categorical," if taken too literally, implies more restrictiveness than may really exist. In some cases it appears that the administration of a categorical program does not follow the categorical pattern:

> Title I of the Elementary and Secondary Education Act clearly was intended by Congress to operate as a formula based categorical program. Yet, during its early years, it might well have been a block grant, thanks to a combination of factors. These included: the looseness of the statutory definition of "educationally deprived children," the Office of Education's reluctance to provide directions regarding appropriate educational programs for this target group, and the vertical links between and among education professionals.[20]

Commonly, the responsibility for insuring the correct use of funds is delegated to state and local governments: The local agency is responsible for using funds correctly, and the state agency is responsible for enforcing correct usage at the local level. "In effect, the state is expected to function as an agent of the Federal Government for purposes of monitoring and enforcing compliance with Federal law." This practice of relying on the states to supervise the use of federal money, rather than on direct federal supervision, raises doubts about the adequacy of federal enforcement.[21]

A recent study is illustrative. In the implementation of national air and water pollution policies, federal administrators are required to achieve national objectives—for which Congress holds them accountable—by relying on state officials. Federal implementation policies permit the states to assume the major responsibility for planning, permitting, enforcement, and grant review. The states are the key actors and are required to establish processes through which they can coordinate local and regional pollution control.[22]

This framework gives the states an opportunity to bargain about the application of national objectives to themselves and their local units. Through negotiation they are able to tailor the implementation of national objectives to state and local goals and political circumstances.[23] Specifically, state administrators make use of the frequent uncertainty of the amount of federal money they will receive; they contend that they cannot plan adequately without an assurance of federal money in time to plan and that consequently they cannot accomplish federal requirements. In effect, state officials use this uncertainty to define pollution problems in terms of state priorities rather than federal priorities.[24] Also recipient states make use of the fact that data on air and water pollution problems are often incomplete or unsatisfactory. When a federal agency proposes specific actions, the state counters by saying that, given the data, the federal proposals are of questionable value— and, since it has been in the business longer, its own solutions are better. These events are better characterized as negotiation and compromise than central direction from "the feds."[25]

Another way in which state and local officials combat federal interference is by taking their disagreement with federal officials to congressmen or to federal bureaucrats in regional offices. In approaching the latter, a tactic commonly employed is to say that "if you are not flexible in your application of the law, we will dump responsibility on you." Other threats are also used. Texas pollution officials reacted to one particular exercise of federal discretion by threatening to send a letter to the regional administrator advising him that they would seek advice from an attorney and their congressman on the propriety of the action taken.[26] And the following came from a Louisiana pollution official:

> If EPA continues to hold up our program on insignificant things in our grant application, we'll go to our congressional delegation. I wanted to go the congressional delegation route last year, but EPA finally came through. But this year is a different matter. EPA is really being nitpicking. They are attempting to slap our wrist like children by letting us know they control the purse strings. Well, I don't think they can get away with it. It's not what Congress intended and we're going to let Congress know how they are treating us.[27]

The author of the pollution study concludes that federal implementation guidelines are adjusted according to problems within the states, the states' abilities to cope with their problems, and how state or local officials perceive them to apply. When a federal agency attempts to pursue national objectives, state and local officials can often block these efforts as being detrimental to them and their programs.[28]

There are other reasons why one must qualify generalizations about federal interference. Many of the specific restrictions are not effective. For example, specifications of allowable uses of funds may be effective in achieving federal objectives, or they may not be, depending on conditions. They will generally be effective if the federally supported activity is recognizably different from other activities undertaken by recipient jurisdictions and if the activity is one that the locality would not have undertaken in the absence of the federal grant.[29] Where these conditions are not met, recipient jurisdictions may use the federal money to displace their own funds and put them to other uses. Similarly, the standard provision that grants "supplement, not supplant" local funds can be circumvented. The nonsupplantation rule is by itself not an effective constraint because the amount that "otherwise would have been expended" cannot normally be ascertained.[30] Even matching requirements are not necessarily as restrictive as they appear. It is true that by requiring local matching the federal government may be able to exert leverage over more funds than it expends for grants. However, the effectiveness of matching depends upon whether the grantee would, in any event, have provided funds equal to or greater than those required by the matching formula. If so, the matching requirement has a zero net effect.[31] Also, record keeping and reporting may not be effective in insuring that federal grants are spent for the purposes intended by the federal government. A grant may be used entirely correctly in the accounting sense; but state or local funds that would have been spent for the same purposes may be diverted to other uses. As is sometimes said, "all money is green." It is most difficult to determine what money is spent for what purpose. Therefore the net economic impact—that is, the difference between the total amount spent for the grant-aided activity and the amount that would otherwise have been spent in the absence of the grant—may be less than the effect recorded on the books. Furthermore, the grantee will have been afforded the opportunity to spend the money freed by the federal grant for purposes having a high priority to him.[32]

Nor do required reports on program activities and accomplishments guarantee that the money will be spent for federally intended purposes. That goal is generally not achieved, for the following reasons: (1) descriptions of planned and actual programs do not contain quantitative information on resource use (meaning that it is hard to ascertain whether the planned use was accomplished or not); (2) information on resource use is not reported in standard or comparable forms by different grantees; and (3) data are rarely included that would permit comparisons of the resources provided to, say, children who are served and those who are not served by the federal program. In short, the planning and reporting requirements do not permit comparative analysis of whether the money was expended as planned.[33]

The point is that federal controls or strings depend for their effectiveness on a variety of conditions. And opportunities exist to substitute federal funds for own-source funds. This "fungibility" is particularly easy to accomplish in larger jurisdictions that provide a wide range of services, that have been spending sizable amounts of their resources in the aided areas, and that have professionally skillful accounting personnel.[34]

Even penalty mechanisms are not as restrictive as one might expect. The usual penalties are withholding or suspension of funds and the requirement that funds spent illegitimately be returned, but these sanctions are so drastic that they are seldom applied. Consequently, the present system is largely one of voluntary compliance.[35]

All these facts should be taken into account in generalizing about federal controls or interference.

BLOCK GRANTS

Block grants are a common focal point of discussions about federal strings—precisely because they are designed to reduce the discretion of federal program administrators and add to the discretion of state and local officials. The key characteristic of block grants is their decentralization of decision-making authority over planning, program choice, and resource allocation. Accordingly, the federal role is not as intrusive. They are lauded for other reasons as well. When a number of categoricals are consolidated into broader programs of assistance, there is the potential to curb the overlap and duplication of the narrowly specified categoricals and thus to lower personnel costs, reduce paper work, and accelerate the flow of funds to the real problems.[36]

While block grants do give wide discretion to recipients in planning for and allocating funds, this decentralization has in practice been limited by a tendency toward "creeping categorization." Partly due to political pressures, Congress has added restrictions to activities within the scope of the block grant, or has established categoricals around it. Health and crime control are two areas that have experienced creeping categorization. Since 1966, eighteen categoricals have been enacted as separate programs and not incorporated within the Partnership for

Health block grant. Also, between 1970 and 1976 Congress added new categories to the Safe Streets Act or earmarked block grants for narrower-than-usual purposes like corrections, juvenile justice, and neighborhood crime prevention. There has thus been a dramatic increase in statutory requirements in the crime control program. This creeping categorization has converted most of the existing block grants into hybrid block-categorical programs and thus reduced the amount of grantee discretion.

Their discretion has been further reduced by the growth of government-wide requirements. Applicants for crime control block grants, for example, must certify their compliance with the provisions of 27 statutes covering such subjects as animal welfare, historic site preservation, clean air, safe drinking water, solid waste disposal, and discrimination.[37]

The block grant design calls for the basic policy decisions to be made in recipient jurisdictions by those who are elected officials or top administrators. Such officials are presumed to be more aware of and accountable to the needs and preferences of the general public than program specialists. The idea is to restore the elected official or chief administrative officer to an authoritative position in the flow of federal aid. However, it is not necessarily true that generalists have the interest, commitment, or capacity to attend carefully to the important decisions relating to a block grant. The federal block grant programs are Partnership for Health, established in 1966 to help states and localities develop comprehensive health plans; the Omnibus Crime Control and Safe Streets Act of 1968; the Housing and Community Development Act of 1974; the Comprehensive Employment and Training Act of 1973, a manpower training program; and Title XX of the Social Security Act of 1974, a program of social services for persons previously covered under aid to the blind, aged, and disabled, and aid to families with dependent children. In fact, when the generalist is a part-time official, when the aided function is not a traditional activity or one heavily supported by own-source revenues, when the program is technical or complex, and when the federal funding is small, "generalists" have not become the key actors in the decision process. In such cases, specialists continue to be highly influential. On the other hand, when the federally aided area is controversial or politically sensitive, generalists may be expected to play a major role. The point is that block grants give generalists the opportunity to become involved in decision making relative to federal grants, but whether they become involved depends on conditions.[38] Therefore, an important attribute of this delivery mechanism may or may not be realized. And if we know that a device will be effective only under special circumstances, we can validly infer that its effectiveness in the real world will be low.[39]

An administrative advantage of block grants is also suggested. Supporters argue that the wide range of activities authorized by a block grant facilitates inter- and intradepartmental coordination at the federal level and enhances the coordination of the activities of counterpart agencies at state and local levels. Experience with existing block grants shows, however, that they do not meet the conditions necessary to achieve a tight system of coordination. If the scope of a block grant encompassed substantially all the federal assistance in a functional area, without a large number of categoricals in the same area, coordination would be greatly encouraged. However, this is not generally the case. The point is that coordination may be confined to only those activities supported by the federal block grant and may therefore fall short of becoming a general system of coordination.[40]

Since all of the existing block grant programs (except crime control) emerged from a consolidation of categorical aids, it is often thought that this device could be used to reduce the duplication of various functionally related programs and the overall number of federal grants as well. The prospects for expanded use of this "middleman" of the federal aid system are mixed, however. Although proponents of block grants have been successful in five instances, there have been several setbacks. In the 1950s and 1960s grant consolidations were proposed in public health and welfare, vocational education, libraries, waste treatment facilities, and other functional areas. All were defeated or ignored. More recently, President Gerald Ford's proposal to replace 59 categorical programs with four block grants for health, education, child nutrition, and community social services suffered the same fate.

Existing block grants are not an unqualified success either. In terms of dollars and constituent support, most of these programs dim by comparison with functionally related formula and project categoricals not incorporated into existing block grants.[41]

Reformers who would give a greater role to block grants have to face the fact that the consolidation of categoricals disturbs vested interests and also that consolidation produces tension in the intergovernmental system as questions are raised about whether various recipients will get more or less under the new program, and how. Of course, the prospects for success are enhanced if existing recipients are provided with some insurance that they will not lose federal dollars through conversion. But experience with the five programs that embody block grant features indicates that appropriations do not significantly increase and may decrease. In crime control, the fiscal year 1978 request for block grant appropriations is slightly less than the fiscal year 1971 expenditure level.[42] This figure suggests the existence of losers.

GENERAL REVENUE SHARING

The State and Local Fiscal Assistance Act of 1972, which established what is commonly considered to be general revenue sharing, was designed to shift still more discretion from Washington to state and local units. This act grants responsibility for spending shared revenue to the elected officials of general-purpose units of government, and it allows them wide latitude in their use of the funds. The State and Local Fiscal Assistance Act marks a departure from the past in other ways too. In its division of funds, the act favors local governments over the states: Local governments receive two-thirds of each year's allocation. The act allows state officals to spend their share of the funds as they choose, with only one restriction—the money cannot be used as state matching funds for other federal aid programs. Local officials also cannot use the money for matching purposes, but they are allowed to spend it for a variety of broad "priority funding categories" defined in the law: public safety, environmental protection, public transportation, health, recreation, libraries, social services for the poor and aged, financial administration, and ordinary and necessary capital expenditures.[43]

Revenue-sharing funds are available to all states, counties, municipalities, and townships. In addition, Indian tribes and Alaskan villages are eligible. The act provides for two alternative methods of dividing funds among the states and their local units. There is a three-variable formula and a five-variable formula, with the formula producing the higher yield to be applied. The three-factor formula uses state population, per capita income of state residents, and total state-local tax effort. The five-factor formula uses in addition the urbanized population of the state and state income tax collections.

The State and Local Fiscal Assistance Act of 1972 is an important development in intergovernmental fiscal relations because it gives state and local officials a substantial amount of federal money with a high degree of certainty and few restrictions on use.[44] In 1976 general revenue sharing was extended for 3.75 years.

COUNTERCYCLICAL AID

Also part of the mix of federal assistance is a very recent program enacted under one section of the Public Works Employment Act of 1976. In July 1976, countercyclical, antirecession aid for state and local governments was authorized at $1.2 billion for five quarters—with allocations based on unemployment rates. One-third of the money goes to states and two-thirds to local governments. Countercyclical aid may be used for the operating expenses of state and local governments.[45]

Proponents were concerned that during recessions state and local governments would be forced to act in a way that is opposite to federal economic policy. When Washington is trying to stimulate recovery by cutting taxes and increasing federal spending, state and local governments face increased welfare rolls and reduced tax revenues, which create pressure to reduce services, lay off employees, and raise taxes. Proponents argued that this legislation was necessary to help stabilize state-local budgets and to prevent state and local governments from making layoffs and deferring projects, decisions that might further aggravate the recession.

Opponents argued that state and local governments would waste the money or spend it in ways that create relatively few jobs.[46] Opponents are also unhappy over the fact that some very wealthy towns have gotten money under countercyclical aid. Palm Springs, California, for example, got over $100,000, and Palm Desert got almost $10,000. Allotments to such less-than-needy communities are made all the more controversial by the fact that the unemployment statistics used to determine their allocations come from a methodology that the Bureau of Labor Statistics (BLS) concedes is not accurate at the local level. The reason is that BLS compiles unemployment statistics through a national survey of 50,000 households, much like a Gallup poll. This sample is big enough to make valid estimates of the national rate but is too small to estimate state and local rates. And most local communities do not keep records of their own rates of joblessness. Federal money given to Palm Springs and Palm Desert was based on a calculation that each had an unemployment rate of 9.2 percent. This was derived by taking the jobless rate for Riverside County—which contains the two towns and some areas of high unemployment—and subtracting any community that kept its own unemployment figures. The city managers of Palm Springs and Palm Desert concede that the 9.2 percent figure is excessive.

The head of the Bureau of Labor Statistics says that he has been warning Congress for years that much federal aid is distributed on the basis of faulty unemployment figures, but no one listens.[47]

FEDERAL ASSUMPTION OF FINANCIAL RESPONSIBILITY

One option regarding federal assistance exists in the realm of potential; it would have the federal government assume full financial responsibility for functions now heavily financed from state and local sources. It has been recommended, for example, that the federal government assume full financial responsibility for all public welfare programs.[48] Ever since the 1930s, some sharing has taken place through categorical aids for assistance to the elderly, dependent children, the blind, and the totally disabled, but not for general assistance. In 1972 a first step toward full assumption of welfare costs was taken when the adult categories of assistance (old age, blind, disabled) were "federalized." Social Security Act amendments provided a federal plan of assistance, established federal definitions of eligibility, and allowed the states to supplement national payment if they wish.

Although these activities fall short of full federal assumption and deal only with the less controversial programs of public assistance, advocates of federal assumption believe that it was a step in the right direction. The argument is that the federal government can bring its superior fiscal power to the aid of the state and local governments by this means and that these programs are already so dominated by federal policy that complete federal financing makes sense. It is also noted that the welfare problem does not respect state boundaries.

An important motivation behind this idea is to relieve the strained financial capacity of state and local governments. The cost of public assistance is an important element of that strain. If the federal government were to assume the entire cost of existing public assistance programs, about two-thirds of the benefits would go to the states. Where much of this load is now carried locally, and this includes some of the most urbanized states, such as California and New York, local fiscal burdens would also be substantially lightened.[49]

Proponents have pointed out on behalf of state and local governments that the funding of public assistance now relies heavily on property and sales taxes, which generally hit the poor harder than those who are better off. In contrast, federal funding would call upon a source that is far more progressive, the income tax.[50]

Federal assumption of financial responsibility, if administrative responsibility is left to the states and localities (which is what the ACIR recommends), implies that categorical or block grant mechanisms would be used to transfer the money. The block grant mechanism would of course give more responsibility to state and local officials.

CONCLUSIONS

The mix of federal aid instruments is changing.

The national government now shares a percentage of its revenues with states and localities on a virtual no-strings basis and is likely to continue to do so (for example, in 1976 general revenue sharing was extended). The block grant has been introduced and extended; and there are those who think that still greater use should be made of block grants in order to widen state and local discretion to use federal funds in a way more relevant to their own priorities.[51]

In any reconsideration of federal aid, it is clear that congressional politics and interest-group politics will be intimately involved. Besides the balance of affected interests, many other questions arise when the mix of federal assistance is addressed. For example, can the most appropriate uses of the different grant types be clarified? Can the program fragmentation that arises from categoricals focusing on narrow activities and specific client groups be curbed through grant consolidations without undermining the ability of categoricals to target federal funds to areas of real need? Can better measures of program need be developed and incorporated into grant formulas, and can Congress avoid the inclusion of conflicting allocational factors in the same grant program? What grant controls should be used, and what grant controls should not be used? Would enactment of legislation authorizing grant consolidations by the president, subject to congressional veto (a procedure comparable to executive reorganization), bring about desirable grant reform? Can "national purpose" as it relates to grants-in-aid be given anything other than a political definition?[52]

There are no easy answers to these questions. But one can be sure that they will be asked, and probably answered—however satisfactorily or unsatisfactorily to the affected interests—in years to come.

NOTES

1. Advisory Commission on Intergovernmental Relations, *Improving Urban America: A Challenge to Federalism* (Washington, D.C.: ACIR, 1976), p. 83.

2. "A Fiscal Note," *Intergovernmental Perspective* 3 (Spring 1977): 20.

3. ACIR, op. cit., p. 83.

4. Joseph A. Pechman, "Financing State and Local Government" (Washington, D.C.: Brookings Institution, 1965), pp. 78–79.

5. Brett W. Hawkins and Robert M. Stein, "Regional Planning Assistance: Its Distribution to Local Governments and Relationship to Local Grant Getting," *Journal of the American Institute of Planners* 43 (July 1977): 279–88.

6. ACIR, op cit., pp. 90–91.

7. Ibid., p. 87.

8. David B. Walker, "Categorical Grants: Some Clarifications and Continuing Concerns," *Intergovernmental Perspective* 3 (Spring 1977): 14–15.

9. Carl W. Stenberg, "Block Grants: The Middlemen of the Federal Aid System," cited in Walker, op. cit., p. 8.

10. Ibid.

11. Walker, op. cit., p. 15.

12. Ibid., p. 18.

13. Ibid. and ACIR, op. cit., p. 88.

14. Stephen M. Barro, "Federal Education Goals and Policy Instruments: An Assessment of the 'Strings' Attached to Categorical Grants in Education," a Rand Working Note Prepared for the Department of Health, Education and Welfare, February 1977, pp. 20–30.

15. See Advisory Commission on Intergovernmental Relations, *Regional Decision Making: New Strategies for Substate Districts* (Washington, D.C.: ACIR, 1973).

16. Walker, op. cit., p. 16.

17. Advisory Commission on Intergovernmental Relations, draft of a chapter on issues in federal grant allocation, April 1977, pp. 39–52, forthcoming in "Categorical Grants: Their Role and Design."

18. ACIR, *Improving Urban America*, op.cit., pp. 87–88.

19. Ibid., p. 87.

20. Walker, op. cit., p. 16. An interesting study that presents evidence in a similar vein is Floyd Stoner, "Implementation of Ambiguous Language: Title I of the Elementary and Secondary Education Act," unpublished Ph.D. dissertation, Political Science, University of Wisconsin—Madison, 1976. See also David O. Porter et al., "How Effective Are Grantor Controls?" in *Transfers in an Urbanized Economy*, ed. Kenneth E. Boulding, Martin Pfaff, and Anita Pfaff (Belmont, Calif.: Wadsworth, 1973), pp. 276–302.

21. Barro, op. cit., p. 22.

22. Robert D. Thomas, "Intergovernmental Coordination in the Implementation of National Air and Water Pollution Policies," in Charles O. Jones and Robert D. Thomas eds., *Public Policy Making in a Federal System* (Beverly Hills, Calif.: Sage Publications, 1976), pp. 129, 131.

23. Ibid., p. 132.

24. Ibid., p. 135.

25. Ibid., pp. 135–37.

26. Ibid., pp. 141–43.

27. Ibid., p. 144.

28. Ibid., pp. 145–46.

29. Barro, op. cit., p. 22.

30. Ibid., p. 23.

31. Ibid., pp. 25–26.

32. Ibid., pp. 16–17.

33. Ibid., pp. 29–30.

34. Ibid. for more details.

35. Ibid., p. 30.

36. Stenberg, op. cit., pp. 9–10; and Stenberg and David B. Walker, "The Block Grant: Lessons from Two Early Experiments," *Publius* 7 (Spring 1977): 54.

37. Stenberg, op. cit., p. 10.

38. Ibid., p. 11.

39. Barro, op. cit., p. 19.

40. Stenberg, op. cit., p. 12.

41. Ibid., pp. 11–12.

42. Ibid., p. 12–13.

43. Robert D. Reischauer, "General Revenue Sharing—The Program's Incentives," in *Financing the New Federalism*, ed. R. P. Inman et al. (Washington, D.C.: Resources for the Future, 1975), p. 83.

44. ACIR, *Improving Urban America*, op. cit., p. 77.

45. Carol S. Weissert, "Restraint and Reappraisal: Federalism in 1976," *Intergovernmental Perspective* 3 (Winter 1977): 11.

46. Ibid.

47. "Palm Springs, Other Wealthy Towns Getting Federal Aid," *Christian Science Monitor,* May 16, 1977.

48. ACIR, *Improving Urban America,* op. cit., p. 16.

49. Ibid., pp. 70–76, 16.

50. Ibid., p. 75.

51. ACIR, *Improving Urban America,* op. cit., p. 16.

52. Walker, op. cit., p. 19.

4

Bias, Benefit, and Other Effects of Federal Aid

Are federal aid allocations fair or not fair? What kind of states and localities receive relatively more federal aid? Is aid "equalizing"—that is, does it reduce disparities among recipient jurisdictions in their fiscal resources, levels of services, or tax burdens borne by their citizens? What are the effects of, and what interests are affected by, changes in federal aid programs?

DISTRIBUTIVE BIAS AND BENEFIT

We first consider how aid is apportioned among recipient jurisdictions. In recent years there has been a lot of controversy about the distribution formulas employed in federal aid. It is alleged that the formulas are unfair to certain cities, or to particular states and regions. According to some, the bias results from premeditated, wholly political actions.[1] However, it is not a simple matter to determine the biases of federal aid. Different methods of analysis yield different conclusions, and the impression is sometimes left that a given method is intentionally chosen in order to reach preferred conclusions. Furthermore, a "bias" is significantly a matter of one's values. Analysis is also complicated by the existence of numerous and sometimes competing "bases of distribution" (or allocational factors)* in the same aid programs. Because these bases may offset each other, the presence of a base in a formula does not necessarily mean that money is allocated according to that base. Admittedly, mutiple-factor formulas reflect the political compromises necessary to enact programs of intergovernmental aid. But it

---

*These refer to variables such as median income, road miles, and percentage of housing that is dilapidated.

71

is important to be aware of a potential cost of this process—namely, the possibility that no single distribution base significantly governs the allocation of aid.

Analysis of how benefits are distributed proceeds along three principal lines. First, inferences about beneficiaries are made from the bases employed in aid formulas. For example, an aid program may be designated beneficial to jurisdictions with poorer inhabitants if a major component of its formula allocates proportionately greater amounts of aid to jurisdictions with lower incomes. We have already noted, however, that the mere presence of a factor in a formula does not necessarily mean that it governs actual allocations to any significant degree. Distributive effects can also be analyzed by making inferences from legislative goals. Allocational intentions may be implied by such goals. However, it should be noted that the design of most aid programs reflects the actions of many interest groups. To accommodate this multiplicity, legislative statements of goals are often very general. Also, implicit or concealed goals may be involved.[2] A third approach is to correlate aid receipts with characteristics of recipient units. This method contributes empirical evidence of the way aid benefits are distributed among different kinds of localities. For example, one might correlate per capita federal aid with per capita personal income and, if a sizable negative correlation emerges, infer both that the aid is equalizing (with respect to income)[3] and that jurisdictions with relatively lower incomes receive relatively larger program benefits.

A recent survey by the ACIR reveals that a variety of allocational factors have been used in distributing federal aid. Again, one must remember that aid money is not necessarily allocated according to a factor that appears in a formula, though it may be. The ACIR focuses on four principles: political fair share (as indicated by population or equal amounts), need for services (or program need), the actual level of services or costs, and fiscal equalization.[4]

Political Fair Share

The concept of an equal share per state is basic to the American political system. It constitutes an important principle in the Constitution and is reflected in the composition of the U.S. Senate. The contrasting principle, equal share per person, is also deeply rooted in the American system and is reflected in the composition of the House of Representatives. Nowadays, greater use is made of population than the equal state shares approach; but, even so, various devices are utilized to protect the financial interests of the smaller states.[5]

There are 28 categorical programs in which total population enters into the allocational formula (1975 figures). In three of these, total population is the sole distributive factor: the hunter safety program, vocational rehabilitation services innovation and expansion grants, and law enforcement and criminal justice basic grants for correctional institutions and facilities. Of course, where an allocational factor is the only formula factor, one can confidently infer that it significantly governs allocations. However, two of these programs include a minimum allocation, and one includes a maximum.[6] Such restrictions generally limit the operation of other formula variables and in this case work to the advantage of smaller states. Among all categorical formula programs—including programs with a variety of allocation formulas—38 categorical formula programs include a minimum entitlement, and there are 14 in which funding in a prior year fixes a minimum allotment. There are also 14 programs that provide a maximum allotment.[7]

Population is a factor in the formulas of four of the five major block grant programs and enters as well into the distribution of general revenue-sharing funds. It enters also into determining eligibility for a number of grants.[8] In addition, total population seems more important than a simple count of its use in grant formulas indicates, since some of the programs with a population factor—including general revenue sharing and some of the block grants—are comparatively large. Further, it appears that many of the measures of "need" used in other grants—for example, various population subgroupings, like percent poor—are highly correlated with total population.[9]

Total population has been criticized as an allocation factor. The key criticism seems to be that population fails to reflect accurately the need for services. For example, its use in block grants for community development has been criticized on the grounds that the number of residents in a city has little relationship to its need for community development activities.[10]

Of course, if total population is regarded as a measure of political equity rather than need, the validity of this criticism disappears. Where population represents political equity, it makes no difference that it is an imperfect measure of need. (It does make a considerable difference, of course, to those who think that grants ought to be distributed according to need and not political equity.)

Another problem with total population is the technical one of accurately estimating the populations of states and cities. Census data collected every ten years can rapidly become inaccurate, due to population shifts, declines, and increases.[11] The city of Milwaukee was so unhappy with the official census report of its 1970 population that it financed a recount, which, unfortunately for the city, showed a smaller count than the Census enumeration. That outcome was far from amusing to Milwaukee officials, who faced a decline in both state and federal aid as a result of having fewer people than previously thought.

We turn next to research evidence of whether larger or smaller jurisdictions benefit from federal aid. Unfortunately, current empirical evidence does not provide an unambiguous answer to the question. There is some evidence that population size does have a guiding effect on the allocation of aid. For example, the ten largest states receive the ten largest grant totals, although not precisely in order of their size.[12] Also, differences in total grant money per capita to state and local governments are comparatively small and have been falling; they were much greater 30 years ago.[13] (Note that "per capita" figures represent a control for population. Small and falling differences, when population is controlled, suggest that population does guide allocations, since controlling it reduces the variation in amounts received among the states.) On the other hand, there is some evidence that population does not significantly guide federal aid money. For example, there is a persisting (but not large) negative relationship between population size and per capita grants to states over the period 1942 to 1972.[14] Thus, the smaller-population states tend to receive slightly higher per capita benefits than do the larger states. This result (states with smaller populations receiving higher per capita grants) holds for many specific types of grants: project grants, formula grants, nonwelfare grants, high matching grants, low matching grants, and grants to local governments.[15] (One might object to this analysis on logical grounds. By using per capita grant awards, one has controlled for population and produced a statistic that is standardized relative to population. Why ascertain if such a measure correlates with population? Evidently, it is because of a special interest in per capita awards independent of total awards.)

Beyond the obvious point that population size is not a powerful guide to federal aid distributions, it is not easy to describe how population relates to aid benefits. Conclusions depend on what evidence is selected. Significantly, it is also unclear whether population is primarily intended as a measure of "need" or "political fair share," or in what programs it is intended as a measure of one or the other. This confusion supports the ACIR's observation that there has been "a failure to sort out clearly the basic purposes for which the national government should extend aid to state and local governments."[16]

The other political fair-share criterion is allocation in uniform amounts. There are 31 programs in which an equal amount of assistance is distributed to each state. In only two of these, however, is "equal amounts" the sole allocational factor: assistance to state institutes for water resources research, and basic grants to the states for the promotion of the arts. In all the other programs having a provision for uniform amounts, the provision operates within a multifactor formula; and there its chief effect is to provide a minimum grant for each state, with additions dependent on the other formula factors. The fair-share principle is also reflected in the even more common practice of imposing minimum or maximum allotments for each recipient; these have already been discussed. However, it has not been pointed out that these provisions probably account, at least in part, for the tendency of the smaller-population states to receive higher per capita benefits than the larger states. This result can be interpreted as reflecting the Senate-like fair share principle.[17]

"Hold-harmless" provisions are another application of the fair-share idea. Included in community development and manpower block grants, these provisions protect recipients against sudden drops in receipts caused by the change from project categorical grants to the new formula block grant.[18] Hold-harmless provisions often phase in losses gradually over a period of years.

Need for Services

Another principle commonly employed in federal grant allocations is "need for services." We have already seen that total population is sometimes regarded as a generalized indicator of this need.[19] Need for services is "by far the most important allocational principle."[20] However, the principle can be general or specific: It can refer to a need for general financial help or to a need for specific services. Need can refer to the general fiscal resources of a jurisdiction, or it can refer to the level of a particular service. In a sense, program need and fiscal need provide competing principles by which allocation formulas may be designed or evaluated;[21] a grant for sewer construction, for example, may do little to help the overall fiscal picture while an unrestricted grant may not get a needed sewer built.

A common measure of need is the count or percentage of some population subgroup based on Census data; examples are "number of school-age children" or "percent urban." Some 55 formulas use a segment of the population as a distribution factor.[22] Various income-related statistics other than per capita income (which is commonly regarded as an indicator of governmental fiscal capacity, not service need) appear in 12 programs. Land area appears in 10 programs. Financial assistance for boating safety takes into account the number of vessels included under the state boat-numbering systems.[23]

Controversy persists over the appropriateness and validity of various indicators of need. Many of the criticisms are self-serving, in the sense that they represent a claim that the needs of one's own state, city, neighborhood, or group are not treated "equitably" under existing formulas. Claims about "better," "more equitable," or "fairer" measures vary with the claimant's social or political controversy.

Additionally, whether a better or more equitable measure of need makes a real difference when employed in an allocation formula depends on what other principles, using what other operational measures, are also employed in the formula. Better or more equitable measures make little difference, other than symbolic, if they are canceled by the operation of other factors.

It is even difficult to talk about this issue without using loaded language. Simple differences are easily transformed into something suggesting bias and unfair political manipulation by the use of words like "inequitable" and "disparity."

There are, however, some clearly dubious practices and oddities. For example, urban population is used in the formula that distributes grants for mass transportation. The formula results in highly unequal aid per transit ride—for example, two cents per ride in New York City and forty-five cents in Grand Rapids, Michigan.[24] Grants under Title I of the Elementary and Secondary Education Act are designed to help students suffering "educational deprivation." The latter is measured in the formula with statistics not on educational performance but on children 5–17 who are from poor families, from families receiving aid to families with dependent children, or living in institutions.[25]

A recent ACIR study concludes that the use of data on population subcategories to determine awards provides only a rough indication of actual service needs. These data also have many of the same problems of currency and accuracy that affect population totals, plus an additional problem. While the Census Bureau provides annual estimates of the total population of each state, such estimates are not made for many subcategories of population. It is therefore all the more likely for these measures to be inaccurate.[26]

Of course, it can be argued that public officials cannot await the development of perfect measures of program need; they must get on with the effort to target federal dollars to adjudged needs. On the other hand, it seems wise to consider that invalid measures may result in supposedly targeted funds not reaching the target. A 1973 study illustrates the problem, by showing that per capita grants in the fields of health, education, and welfare are haphazardly related to percent of poor families. For public assistance grants, the correlation is only .09, for health grants .06, and for education grants .10. For health, education, and welfare generally, it is only a modest .28. The authors conclude that there is no consistent pattern of distribution to states where there are poor persons and poor governments, despite the fact that grants in these fields are intended to benefit poor persons.[27] Another study concluded that expenditures for water pollution control appeared to be independent of the location of water pollution.[28]

Such studies raise doubts about whether the beneficiaries of federal aid programs are necessarily the jurisdictions in need of assistance, even as this is defined by the programs themselves. Consequently, one cannot always be confident about what kind of jurisdictions actually receive relatively more aid benefits. And even if we know with certainty the characteristics of states or localities that benefit from some federal aid program, it does not follow that we know about the pattern of resource use within these jurisdictions. Is the money used to meet needs? According to whose definition? We do know that the opportunity exists for states and localities to substitute federal dollars for purposes determined by themselves.

A recent, extensive, and systematic study of the relationship between need and federal aid has not clarified the picture. It employs three rough indicators of general service need: per capita income, percent of population living in urban areas, and total population. Greater need is represented by lower-income, more urban, and larger populations. The question is, Do federal grant moneys respond to interstate variations in need? The study first looks at the correlation between per capita federal grants and income, urbanization, and population size in the years 1942, 1962, 1967, and 1972. These correlations suggest that states with higher incomes tend to benefit from federal grants. This is the opposite of responding to need, but the relevant correlations are very small. Only for one year, 1942, is the correlation even moderately large (.31). Other correlations suggest that rural states are the principal beneficiaries of federal grants; there is a persistant negative correlation between urban population and grants per capita. However, the correlations are again tiny, none exceeding −.21. Finally, the correlations indicate that the states with smaller populations get more grant money per capita.[29] What emerges from this set of correlations is little evidence that federal grants respond to state needs.

Complications arise when this same study examines "various cuts of the grant system." Although the relationship of per capita income to total per capita federal aid is positive (1972), the relationship between per capita income and per capita formula grants is negative, although very small (−.11). The relationship is also negative for project grants, grants to state governments, high-matching grants, low-matching grants, no-matching grants, high-matching formula grants to states

(–.83), low-matching formula grants to states, no-matching formula grants to states, high-matching project grants to states, low-matching project grants to states, no-matching project grants to local governments, and undetermined project grants to local governments. On the other hand, the relationship is positive for grants to local governments, low-matching formula grants to local governments, no-matching formula grants to local governments, no-matching project grants to states, high-matching project grants to local governments (.33), low-matching project grants to local governments, and low-matching project grants to state and local governments. It is not easy to see a pattern in all this. Per capita income is positively related to aggregate per capita federal grants, but in 13 of 21 "cuts" of the aid system income and grants are negatively related.[30]

It is clearer that federal grants tend to favor rural and less populated states and localities. However, even here the degree of favoring is not large.

There is little wonder that the ACIR has recommended that executive departments and agencies be required to review periodically "the adequacy of the need indexes employed in their respective grant programs."[31]

Reimbursement Programs

Still another principle for distributing federal aid is the reimbursement of state and local expenditures. The prototypical grant of this kind is the open-ended matching program described in Chapter 3. Such a program means that more federal assistance goes to jurisdictions that provide a higher level of service. In their pure form, these grants reimburse all allowable expenditures without limit, and this means that the amount of federal aid depends on the level of activity undertaken by the grant recipient. The level of activity in turn depends on recipient resources and policy choices. Such a program obviously permits a great deal of flexibility to recipient jurisdictions.[32]

The reimbursement principle is employed in a small number of grants, but these include some of the most significant ones. There are 27 programs in which the allocation of a federal categorical grant depends wholly or in part on the level of recipient expenditures. Another 15 grants do not reimburse expenditures but reimburse on the basis of program level. However, level of program or expenditures is only one of several allocational factors in many of these programs. Many such grants are not fully open-ended, but they do retain the basic reimbursement principle of rewarding those recipients with higher levels of expenditure or service.[33]

In fiscal terms, the most important reimbursement programs are the open-ended programs of aid to families with dependent children and Medicaid. Under Medicaid the federal share of expenditures ranges from 50 to 83 percent, depending on per capita income in the state. The states determine recipient eligibility (under federal regulations) and many of the services to be provided. In fiscal year 1976, these two programs alone accounted for nearly one-fourth of all grant-in-aid dollars.[34]

Reimbursement programs are said to offer an appropriate means of sharing costs between Washington and state or local governments in proportion to the benefits that accrue to each level. The phenomenon that economists call "externalities" is an important part of the defense of reimbursement grants. This means that the benefits of some services or programs spill out beyond the boundaries of the jurisdiction providing the service. Pollution control is a good example. In the absence of financial aid, states and localities are likely to provide less of this activity than would be desirable from a national standpoint. This situation might be remedied by a properly designed cost-sharing or reimbursement grant. However, the question of what services involve important externalities cannot be answered without dispute. Some contend that the welfare field is one in which interjurisdictional externalities are relatively unimportant, but it can be argued that the existence of unemployed and poor people has adverse effects beyond the borders of the jurisdictions in which they live.[35]

The flexibility of open-ended programs can result in standards of service that vary widely among recipients. These differences can be attacked as "disparities" or defended as reflecting legitimate variations in the preferences of citizens in various parts of the nation. Some people would argue that it is not right to reimburse substandard or inadequate state or local services. In addition, reimbursements may operate to benefit wealthier jurisdictions disproportionately. Finally, because the magnitude of expenditures is determined by recipient choices, reimbursement grants add to the uncontrollability of federal budget outlays.[36]

Fiscal Equalization

Still another principle used in the distribution of federal aid is fiscal equalization. It involves distributing federal grants in a way that tends to compensate for the differences that exist in the abilities of states and localities to finance public services from their own resources. In this way, federal intergovernmental aid becomes a tool for improving fiscal balance among recipients. By recognizing differences in the recipients' relative capacities to finance services from their resources,[37] the grant principle of fiscal equalization in effect involves taking from the haves and giving to the have-nots.

Fiscal equalization has never been the sole criterion by which federal aid is allocated. Instead, it has been used as one factor among many in federal distribution formulas.[38] Of course, one cannot be certain that the presence of an equalization factor in a formula that includes a number of other factors results in a distribution that is equalizing. That depends on how many other factors there are in the formula, how they are measured, and how they interact.[39]

Currently, 19 formula-based programs include a per capita income factor. Five are in vocational education; two are environmental grants; and all the other equalizing grants are in the fields of education, social services, health, and public assistance. It should be noted, however, that even in these fields only a small number of all federal grants take per capita income into account in determining grant awards. And there is no obvious rationale to account for the use of fiscal equalization in some of these programs and not in others.[40]

None of the five block grant programs include a measure of fiscal capacity, but per capita income does enter into the distribution of general revenue-sharing funds to states and localities. In three additional programs, per capita income affects the size of the required state and local matching contribution: public library construction, library services, and the national school lunch program. In two grant programs —child welfare basic grants to states and community mental health centers construction—income enters into both the allocation and matching provisions.[41]

Research indicates that the overall effect of federal aid has never been more than mildly equalizing, and often it has tended to benefit wealthier states and localities.

As operationalized, the principle of fiscal equalization involves measuring the fiscal capacity of recipients—such as per capita personal income—and lowering federal aid amounts as this capacity increases. Equalization thus implies a negative correlation between fiscal capacity and grant awards. We have already noted that in 1972 there was a slight positive relationship between per capita federal grants and state per capita personal income.[42] There is other evidence that grants have been counterequalizing, at least to states (meaning that the wealthier states generally got more, not fewer, benefits). This was especially clear in the 1940s.[43] In the 1950s and early 1960s, grants became more equalizing, although to a very small degree. In 1961-62, for example, the ACIR reported a weak inverse relationship (-.04) between per capita grants and per capita income.[44] However, by 1964 the statistical relationship had again become positive. Indeed, research by Deil S. Wright shows that, from 1940 to 1964, there was no consistent equalizing effect of federal grants.[45]

A 1975 study reveals that the highest-income states received the largest amount of federal aid per capita, middle-income states received the least, and the low-income states received an intermediate amount.[46]

There is evidence of a mild degree of equalization in programs of federal assistance to education (combined allocations for ten assistance programs).[47] Also, there is a slight negative relationship (–.299) between general revenue-sharing payments and income.[48]

Of course, not everyone thinks that federal aid ought to be allocated in a capacity-equalizing way. Equalization formulas worsen the situation complained of by those who say that the jurisdiction that pays the tax has a vested right to the receipts. It is also argued that because the income levels of the states are converging with the passage of time, the need for fiscal equalization is declining. Additionally, fiscal equalization can conflict with some other widely accepted principles for allocating federal aid. Jurisdictions that are "needy" in terms of particular services may not be "needy" financially. In such cases, it is difficult to decide which principle should be paramount.[49] There is also the measurement issue. A considerable debate, some of it highly technical, rages regarding how best to measure fiscal capacity. A new method suggested by the ACIR takes into account the revenue-raising potential from a variety of tax sources besides income.[50]

The "Urban Crisis" View of Aid Distribution

Students of the distribution of federal aid are often interested in the way aid impacts on big cities and their problems. Although federal aid to cities has increased over the years, there is little evidence that it has materially slowed down (let alone reversed) the forces that work to increase metropolitan fiscal disparities and strain the fiscal abilities of big cities. Cities are faced with dwindling tax resources, increasing proportions of "high-cost citizens," expenditure demands, inflation, and the growing ability of employee unions to push salary and fringe benefits higher.

Of course federal aid programs have helped the cities; but some argue that this has been a by-product of policies designed to help poor people rather than a result of programs designed to help burdened jurisdictions. Because the poor tend to cluster in central cities, federal aid programs with a poverty orientation are bound to have some sort of interlocal equalization effect. As the ACIR said in 1976,

Nevertheless, even after all of the state and federal aid programs with the most indirect equalization effects are thrown on the scales, the fact remains that intergovernmental financial help has yet to come in sufficient magnitude to turn the fiscal tide for the nation's hard pressed central cities. Nor does it promise to do so in the face of the national recession of the mid-1970s."[51]

There are, of course, people who think the federal government should not attempt to save the cities or equalize fiscal capacities among jurisdictions in metropolitan areas. The ACIR is not one of these. It holds that national urban problems are a legitimate target of federal efforts. But urban problems cannot be solved if one partner in the federal system has the bulk of the resources and the other two have the bulk of the expenditures to meet.[52] Accordingly, the ACIR recommends that the federal government continue to share a percentage of its revenues with the states and localities on a no-strings, general revenue-sharing basis; that greater use be made of broad block grants that permit more state and local discretion; that the federal government assume full financial responsibility for all public welfare programs; that the federal government encourage a more effective state tax system through federal income tax credits for state income taxes paid; that business-type activities on federal property be subjected to state and local sales and excise taxes; and that military pay be subject to state and local income taxes and withheld at the place where earned.[53]

Recently, Congress has begun to turn its historically-less-than-pro-city gaze on big-city woes. In September 1976 the House Committee on Banking, Currency, and Housing began two weeks of hearings on big-city problems ranging from taxation to housing, transportation, plant site selection, and federal subsidies. Its chairman announced that a major review of urban policies was necessary to draft legislation to "stop the erosion" of urban life.[54] At that time, President Gerald Ford was arguing for consolidation of categoricals into block grants, and candidate Jimmy Carter was talking about boosting housing programs through direct subsidies and low interest loans, and about job programs.[55] A few months later the U.S. Senate, "a bastion of rural power," showed signs of responding to urban problems. It voted 79 to 7, with only conservative Republicans in the negative, in favor of revising the formula for community development grants to give a preference to communities with higher concentrations of older housing, thus plowing millions more federal dollars into the aging cities of the Northeast and Midwest.[56] The *Christian Science Monitor* editorialized that this shift of federal housing dollars to the aging cities of the North was "justified and welcome." It also noted that the change reflected a growing recognition in Washington of the worsening plight of America's cities, even among legislators from the southern, once rural, states.[57]

On the other hand, the problems of cities may not be amenable to solution by intergovernmental aid. A recent study by the General Accounting Office concludes that federal aid changes to eliminate "inequities" in the allocation of grant funds are but a drop in the bucket to the biggest cities like New York. New York City, because of the loss of manufacturing jobs and therefore people, "simply does not earn enough money to support the population that remains." To solve New York's long-term economic and social problems, it is crucial to attract private employment. And this cannot be done by federal aid revisions alone, nor even by belt tightening. It requires such things as wider tax borders to include fleeing commuters and an improved education system. But national awareness of the problem cannot hurt, and lawmakers in Washington are manifesting more urban awareness than they have historically. And city officials are acknowledging this change away from what Seattle Mayor Wes Uhlman—referring to mortgage loans, urban renewal, and interstate highways—has called "$300 billion spent in 45 years to move people out of cities, tear down their homes and business places, and make it easier for them to drive away."[58]

By itself, of course, all this activity does not mean that the problems of the cities are going to be solved, or even resolutely addressed by the federal government in the face of citizen attitudes toward taxes, "Sunbelt-frostbelt" rivalries, and the viewpoint that city problems address themselves first to the states and only in an emergency, if then, to the national government.

Concluding Comments on Distribution

Neither the distribution principles employed by the federal government in their variety nor the distributive consequences determined by empirical research indicate a clear system of priorities. They indicate a patchwork, no doubt the result of political bargaining, horsetrading, and the adoption of one aid program without express consideration of its possible effects on other programs. In viewing the overall aid system, the ACIR describes it as manifesting "the absence of a consistent set of distributional principles," "ad hoc decision making," and "contradictory relationships" (discovered by correlation analysis).[59]

However one wishes to characterize the distribution of federal aid, and however one bemoans its lack of system, existing arrangements are not the result of a congressional conspiracy. What seems to be at work is happenstance and not policy. Most grants rely on two or more allocational factors. The overall result is that recipient states and localities do not receive federal aid in a way that closely follows any of the commonly employed principles or that clearly benefits any one kind of jurisdiction compared with another. Thus the charge of unfairness can be raised by nearly any jurisdiction, depending on what equity test is applied.[60] Intergovernmental aid is par excellence the subject of self-serving argument.

STIMULATION, DISTORTION, OR SUBSTITUTION

Another question about the effect of federal aid is whether it "skews the budgets" and "distorts the program priorities" of recipient governments. The charge is that aid pushes recipients away from the expenditure amounts and program emphases they would normally prefer and pushes them toward the aided functions, which are unnaturally attractive because their costs can be shared. This charge is backed by reference to studies showing that federal grants tend to have a "stimulative effect" on state-local outlays.[61]

Typically, a stimulative effect is defined for research purposes as one in which a dollar of federal aid is associated with more than a dollar of grantee spending.[62] If this stimulative pattern materializes, the inference is sometimes made that a distortion effect has taken place in grantee decisions. But a different inference is sometimes made from the same stimulative pattern—that the program activities that the grantor wanted to affect have been affected additively, meaning over and above the grantee's own-source spending.

A grant effect is called "substitutive" if federal funds are diverted to grantee purposes. In research this is often defined as a dollar of grant money associated with less than an additional dollar of grantee spending inclusive of federal aid. If this substitutive pattern materializes, the inference is made that federal dollars "were used, in part, either to replace own-source State-local expenditures (the latter being freed for other program areas) or to reduce State-local taxes."[63]

The ACIR reports that studies have generally, although not uniformly, found that federal grants tend to stimulate state-local expenditures.[64] Its own study with 1972 data also finds a stimulative effect. Like the earlier studies, ACIR's evidence points to varying degrees of stimulus. And the form of grant makes a difference in stimulus—whether formula, project, high-matching, or other—but all lead to a stimulative response by the state-local sector.[65] The possibility exists, of course, that stimulative effects are primarily in the form of increased wages, with little stimulation in terms of employee numbers. However, the evidence is that the major impact of federal grants is on public-sector employment levels, so that the overall effect of the grant system is to stimulate state-local spending for additional employees—that is, to increase service levels rather than public-sector wages. Again, this effect differs for the various types of grant instrument, but the overall effect is stimulative.[66]

The ACIR is careful to note that its study is based on the grant aggregate (for all and various types of grants) and total state-local expenditures. This does not permit one to infer a stimulative effect on particular program activities, or on any particular recipient government.[67] Indeed, with all the logical and methodological questions that surround efforts to determine stimulative or substitutive effects, one is uneasy about what can be inferred. Difficult measurement issues intrude. The usual test of stimulation has been mentioned. A stricter test holds that stimulation occurs only when state-local spending (including federal aid) increases more than the amount of the federal grant plus that required by matching provisions.[68] By implication, budgetary distortion occurs or may occur when this happens.

But logically a more-than-a-dollar-spent-for-a-dollar-received effect could manifest itself (regarding any or all programs) but not signify a distortion of grantee priorities if the "more than" reflected what the grantee intended to spend anyway. Distortion is not even certain where there is no opportunity to substitute federal for local money, because the grantee may wish to spend in a manner that evidences stimulation.

Of course, the opportunity to substitute federal for local money is widespread. It clearly exists whenever the grantee performs a wide range of services, receives intergovernmental aid from many grant sources,[69] and possesses skilled accountants. It therefore exists in all the states and in the larger local jurisdictions.

A seemingly more direct way of getting at distortion focuses on the difference between the amount spent and the amount that would otherwise have been spent in the absence of the grant. If that difference is equal to or more than the amount of the grant, it can be concluded that the funds have been used for the purpose intended by the grantor and not substituted for grantee purposes.[70] If the difference is smaller, grantee purposes have guided the use of the grant money; the program priorities of recipients have not been distorted. By implication, distortion can be ascertained when one learns the spending intentions of the potential grantee in the absence of grant money. But intentionality is exceedingly hard to measure, especially, as in this case, when plans may be highly tentative and when the grantee may have reason to hide his true intentions. If he reveals them, he may be admitting that he is using federal funds to substitute for local money. Where there is a "supplement not supplant" requirement, that is illegal.

Efforts have been made, using time-series analysis or other techniques, to predict what a recipient's expenditure pattern would have been had the grant not been received. It is doubtful, however, that any projection based on past decisions can accurately reflect what expenditures would have been. With such techniques, the answer to the question of what expenditures would have been is largely a function of the assumptions one makes.[71]

One student of federal grants states that "the amount that 'would otherwise have been allocated' is a hypothetical construct. It cannot be measured or observed."[72]

With all these problems and issues, it seems unwise to speak very confidently about federal grants causing distortion effects, even though there is evidence of aggregate stimulative effects. Distortions no doubt occur, but research has not yet presented a very clear picture of them.

EFFECTS OF THE AID PROGRAMS OF THE NEW FEDERALISM

The main idea of the "new federalism" was to replace categorical aids with alternative programs that gave more discretion to states and localities. Block grants and general revenue sharing were the two main proposals.

Community Development Block Grants

One of the most important block grants was directed at city problems. It consolidated seven existing categorical aids, the largest of which was urban renewal (which has distributed over a billion dollars annually). Other urban programs lumped into the "community development block grant" (CDBG) were model cities, water and sewer grants, land acquisition, neighborhood facilities, open space land, rehabilitation loans, and public facility loans.[73]

An important feature of the new program is a change from competition for funds (under the older project, categorical program) to a system of local entitlements in which community development money is distributed by formula. The components of the formula are population, poverty population counted double, and overcrowded housing. The money can be used for any purpose authorized by the total of categorical programs that were replaced. Funding is automatic unless the secretary of Housing and Urban Development (HUD) determines that the proposed activities are "plainly inappropriate."[74] In addition, the money goes to general-purpose governments at the local level and not to autonomous or semiautonomous units like redevelopment agencies, model city agencies, or housing authorities. This has not made the independent agencies happy, but it has meant that officials of general-purpose governments have more revenue with which to meet needs as they see them. In general, the program is defended by those who support greater state and local control over federal money for community development and who believe that community development dollars should not go to particular localities just because they are adept at grantsmanship. Opponents have expressed doubt that the money will be spent in aid of low- and moderate-income individuals and their communities.[75]

What about the effect of community development block grants? Raymond A. Rosenfeld examined the effect of changing community development aid from project categorical programs to the block grant approach in 147 metropolitan entitlement communities. He compared census tracts that benefited under one or more of the old categorical programs with the census tracts targeted by city officials for block grant funds[76] and found that nine-tenths of the categorical neighborhoods were included in plans for block grants. Furthermore, the activities planned for these neighborhoods substantially resembled the original plans. On the other hand, the new programs also included a number of census tracts not covered by categorical programs. This increased coverage is picking up some lower-income neighborhoods that were formerly excluded from federal community development plans, but it is also picking up an even larger number of wealthier neighborhoods. Rosenfeld expressed concern that if activities in the former categorical neighborhoods are phased out as projects are completed or commitments fulfilled and if spending patterns continue along present lines, the percentage of CDBG funds directed to low- and moderate-income areas will decrease.[77]

What is the explanation for the expansion of community development funds into higher-income city neighborhoods? One good possibility is that elected officials in cities are more concerned about their electoral standing with moderate and well-to-do voters than with poorer voters. Another possibility is that the lack of citizen participation in poorer neighborhoods makes it easier for officials to spread funds for community development. There is some evidence that the allocation of money under the Economic Opportunity Act of 1964 was associated with citizen participation efforts.[78] In any case, the expansion of funds to include higher-income groups supports the reservations of the opponents of the community development block grant program.

Other studies also support the opponents. An intensive study of 79 California cities with a population of more than 25,000 reveals some substantial resource shifts of the sort that make opponents unhappy. For example, compared with allocations under the old categorical programs, the new program shifts funds away from cities with higher percentages of blacks. It also hurts cities that have more old and overcrowded housing, those with larger concentrations of residents below the poverty line, and those under greater fiscal pressure.[79] The authors conclude that the shift in funds under the block grant program does not target federal revenues to city needs as these are usually defined;[80] in fact, it does a poorer job of matching resources to needs than did the categorical system.[81]

Conclusions of this type are not confined to California cities. National studies by the Brookings Institution and by Harvard-MIT reach similar conclusions. The Brookings study indicates that of the 20 worst-off cities in the country, all but two would be getting less federal aid in 1980 than they got a decade earlier under the old categorical programs. The chief beneficiaries would be cities such as Fort Lauderdale, Dallas, Phoenix, and Miami. Fort Lauderdale would get four times as much money as before, while Newark, New Jersey would lose more than half of what it used to get. Brookings attributes this shift to a formula that distributes funds to the disadvantage of cities with declining populations. The Harvard-MIT report concludes that the new approach to community development has reduced federal strings, but it has done so at the expense of the poor.[82] The results of these studies justify some of the warnings heard when Congress, spurred by the Nixon administration, began dismantling the more precisely targeted categorical grants in favor of revenue sharing and block grants.[83]

The original act expired in the fall of 1977, and it was clear that the program was due for a change. New funding formulas were supported by the Carter administration and by groups that have recently sprung up to help revitalize the Northeast, such as the Coalition of Northeast Governors and the Northeast-Midwest Economic Advancement Coalition. These groups have focused on winning changes in grant formulas, since formula grants are, in the words of one official, "the most susceptible to alteration of all forms of the federal outlays."[84] One of the proposals to change the formula involved taking account of age of housing and population lag. In June 1977, such a bill passed the House of Representatives; if signed into law, it would have nearly doubled the amount of federal community development money going to Boston by 1980. It would have more than doubled the funds going to other ailing northeastern and midwestern cities such as St. Louis, Buffalo, and Detroit. The "least needy" cities—such as Dallas, Albuquerque, Phoenix, and

San Jose—would continue receiving about the same amount as they would have otherwise.

Passage of the bill was "hailed by advocates of the northeastern block as a victory for their emerging sense of regionalism."[85] On June 7, the U.S. Senate, a long-time bastion of rural power, approved a revised formula for community development that was even more generous in directing federal dollars to older cities.[86]

In late September, House and Senate conferees retained formula factors—such as the amount of pre-1940 housing—that will benefit the older cities. Thus a significant change in the allocation of federal community development funds occurred and in the direction of cities experiencing the greatest amount of urban decay. Since these cities are also centers of poverty and poor housing, this change should make critics of the original community development act a good deal happier. President Carter signed the revised bill into law on October 12, 1977.

General Revenue Sharing

Another program of the new federalism has generated even more interest and debate: general revenue sharing. We will focus on certain effects that are interesting because of their political implications.

It is clear, for example, that despite some restraints on the use of revenue-sharing money, state and local policy makers have enjoyed wide discretion. Governors, legislators, mayors, county officials, and city managers indicate that they have experienced little or no difficulty in putting the money where their governments need it most. State and local officials evidently enjoy this latitude for specific reasons. One is that it is virtually impossible to distinguish federal revenue-sharing dollars—or any other federal dollars—from state or local dollars once states and localities have the federal money.[87] "Because revenue sharing dollars can be substituted for equal amounts of state and local revenue from their own sources, many of the conditions for the use of revenue sharing funds are largely cosmetic in character. . . ."[88] In addition, Congress and the president intended revenue-sharing dollars to be used for a wide variety of purposes. In fact, the basic idea of the program was to surmount the kind of expenditure limitations imposed by categorical forms of aid. Besides the flexibility indicated by the act itself, states and localities have received assurances that they would not be told how to spend the money. One such assurance came from President Nixon at the time he signed the act into law.[89]

There are, however, definite patterns to the use of federal revenue-sharing dollars by states and localities. The largest part of state expenditures has been concentrated in education; among cities, the concentration has been in public safety. An interesting study of the use of revenue-sharing funds in Rochester and Irondequoit, New York illustrates another pattern—use of the money to reduce taxes or avoid tax increases. In Rochester, revenue-sharing funds were openly touted as a substitute for money that would otherwise have accrued only from a tax increase. In Irondequoit, the concern was with stabilizing tax rates.[90] Similarly, in a survey of over 1,500 state officials the most frequently mentioned state use of revenue-sharing funds (except for passing money on, as required, to local governments) was to avoid tax increases. Thirty-nine percent made this response, and another 16 percent said that the funds were used to reduce taxes. "Increased capital outlays" was the third most important perceived impact. It was in the poorer Southern states that revenue sharing seemed to affect capital outlays most. The majority of responding officials in Alabama, Arkansas, Georgia, Mississippi, Missouri, and West Virginia indicated that this was a major impact in their states.[91] There is also evidence that general revenue-sharing funds have been used for capital outlays in local governments.[92]

Nathan, Manvel, and Calkins interviewed officials in a sample of 65 recipient governments, including 21 counties, 29 municipalities, and six townships, to ascertain the use of revenue-sharing funds. They found significant differences between state and local governments with regard to use of funds. States tended to use revenue sharing as a substitute for the other forms of revenue; local governments were more likely to treat revenue sharing as new spending. Revenue-sharing funds thus seem to be additive for local governments and substitutive for the states.

The most important additive effect of revenue sharing found by the survey associates was the use of revenue-sharing funds for new capital expenditures. Forty-two of the 63 units devoted some of these new resources to capital purchases. An important correlate of the use of revenue-sharing funds for capital spending was the fiscal condition of the recipient. The survey classified recipient fiscal condition as under extreme, moderate, little, or no fiscal pressure. None of the 14 high capital spending units were under extreme fiscal pressure, and only three were facing moderate pressure. Most of the units devoting 50 percent or more of revenue-sharing funds to new capital expenditures were facing little or no fiscal pressure, tended to be smaller in population, and were largely located in the South and West.[93]

General revenue sharing has had a modestly equalizing effect on the fiscal capacities of rich and poor states. Thus, states with relatively low fiscal capacities have received relatively more general revenue-sharing funds than those with higher capacities. To illustrate with states at extreme ends of the income distribution—Connecticut, with a 1973 per capita income of $5,889, received a per capita revenue-sharing allocation of $24.39 while Mississippi, with a per capita income of $3,-448, received $44.12.[94]

Revenue-sharing funds provide more aid to central cities than to suburban communities. When the per capita entitlements of central cities are compared with the estimated average per capita entitlement of all suburban cities in the same county, central cities get 1.5 to 3 times as much as their suburbs. For example, the city of Milwaukee received $19.38 of per capita entitlements, while suburban municipalities in Milwaukee County received on the average $6.47, and the richest suburb, Fox Point, received $4.55. The latter was actually larger than Fox Point would have received in the absence of a provision that no local government should receive less than 20 percent of the statewide average per capita local entitlement. Indeed, the equalizing effect of general revenue sharing is blunted by this provision and another one that says no local government can receive more than 145 percent of the average local entitlement. Revenue sharing's capacity to reduce local fiscal disparities in metropolitan areas would have been greater had Congress not limited its equalization impact in this way. According to a special study by the Office of Revenue Sharing, removal of the 145 percent limitation would substantially increase revenue-sharing allocations to various large cities as follows: Boston would get 41 percent more, St. Louis 68 percent more, and Philadelphia 57 percent more.[95]

There are allegations that revenue sharing has short-changed the poor and elderly by allowing state and local governments to spend funds on other targets, but the fungibility of revenue-sharing dollars made it impossible to tell precisely what groups benefited from revenue-sharing money. "It is virtually impossible for any researcher to state authoritatively that revenue sharing dollars were or were not used for programs benefiting disadvantaged people."[96]

Revenue sharing also has been analyzed in terms of specific incentives that arise from the provisions of the distribution formula. For example, because tax effort by state and local governments is a factor in the distribution of funds, the formula rewards states that raise their taxes faster than the national average and local governments that raise their taxes faster than the statewide average. Unfortunately for the states, the benefits accruing from an increase in taxes cannot be captured exclusively by the state which raises its taxes, since two-thirds of the resulting increase in revenue-sharing entitlement would automatically be spread among that state's local governments.[97]

There is also an incentive for states to raise more of their total revenue from the income tax. (State income tax collections figure in one of two alternative formulas.) At least 15 states could benefit from this provision. Importantly, they could do so without increasing overall tax burdens. All a state has to do is change its revenue structure—that is, collect more of its total revenue from the income tax and less from other sources such as the sales tax. Furthermore, the fact that two-thirds of the increased entitlements will have to be shared with local governments is not necessarily a disadvantage. To the state government, such increases may simply substitute for an expansion of state intergovernmental aid. There is, however, no evidence that the tax incentive has to date significantly influenced state taxing behavior.[98]

It may be noted also that taxes increase revenue-sharing entitlements, but fees and user charges do not. Thus in the future, when a state or community is faced with a choice of raising user charges or financing services from increased general taxes, the latter course might be chosen because it would bring an increase in the area's revenue-sharing entitlement. Another possibility is for general-purpose local governments operating school systems to earmark charges and fees for education, for the following reason: Under the current formula, school taxes levied by general purpose governments are excluded from consideration in the distribution formula. Therefore, if the general-purpose government could earmark all its fees and charges to support its schools and shift an equivalent amount of property tax receipts supporting the schools into the general fund, it could, by what amounts to a relabeling procedure, increase its entitlement for revenue sharing. However, state laws may currently be a deterrent to this action. State school aid is sometimes keyed to local tax efforts for education, and financing the schools entirely from user charges and fees might result in zero tax effort.[99]

Because all general-purpose governments are eligible to receive revenue-sharing funds, revenue sharing has "propped up certain duplicative and obsolete local governments."[100] Many reformers believe that small, fiscally limited, and administratively questionable units of government should go out of business and merge to form larger, more fiscally and administratively capable units.

On the other hand, because only general-purpose governments receive revenue-sharing money and since only the taxes collected by such units are considered in intrastate distributions, there exists a strong bias against special-purpose units of government and their taxes. Mergers of special-purpose units might be expected under this incentive. Independent special-purpose units may be resorbed by coterminous general-purpose units, so that the latter could count the tax revenues raised by the former in determining entitlements. The idea would be to make an independent special district into a dependent special district—that is, one whose powers are legally subordinate to the general purpose government. Alternatively, instead of independent special districts relying on their own tax receipts, they could rely on intergovernmental transfers from general-purpose local governments. Both a merger and a shift to local transfers would increase the revenue-sharing entitlements of the general-purpose governments. Indeed, these incentives in the revenue-sharing formula have not gone unnoticed. In Maryland, for example, a number of special park and planning districts and water and sewer commissions have been merged into county governments. One of the arguments used by advocates of this merger was that the taxes levied by the districts would be counted in the revenue-sharing formula if the special districts were abolished.[101]

Other incentives also manifest themselves in the revenue-sharing program, as Robert D. Reischauer convincingly shows. But this brief review makes it clear that the grant is far from neutral in its benefits.[102]

Despite conflicts about the principle of revenue sharing and the program's effect, general revenue sharing has been extended. In October 1976, it was extended for 3.75 years at a base authorization of $6.65 billion for each fiscal year. Funding is guaranteed and not subject to annual appropriations. The distribution formula in the 1976 legislation is the same as in the original law. However, priority funding categories that applied to local governments (although not to the states) and the prohibition against using revenue-sharing funds as a match for other federal grant funds have been eliminated.[103] Municipalities must now hold proposed use hearings unless they receive less than $10,000 or the entire allotment goes to one project.[104] Revenue sharing is with us still and promises to remain.

Concluding Comments on the Programs of the New Federalism

The consequences of transferring authority from the national level to state and local levels is of special interest to groups whose strengths differ from one level to another. Labor unions and other groups representing large cities, the poor, and minorities have long been more effective in Washington than in the state capitals. And these groups have been particularly concerned about the political implications of the new federalism. Also, important rivalries among local units of government are in evidence. Not all big cities like making urban counties eligible for community block grants, for example. Also, some of the best known of the independent agencies, such as community action agencies established under Office of Economic Opportunity programs and the community development agencies of model cities, have long been in conflict with mayors and other elected officials over how to spend money for social programs and community redevelopment. Despite the fact that they represent a good deal of professional expertise, they are being shunted aside.[105]

NOTES

1. David B. Walker, "Categorical Grants: Some Clarifications and Continuing Concerns," *Intergovernmental Perspective* 3 (Spring 1977): 17.

2. David W. Schodt et al., *An Evaluation of Selected State-Local Relationships in Wisconsin* (Madison, Wis.: Governor's Commission on State-Local Relations and Financing Policy, 1976), pp. 8–9.

3. See Deil S. Wright, *Federal Grants-in-Aid: Perspectives and Alternatives* (Washington, D.C.: American Enterprise Institute for Public Policy Research, 1968).

4. Advisory Commission on Intergovernmental Relations, draft of a chapter on issues in federal grant allocation, April 1977, forthcoming in "Categorical Grants: Their Role and Design."

5. Ibid., pp. 9–10.

6. Ibid., p. 10.

7. Ibid., p. 22.

8. Ibid.

9. Ibid., p. 16

10. Ibid.

11. Ibid., pp. 18–21.

12. Ibid., p. 12.

13. Ibid., pp. 11, 14.

14. Advisory Commission on Intergovernmental Relations, *Federal Grants: Their Effects on State-Local Expenditures, Employment Levels, Wage Rates* (Washington, D.C.: ACIR, 1977), p. 33.

15. Ibid., pp. 8, 33–36.

16. Advisory Commission on Intergovernmental Relations, *Improving Urban America: A Challenge to Federalism* (Washington, D.C.: ACIR, 1976), p. 37.

17. ACIR, draft chapter, op. cit., pp. 21–23.

18. Ibid., p. 23.

19. Advisory Commission on Intergovernmental Relations, *The Role of Equalization in Federal Grants* (Washington, D.C.: ACIR, 1964), pp. 46, 63.

20. ACIR, draft chapter, op. cit., p. 25.

21. Ibid., p. 38.

22. Ibid., p. 25.

23. Ibid., p. 26.

24. Ibid., p. 27.

25. Ibid., p. 35.

26. Ibid., p. 28.

27. Cited in ibid., p. 30.

28. Cited in ibid., p. 31.

29. ACIR, *Federal Grants*, op. cit., p. 33.

30. Ibid., pp. 8, 34.

31. ACIR, *Role of Equalization*, op. cit., p. 79.

32. ACIR, draft chapter, p. 39.

33. Ibid., pp. 41–42.

34. Ibid., p. 45.
35. Ibid., pp. 47–48.
36. Ibid., pp. 49–52.
37. ACIR, *Role of Equalization,* op. cit., p. 48.
38. ACIR, draft chapter, op. cit., p. 53.
39. Ibid., p. 59.
40. Ibid., p. 57.
41. Ibid., p. 58.
42. ACIR, *Federal Grants,* op. cit., p. 33.
43. Ibid.; and ACIR, draft chapter, op. cit., pp. 53–54.
44. ACIR, draft chapter, op. cit., p. 54.
45. Ibid., pp. 55–56.
46. Cited in ibid., p. 60.
47. Cited in ibid., p. 62.
48. Cited in ibid., p. 66.
49. Ibid., p. 67.
50. Advisory Commission on Intergovernmental Relations, *Measuring the Fiscal Capacity and Effort of State and Local Areas* (Washington, D.C.: ACIR, 1971). See also John S. Akin, "An Improved Method for Estimating Local Fiscal Capacity," *Review of Regional Studies* 4 (Fall 1974): 29–43.
51. ACIR, *Improving Urban America,* op. cit., p. 36.
52. Ibid., p. 16.
53. Ibid.
54. Guy Halverson, "Congress Turns Its Gaze on Big-City Woes," *Christian Science Monitor,* September 14, 1976.
55. Ibid.
56. Peter C. Stuart, "Historic Shift to Aid for Older Cities," *Christian Science Monitor,* June 9, 1977.
57. "To rescue the Cities," *Christian Science Monitor,* June 10, 1977.
58. Ibid.; and Peter C. Stuart, "Washington Rediscovering America's Needy Cities," *Christian Science Monitor,* November 18, 1977.
59. Walker, op. cit., p. 17.
60. Ibid.
61. Ibid.
62. ACIR, *Federal Grants,* op. cit., p. 2.
63. Ibid.
64. Ibid., p. 5.
65. Ibid.
66. Ibid., pp. 5, 53.
67. Ibid., p. 2.
68. Ibid., p. 9, footnote 1.
69. Walker, op. cit., p. 17.
70. Stephen M. Barro, "Federal Education Goals and Policy Instruments: An Assessment of the 'Strings' Attached to Categorical Grants in Education," a Rand working note prepared for the Department of Health, Education and Welfare (HEW), February 1977, p. 16.
71. Robert D. Reischauer, "General Revenue Sharing: The Program's Incentives," in *Financing the New Federalism,* ed. R. P. Inman et al. (Washington, D.C.: Resources for the Future, 1975), p. 56.
72. Barro, op. cit., p. 10.

73. ACIR, *Improving Urban America*, op. cit., p. 89; and Jeffrey L. Pressman, "Political Implications of the New Federalism," in *Financing the New Federalism*, ed. R. P. Inman et al. (Washington, D.C.: Resources for the Future, 1975), p. 25.

74. Richard DeLeon and Richard LeGates, *Redistribution Effects of Special Revenue Sharing for Community Development* (Berkeley: Institute of Governmental Studies, 1976), p. 1

75. Pressman, op. cit., pp. 25–28.

76. Raymond A. Rosenfeld, "Implementation of the Community Development Block Grant Program: A Neighborhood Focus," paper presented at the 1977 meeting of the Southwestern Political Science Association, Dallas, March 30–April 2, 1977.

77. Ibid.

78. Robert Stein, "The Community Action Program: A Study of Impact in 100 U.S. Cities," (M.A. thesis, University of Wisconsin—Milwaukee, 1974).

79. DeLeon and LeGates, op. cit., pp. 13–15, 16.

80. Ibid., p. 18.

81. Ibid., p. 21.

82. "Poorer Cities Losing U.S. Aid," *Milwaukee Journal*, February 14, 1977.

83. "Fixing Flaws in Federal Grants," *Christian Science Monitor*, February 18, 1977.

84. Chris Kenrick, "Northeast Stands to Gain from Community-Aid Bills," *Christian Science Monitor*, May 10, 1977.

85. Chris Kenrick, "Emerging Northeast Lobbies Get Federal Funds Flowing," *Christian Science Monitor*, June 3, 1977, and "Northeast Stands to Gain," op. cit.

86. Stuart, "Historic Shift to Aid," op. cit.

87. Advisory Commission on Intergovernmental Relations, *General Revenue Sharing: An ACIR Re-evaluation* (Washington, D.C.: ACIR, 1974), p. 2.

88. Ibid., p. 10.

89. Ibid., p. 2.

90. Sarah Liebschutz, "General Revenue Sharing as a Political Resource for Local Officials," in *Public Policy Making in a Federal System*, ed. Charles O. Jones and Robert D. Thomas (Washington, D.C.: Sage, 1976), pp. 112–15.

91. Deil S. Wright et al., *Assessing the Impacts of General Revenue Sharing in the Fifty States: A Survey of State Administrators* (Chapel Hill: Institute for Research in Social Science, 1975), pp. V1–V27.

92. Liebschutz, op. cit.

93. Richard P. Nathan, Allen D. Manuel, and Susan E. Calkins, *Monitoring Revenue Sharing* (Washington: Brookings Institution, 1975), pp. 181–233.

94. ACIR, *General Revenue Sharing*, op. cit., p. 3.

95. Ibid., pp. 3–5.

96. Ibid., p. 11.

97. Reischauer, op. cit., pp. 59, 62.

98. Ibid., pp. 67–70.

99. Ibid., p. 72–73.

100. ACIR, *Improving Urban America*, op. cit., p. 81.

101. Reischauer, op. cit., p. 75.

102. Ibid., p. 87.

103. Carol S. Weissert, "Restraint and Reappraisal: Federalism in 1976," *Intergovernmental Perspective* 3 (Winter 1977): 12.

104. Mary Glindinning, "Public Shows Little Interest in Revenue Sharing Funds," *Milwaukee Journal*, October 14, 1977.

105. Pressman, op. cit., pp. 32–36.

5
The Mix of State-Local
Revenue Sources

This chapter describes the range of state and local revenue instruments[1] and stresses the jointness of state and local governments. With few if any exceptions, the programs of each level affect and are affected by activities of the other level. The state not only determines the means local units may use to raise revenue but also establishes the legal duties of local governments. On the other hand, the state depends on local units of government to provide a multitude of services that state policy requires. The two levels of government have mutual interests in serving the same population, and they have a common responsibility for formulating and administering programs to achieve public objectives.[2]

TAXES

There is a trend toward diversifying state and local tax sources. In 1942 sales taxes produced about 7 percent of total state-local tax revenue (not of all revenue), but by 1975 they produced over 20 percent. Individual income taxes have similarly risen, from about 3 percent in 1942 to 15 percent in 1975. Simultaneously the proportion of state-local tax revenue contributed by property taxation has declined from 53 percent to about 37 percent.[3]

In 1960, there were 31 states that had a personal income tax, 35 had a sales tax, 19 had both, and four had neither. By 1976, all but nine states (Connecticut, Florida, Nevada, New Hampshire, South Dakota, Tennessee, Texas, Washington, and Wyoming) had a broad-based personal income tax; and only five states (Alaska, Delaware, Montana, New Hampshire, and Oregon) were without a general state sales tax. Every state except New Hampshire had at least one of these two major taxes.[4]

Figure 5.1 goes beyond property, sales, and income taxes. It notes the change in reliance on a wide variety of revenue sources between

FIGURE 5.1: Diversification of State and Local Revenue System with the Relative Decline in Property Taxes and Relative Increase in State Income Taxes and Federal Aid, Fiscal Years 1954 and 1974

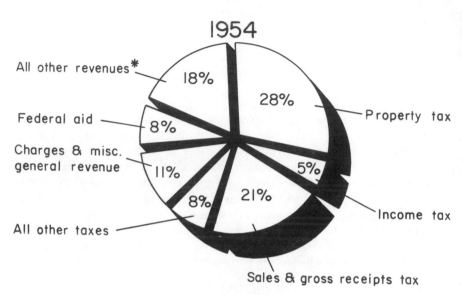

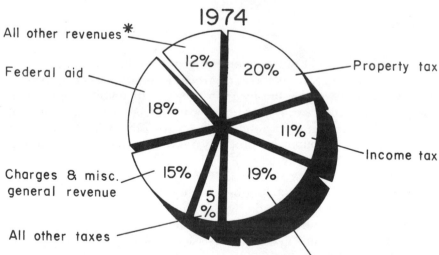

*Includes utility, liquor store, and insurance trust revenue.

Source: Advisory Commission on Intergovernmental Relations, *Improving Urban America: A Challenge to Federalism* (Washington, D.C.: Government Printing Office, 1976) p. 52.

1954 and 1974. The percentages shown in Figure 5.1 should be understood as proportions of total revenue—that is, income from all sources, not just from taxes. Increasing balance among the principal tax sources is suggested. The 1976 estimate suggests even more balance. Federal aid accounts for 19.9 percent; property tax 18.5 percent; sales and gross receipts 18.7 percent; income tax 11.1 percent; charges and miscellaneous 15.4 percent; and utility, liquor store, and insurance trust revenue 12.5 percent. In the past 20 years, in short, increased reliance on federal aid, income taxes, and fees and charges has produced a far more diversified state-local revenue system.[5]

Left out of the picture so far is state intergovernmental aid. Local governments have come to depend more heavily on both federal and state aid.[6] State aid has registered a steady increase in relation to local own-source revenue in the last 20 years. This is true even when inflation and population growth are considered.[7]

While the states have strengthened their own revenue systems by diversifying tax sources, they have been slower to permit local governments to do so.[8]

Both state aid and the diversification of local government revenue sources will be considered below.

Property Taxes

When all revenue is examined, property taxes no longer produce the largest share of total state and local revenue. Federal aid does. But property taxes are still a very significant element of the state-local revenue system. In most states, even though other sources have grown in relative importance, the property tax still yields more than any other single item of state-local own-source revenue. In addition, the property tax dominates local revenue from own sources; it is the principal tax instrument available to local governments. But the property tax is not only important, it is also controversial. Reformers seek to "rehabilitate" it, both from Washington and from the state capitals. Taxpayers are unhappy with it. ACIR surveys over a four-year period show that the local property tax is widely regarded as the least fair tax.[9]

Reformers and taxpayers alike express concern over a number of features of the property tax system. Among them are a desire to bring property assessments into closer alignment with the market values of real property, to provide more information about changes in assessment levels, to revamp procedures for appealing such changes, and to improve the professional qualifications of assessors.[10] But above all of these is a general desire for property tax relief.

In recent years criticism has mounted. The property tax is said to be overworked by local governments and also to place a relatively greater burden on those least able to pay it.[11] In addition, the uneven distribution of taxable property values among local governments is often cited as the most important cause of the disparity that exists among localities in their abilities to provide services.

With minor exceptions, all real property is taxable in all of the 50 states. In addition most of the 50 states place some form of tax on tangible personal property. The latter may include "all personal property" or very specific items, such as aircraft or automobiles. In many states the value of personal property is not assessed by any public agency. Instead, the value is determined by the taxpayer's own declaration, a system that is not reliable and is often criticized for giving people an incentive to cheat.

Common exemptions from property taxation include property owned by schools, churches, governments, libraries, cemeteries, and nonprofit organizations. Local units of government are usually subject to many restraints on the types of property to be taxed and rates of taxation.

Sales Taxes

Most states have adopted sales taxes, although rates and provisions vary widely. In some states food and medicine are exempt from sales taxes, while in others they are not. The purpose of such an exemption is of course to reduce the burden of the tax on the lower-income taxpayer. Sales taxes are selectively applied to various consumables such as motor fuel, insurance, amusements, alcoholic beverages, and tobacco. All 50 states and the District of Columbia tax motor fuels.

Some states are heavily dependent on the general sales tax for their revenues. Mississippi and Alabama were discussed in an earlier chapter as examples of this approach to taxation.

Local sales taxes have also grown steadily. More than 4,800 local jurisdictions in the United States employ a sales tax. The vast majority (over 4,100) are municipalities, although they are joined by 662 counties, 52 school districts (all in Louisiana), six boroughs (all in Alaska), and five rapid transit districts. The heaviest concentration of sales tax use at the local level is in five states: Illinois, Texas, California, Oklahoma, and Alabama. In all, 29 states authorize a local sales tax. In some localities sales taxes make a sizable contribution to total local revenue. In 1976 the sales tax contribution was 67 percent of total city taxes in Tulsa. At the other extreme was Kansas City with only 5.6 percent and Buffalo with 7.2.[12] Twenty-two of the 48 largest cities got no sales tax revenue at all.

Reformers who address sales taxes are concerned about a number of issues. One is that general-purpose local governments have authority to adopt a sales tax (or an income tax or both) in order to achieve a more balanced and diversified use of the basic tax instruments. Another concern is that where local sales taxes are employed, the same items be taxable by both state and local units to simplify administration.[13] Also, it is commonly urged that local sales taxes be state collected and administered and that priority use of the tax be given to local governments having the widest jurisdictional reach, such as the county, with some provision for sharing revenues with their contained municipalities. There is also concern about too great a variation among local jurisdictions in sales tax rate. If variations become extreme, business location decisions and consumer buying habits may be affected. In a sense, this issue is related to the previous one in that the larger the geographic coverage of a tax, the more difficult it becomes to search out jurisdictions with lower taxes.[14]

Naturally, a local sales tax will be most lucrative for localities possessing concentrations of business activity. In other words, there are inequalities in revenue-raising capacity among local jurisdictions that may use this source. And these inequalities may worsen disparities in total funds available to support public services. Disparities of this kind can be reduced by programs of state aid based on something other than simply returning state-collected revenue to its place of origin.

When confronted with the need to raise local revenue yields, there is evidence that local taxpayers favor sales and income taxes over property taxes.[15]

Income Taxes

As mentioned earlier, income taxes have become an increasingly important part of the state-local revenue picture. Nearly all states tax incomes, either of persons or corporations, or of both. Rates vary from less than 2 percent to almost 20 percent. While most states tax both corporate and individual incomes, most do not impose a graduated tax on corporate income; they tax at flat rates between 3 and 12 percent. Also, there are differences among states in what portion of a corporation's income is taxable.

In ten states, local governments are allowed to levy an income tax. Several of the nation's largest cities impose a local income tax, among them Baltimore, Birmingham, Cincinnati, Cleveland, Detroit, Kansas City, New York, Philadelphia, Pittsburgh, and St. Louis. Most of the local income taxes are concentrated in Alabama, Missouri, Ohio, Pennsylvania, and Kentucky. The typical local income tax does not reach "unearned income"—that is, income from dividends, interest, capital gains, estates, and trusts. In this respect it has a base different from those of federal and state income taxes.

As to tax rate, some local option is the pattern. For example, Maryland permits a range of surcharges to the state tax—not less than 20 percent nor more than 50 percent—while Indiana permits a choice of rates up to 1 percent. Another aspect of the tax rate is the choice between flat and progressive structures. The general practice has been to follow a flat-rate approach. However, some of the more recently adopted local income taxes use a graduated rate. Wilmington, Delaware, and New York City follow this practice. Of course, where the local tax is a surcharge on the state tax, the former has the same progressivity or lack thereof as the latter. This surcharge type of tax, or "piggyback" tax, is the easiest local income tax to administer.[16]

One of the principal attractions of the local income tax to cities is the ability of that tax to reach individuals working in the city but residing elsewhere. The usual argument here is that commuting workers impose service requirements—such as for police, parking facilities, and street maintenance—beyond those which are needed for local residents alone. Many points of dispute exist over this issue. Some people do not believe that a commuter should pay any local income tax to the jurisdiction in which he or she works. But if it is agreed that such a tax should be paid, can the costs that the commuter imposes on the taxing jurisdiction be fairly estimated? And should the commuter pay some of all costs incurred by the jurisdiction where he or she works, including such functions as education and welfare, or should he or she simply pay for those services that (more or less) are directly consumed by him or her? There is also the question of "double taxation." It certainly would not be fair to tax the commuter fully both in the place of residence and the place of employment.

Like other local tax instruments, a local income tax may have migration effects on both individuals and businesses—that is, people may move to avoid them. However, it is commonly thought that small tax rates imposed by local governments are not likely to be a deciding factor in location choice. And since most local income taxes are applied to income earned where one works, regardless of residence, moving one's residence is not likely to help.[17]

Minor Taxes and Charges

In addition to the major revenue sources so far discussed, there are a number of minor taxes and user charges that are important in the aggregate to the state-local revenue picture. Many states impose a tax on domestic corporations at the time of their organization, and almost every state imposes a franchise fee on corporations. This fee is for the privilege of carrying on business in the state or for existing in the state as a corporation. (New York State places an unusual amount of emphasis on the franchise tax.) Also, many states impose special taxes on banks and other financial institutions. There are also license taxes for the privilege of removing natural resources from the ground and taxes on stock transfers, gifts, inheritances, and estates.

User charges are not the same as taxes; they are charges levied on the user of a particular good or service, per unit thereof. Such charges have a number of important advantages. They allocate financial burden among individuals in close relation to the quantity of good or service those individuals choose to consume. Because they function as prices, user charges compel the individual to consider costs to himself and also, ideally, those costs that his actions impose on the system. Finally, user charges yield information about the demand for government services. When producers of the services combine this information about demand with estimates of the marginal cost of each service, they can make more efficient decisions about what quantity to produce, the capital investments to make, and the changes in service that are needed. The case for employing user charges is strongest if (1) the benefits of the service are easily identified with the individual recipient, rather than the whole community, (2) charges can be easily collected, and (3) the charges do not constitute inequitable burdens on individuals.[18]

User charges are not without their disadvantages, however. The federal government and many, if not all, states allow personal deductions for the major taxes levied by local governments, but no comparable deductions are allowed for user charges; hence no portion of the cost of providing these services can be "exported" to other levels of government. (Businesses are allowed to deduct both charges and taxes as income-related expenses.) Second, federal revenue-sharing funds and some state aid payments are based on tax efforts; and this procedure is defined in terms of taxes excluding user charges. In addition, user fees have been criticized as regressive. Strict application of the benefit principle to finance all services ignores ability to pay.[19]

The actual range of user charges employed by local governments is quite wide. In Wisconsin, for example, they are used for services like water, sewage disposal, electricity furnished by municipal utilities, garbage and trash collection, and for special activities like snow removal and weed control. There also are fees and charges imposed by bus lines, airports, swimming pools, and zoos. Other examples of common user charges include parking meters and permits for various kinds of activities.[20]

EARMARKING

Earmarking is the practice of designating specific revenues for financing specific goods or services. The practice is extremely widespread: Earmarked taxes form an integral part of the revenue/expenditure systems of all 50 states, with over 40 percent of state taxes earmarked.[21] If the revenue/expenditure systems of local governments are also included, the percentage is much higher—especially if the revenues of local school districts are considered to be earmarked.

Normally, earmarking is a term used to describe the marriage of a single tax or revenue source to a single public service within a multitax, multiservice unit. However, an identical effect is created when special-purpose districts are tied to a single tax source. Thus, school districts, fire districts, sanitation districts, airport districts, and so on are often considered to be financed by earmarked revenue.

There is support for the practice. One argument views the marriage of a revenue source to the provision of a public service as a way to improve taxpayer participation in public expenditure decisions— either directly or through legislative representation. The taxpayer, in voting a levy of earmarked funds, is able to express an opinion on the amount of funds to be devoted to a specific purpose—whether it be public education, parks, fire protection, or other purposes. Thus the taxpayer/voter can make a rational choice based on his perception of the cost and effectiveness of a service.[22]

Another rationale for earmarking is that it links the benefits received by users of a governmental service to the taxes collected from them. A tax on motor fuels may be directly linked to the provision of highways. The level of public spending for highways is thus directly linked to highway use in a manner roughly equating benefits and payments for each user.[23]

Nevertheless, the practice of earmarking has traditionally been attacked both by scholars and interest groups.[24] Students of public finance often argue that earmarking is inefficient, that it inhibits quick adjustments to changes in costs and changes in demand. The practice is criticized for making the tax structure more regressive and for impeding the attainment of optimum levels of service.[25]

Earmarking is sometimes applied to trivial situations. The Montana constitution, for example, requires that the proceeds of a tax on livestock be used to pay bounties for the destruction of predatory animals.[26]

While improper or trivial earmarking can be a serious problem, concentration on these issues presents a distorted picture of state and local revenue/expenditure systems. The practice of earmarking, though still relatively common, is decreasing[27]—at least on a percentage basis. The continuing trend toward increased intergovernmental transfers has undoubtedly decreased the impact of earmarking on expenditure patterns. Federal intergovernmental transfers for education, for example, increased from $950 million in 1960 to $5,844 million in 1970[28] to $9,254 million in 1976. Today, we typically find a mix of earmarked and other revenues providing for the earmarked function. These other revenues are usually supplementary appropriations from the general fund or grants-in-aid.[29]

Since the earmarking of gasoline tax receipts and vehicle license fees for highway expenditures is one of the most common forms of earmarking by the states, it can serve to illustrate the impact of earmarked funds.

In Wisconsin highway revenues are generated by a tax on motor fuels and by motor vehicle registration fees. These revenues are placed in a segregated highway fund, and they are allocated for construction and repair costs at both the state and local levels.

The basic system of highway fund distribution was established in 1925. At that time, the aids system provided $25 per mile for town and village roads and from $50 to $200 per mile for city streets, the amount being determined by city size. The amounts were increased in 1931 and again in 1939 to their present levels ranging from $65 to $520 per mile. Under the 1925 law, counties also receive aid based on the number of vehicles registered in the county and the highway mileage in the county. Since 1947 supplemental funds have been made available to all units of government.

Funds may be utilized for the improvement and maintenance of local roads and streets (including snow removal). Aid to counties may also be used to match federal funds for the improvement of the county highway system. In practice, highway funds function as general aid or a form of revenue sharing. State statutes give local units complete discretion in the use of the funds within the limits described above; and there are no state audits of how the recipients of highway aids actually spend the money. Local governments may accrue a surplus of aid money in one year by claiming that they will spend it in the next. Local governments do not operate under standardized accounting methods or even on the same fiscal years. Finally, the substitution of state for local funds cannot be calculated.

While outdated formulas raise doubts about bias in the distribution of these highway funds, the amount of aids allocated does not come close to meeting the road and street needs of Wisconsin local governments. The Wisconsin Department of Transportation, for example, estimates that cities and villages would need $666.4 million in funds during the period 1975–79. Yet only $30.6 million was allocated to cities and villages for highways during fiscal year 1975. Thus state aid from the segregated fund falls far short of expenditures. From the perspective of local units the segregated fund merely provides a minimum guarantee in the form of basic highway aids.

The practice of earmarking revenues, then, does not seem to be cause for great concern in light of today's trends in fiscal federalism. If the Wisconsin case is at all typical, earmarked revenues distributed through intergovernmental transfer only form a small base for expenditures and thus hardly distort local spending priorities.

STATE INTERGOVERNMENTAL AID

Although it is spending to state governments, state aid is revenue for the receiving local units.

Three main approaches are used by state governments to provide financial assistance to their localities. First, financial responsibility may be directly assumed by the state, thereby freeing local financial resources for other purposes but running afoul of the philosophy that government should be "close to the people." Second, states may authorize local governments to use a variety of tax, fee, and charge instruments. This is the revenue diversification approach. The third approach is the grant-in-aid device.[30]

State governments vary widely in their relative reliance on the three aid approaches. Hawaii is a strong user of the direct provision of services approach, while the two largest states—New York and California—stress intergovernmental aid. In terms of local revenue diversification, 27 states currently authorize a local sales tax, and ten states authorize local income taxes.[31]

State intergovernmental expenditure as a percent of total state general expenditures varies considerably among the states. Not unexpectedly, it is smallest in Hawaii—2.1 percent in 1975. In Wisconsin it was 50.2 percent. New Hampshire's figure was 19.1 percent. The U.S. average was nearly 38 percent; thus, more than one-third of the average state budget goes to support locally provided services.[32]

If the intergovernmental aid and direct state servicing approaches to providing state assistance are meaningful alternatives, one might expect a negative or inverse correlation between the two approaches. In a recent ACIR study, the expected negative relationship showed up for highway and welfare expenditures only. For these functions there is thus some evidence that direct state spending and state aid are substitute approaches. However, the expected relationship was not evident for education or for all state functions together. This may be because there has been a generally upward trend both in state direct expenditures and state intergovernmental aid.[33]

The relative importance of state aid in the local revenue system reflects in significant part the growth and transfer of welfare financing to upper levels of government during the 1930s and in part the striking growth of educational aid in the last two decades.

The strongest trend in state aid has been the relative decline in state support of public highways. State aid is now and always has been dominated by the education function, although since 1967 the relative importance of the education function has declined somewhat. General local government support, or state revenue sharing as it is also called, shows a generally upward trend since 1966.[34]

As for recipients, the largest portion of state aid is channeled to school districts to support public education. Counties and cities are the second and third largest recipient governmental units,[35] as shown in Figure 5.2.

State grants-in-aid take a variety of forms. The basic types are general or targeted, matching or nonmatching, and related or not related to local fiscal capacity. General aids (or shared revenue/shared taxes) are usable for any purpose the local unit chooses. Target aids are to be spent for specified purposes. Matching aids require local units to spend a predetermined amount of their own revenue for each dollar of state aid. Aids related to fiscal capacity consider the revenue raising ability of the local unit in determining the amount of the allocation.[36]

A variety of objectives are sought by states in extending financial assistance to their localities. One view of general aids is that they should be used to substitute for local property tax levies. State-raised taxes are held to be superior on two counts: The state has a greater capacity to tax, and the state-raised tax is usually less regressive. Another objective of general aid is to achieve a basic level of services. Some people argue that citizens have a right to certain basic services regardless of the locality in which they happen to live. And unrestricted aid is held to be the proper device for pursuing this objective because the needs of local governments are so varied that it is desirable to have a program that allows local officials to decide on their own service priorities. (On the other hand, if one can specify the "basic services" to which people have a right, then targeted aids could be used to meet them directly.) A third objective of general aid is fiscal equalization. The idea is to use state aid to help equalize the ability of local units to raise taxes and/or provide services. General aid programs may therefore help in the financial deliverance of cities or other units having relatively low fiscal capacities. Equalization aids may be distributed with the specific intent that equal revenue effort (measured by the ratio of taxes to income or to

FIGURE 5.2: State Payments to Local Governments, by Type of Government, 1974—$45.6 Billion (in millions)

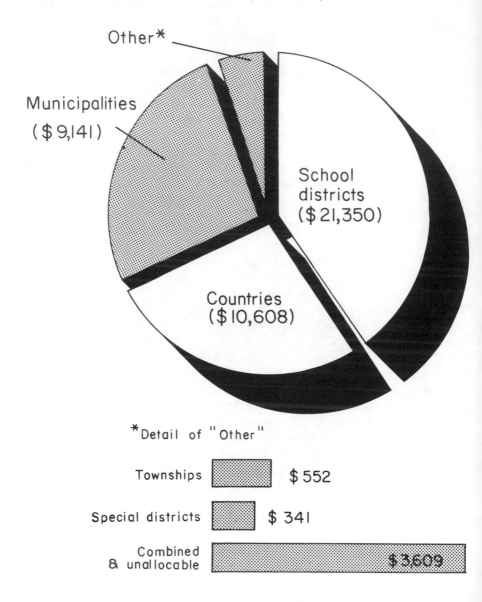

Source: Advisory Commission on Intergovernmental Relations, *Improving Urban America: A Challenge to Federalism* (Washington, D.C.: Government Printing Office, 1976), p. 66.

property wealth) will yield equal amounts of revenue, or equivalent levels of service.[37]

The principal objectives of targeted aids are as follows. Sometimes both the state and the local units share an interest in providing a certain service. When this happens, the state may wish to encourage and support local governments that choose to carry out this activity. State aid is then directed at the sharing of costs for this function. More specifically, the state may wish to provide each locality with an amount of aid sufficient to provide some minimum level of the particular service.[38]

Where there are so-called spill-over effects from the provision of a service, local governments may not find it feasible to provide the service. Examples are the alleviation of air and water pollution, planning, and mass transit systems. The benefits of such services spill over the boundaries of the units of government providing them, and as a result some of the benefits are received by residents of other jurisdictions— who need not pay for them. State aid is a partial solution to this problem. The principle involved is to compensate the unit providing the service for benefits received outside that unit.[39]

Wisconsin's program of state aid provides an example of the variety of forms that aid may take. Wisconsin is not typical, however. It is a leader in the percentage of state expenditures devoted to intergovernmental transfers and also places greater emphasis on unrestricted aid than most other states. Additionally, the state of Wisconsin has a strong record of reforming government, and that record extends to intergovernmental aid. Wisconsin had adopted all five measures recently cited by the ACIR in a report on the progress of state aid reform.[40] Thus Wisconsin's system of state aid is a better indicator of the variety of instruments available than is the typical state system.

State intergovernmental aid in Wisconsin falls into three types of programs: targeted state aids, (unrestricted) shared taxes, and property tax relief.

The amount allocated for targeted aids is determined by a statutory formula and depends on legislative appropriation rather than on the yield of a particular tax.[41] The major targeted aids in Wisconsin are for welfare and health programs (paid to counties), natural resource aids (paid to counties and municipalities), transportation aids (also paid to counties and municipalities), and education aids (paid to school districts). In addition, there are "general government aids" paid to counties to help defray the costs of basic county activities. These include payments made to regional planning commissions for planning studies.

Shared taxes are distributed by statutory formula from specific percentages of the state individual income, corporate and franchise income, utility, liquor, and other state taxes. The distribution formula consists of three parts, each with its own specific formula: a per capita payment, which is an amount paid to each municipality and county on the basis of its estimated population; the special utility payment, which is an amount paid to each municipality and county having certain types of utility property located within it; and the "aidable revenues" payment, which is an amount paid to each municipality on the basis of its three-year average general property tax and other locally raised revenues in comparison to the other municipalities of the state. Counties receive shared tax payments based on a similar formula.[42]

Typical revenue-sharing objectives are pursued by the state of Wisconsin in its shared tax program. One is that a basic level of services be financed from revenue sources more progressive than the property tax. Another recognizes the fact that some communities are more greatly endowed with wealthy or burdened with low-income taxpayers than others. A portion of the shared taxes is thus distributed in a manner that seeks partially to neutralize disparities in local revenue-raising capacity. This is the aidable revenues component.[43]

Property tax relief, the third major state program, is represented by four subprograms: personal property tax relief, general property tax relief, "homestead credit," and manufacturing machinery and equipment property tax exemptions. General property tax relief is the amount paid to municipalities to reduce the property tax on real estate and personal property other than farmers' livestock and merchants' and manufacturers' inventories. These payments appear finally as credits on individual property tax bills. The amount of relief allocated to each municipality depends on the property tax effort for all purposes relative to the statewide average tax effort (measured by full value property tax rate). And the amount of relief received by each taxpayer within the municipality depends upon the assessed value of his or her taxable property.[44]

Personal property tax relief is the amount paid to each municipality to reduce its property tax on farmers' livestock and merchants' and manufacturers' inventories. These amounts also are shown as credits on the appropriate tax bills.[45] Currently, Wisconsin provides payments equal to an average of 80 percent of the tax liability on this property.

The "homestead credit" program provides a direct payment to individual owners and renters with household incomes up to $7,500 for the purpose of offsetting a certain portion of their property tax liability. The amount of credit depends on tax liability and income. The basic principle of this so-called circuit-breaker legislation is to stop the flow of property tax funds from taxpayer to tax collector when the property tax reaches a certain percent of personal income—a level that the state deems excessive.[46] In contrast to the general and personal property tax relief programs, whose purpose is to lower the overall level of local property taxes, the goal of Wisconsin's homestead credit program is to lessen the regressivity of the property tax by providing credits to low income taxpayers.[47]

Wisconsin has exempted manufacturing machinery and equipment from local property taxes in order to foster a more attractive climate for industrial location. The state therefore compensates each municipality and county by an amount equal to the potential tax yield on manufacturing machinery and equipment that has been exempted from property taxation.

In the next chapter we turn to issues that have arisen concerning state aid and the other revenue sources. There is a growing interest in change relating to sources of revenue—such as greater state and local use of income and sales taxes, reform of the property tax, and improvement of state aid programs.

NOTES

1. Wisconsin Commission on State-Local Relations and Financing Policy, "Local Government Revenue Sources: Alternative Revenue Sources," Issue Paper no. 15 (Madison: the Commission, July 1976), p. 17.

2. Wisconsin Commission on State-Local Relations and Financing Policy, *Final Report of the Commission on State-Local Relations and Financing Policy* (Madison: the Commission, 1977), p. 27.

3. Advisory Commission on Intergovernmental Relations, *Improving Urban America: A Challenge to Federalism* (Washington, D.C.: ACIR, 1976), p. 50.

4. Ibid., p. 51.

5. Advisory Commission on Intergovernmental Relations, *Significant Features of Fiscal Federalism, 1976 Edition* (Washington, D.C.: ACIR, 1976), p. 3.

6. Ibid., pp. 3–4.

7. ACIR, *Improving Urban America*, op. cit., p. 61; and Advisory Commission on Intergovernmental Relations, *The States and Intergovernmental Aids* (Washington, D.C.: ACIR, 1977), pp. 7–10.

8. ACIR, *Improving Urban America*, op. cit., p. 54.

9. Ibid., pp. 55–60. See also Wisconsin Commission, *Final Report*, op. cit., chaps. 9 and 10.

10. ACIR, *Improving Urban America*, op. cit., pp. 57–60.

11. Wisconsin Commission, Issue Paper no. 15, op. cit., p. 5.

12. Ibid., pp. 6–7.

13. Ibid., p. 7.

14. Ibid., pp. 7–8; and ACIR, *Improving Urban America*, op. cit., p. 54.

15. ACIR, *Improving Urban America*, op. cit., p. 54.

16. Wisconsin Commission, Issue Paper no. 15, op. cit., p. 9.

17. Ibid., pp. 9–10.

18. Ibid., pp. 10– 11.

19. Ibid., p. 11; and Wisconsin Commission on State-Local Relations and Financing Policy, "State and Local Sources of Funds," Alternative Paper no. 10, part 2 (Madison: the Commission, November 1976), pp. 19–20.

20. Wisconsin Commission, Issue Paper no. 15, op. cit., pp. 11–12.

21. Per Eklund, "A Theory of Earmarking Appraised," *National Tax Journal* 25 (June 1972): 223; and Walter W. McMahon and Case M. Sprenkle, "A Theory of Earmarking," *National Tax Journal* 23 (September 1970): 255.

22. James M. Buchanan, "The Economics of Earmarked Taxes," *Journal of Political Economy* 71 (October 1963): 457–69.

23. James A. Maxwell and J. Richard Aronson, *Financing State and Local Government*, 3d ed. (Washington, D.C.: Brookings Institution, 1977), p. 221.

24. Buchanan, op. cit.; and *A Handbook of State and Local Taxes* (Washington, D.C.: Congress of Industrial Organizations, 1954), pp. 102–4.

25. McMahon and Sprenkle, op. cit., p. 261.

26. Maxwell and Aronson, op. cit., p. 22.

27. McMahon and Sprenkle, op. cit., p. 255.

28. Advisory Commission on Intergovernmental Relations, *Federal-State-Local Finances: Significant Features of Fiscal Federalism* (Washington, D.C.: ACIR, 1974), p. 70.

29. Eklund, op. cit., p. 226.

30. ACIR, *States and Intergovernmental Aids*, op. cit., p. 1.

31. Ibid.

32. Ibid., pp. 2–3.

33. Ibid., p. 4.

34. Ibid., p. 11.

35. Ibid.

36. Wisconsin Commission on State-Local Relations and Financing Policy, "State and Local Sources of Funds," Alternative Paper no. 10 (Madison: the Commission, October 1976), p. 14.

37. Wisconsin Commission on State-Local Relations and Financing Policy, "State Aids to Local Governments: Policy Considerations," Issue Paper no. 16 (Madison: the Commission, July 1976), pp. 1–4.

38. Ibid., p. 3.

39. Ibid.

40. ACIR, *Improving Urban America*, op. cit., p. 68.

41. Wisconsin Commission, *Final Report*, op. cit., chap. 9, p. 1.

42. Ibid.

43. Ibid., p. 4.

44. Ibid., p. 1.

45. Ibid.

46. ACIR, *Improving Urban America*, op. cit., p. 57.

47. Wisconsin Commission, *Final Report*, op. cit., chap. 9, p. 1.

6

Selected Current Issues in the Use of State and Local Revenue Sources

Richard D. Bingham, Brett W. Hawkins, and Kraig Rodenbeck

This chapter addresses issues that arise when changes are contemplated or made in the way the principal tax sources are used. For example, what are the pros and cons of a local sales tax? What are the pros and cons of expanding state programs of property tax relief? What considerations of bias and benefit arise from programs of state aid? What conflicts of interest occur over these and other issues?

Three main topics organize this chapter: property-related revenue issues, local revenue diversification, and state aid. Many subtopics are also addressed. In order to place these issues within a political context, we will make frequent reference to the way the issues are being confronted in Wisconsin. Other settings will be mentioned when needed to show alternatives not explored in Wisconsin, but Wisconsin will get much of the attention.

PROPERTY-RELATED REVENUE ISSUES

The popular and sometimes emotional issue of property taxation will be approached from four different directions: (1) pressures on property taxes stemming from school costs, (2) pressures from state-mandated services, (3) relief from property taxes, and (4) property tax base sharing for purposes of reducing disparities among localities in their abilities to finance public services.

The Pressure of Financing Local Education

A subject of perennial interest to property tax reformers is elementary and secondary education, since school districts are big consumers of property tax revenue. From 1942 to the early 1970s, the share of the property tax dollar claimed by education has grown from about one-third to about one-half—leaving municipalities, counties, and townships a smaller share to use for other services. It is expected that educational costs will remain high even if enrollments decline.[1]

Noting that education is a service with a high spillover benefit and that the property tax burden has grown to a point where it is nearly intolerable in many jurisdictions, the ACIR recommends that the schools be financed from statewide taxes of a type more responsive to economic growth and less regressive in impact—that is, from sales and income taxes.[2] The ACIR believes that "in the long run substantially all the non-Federal financing of elementary and secondary education should be shifted from the local property tax to the superior tax resources of the state governments."[3] Hawaii has already assumed complete responsibility for both the financing and the operation of schools, and a number of other states—New Mexico, North Carolina, Delaware, and Louisiana, among them—are within striking distance of the ACIR recommendation. By 1975, about two-fifths of the states had begun to increase state funding and thereby move away from overreliance on the property tax for school purposes.[4]

As an intermediate step, the ACIR recommends that regional or county property taxing districts be authorized to provide most of the financing of metropolitan schools. The typical metropolitan area has more than a dozen school systems per county; and these systems differ widely in their financial capacities to support education programs (and hence in the tax rates they must impose). In order to achieve larger and therefore less fiscally divergent school-administering units, the ACIR even recommends that a state agency be authorized to mandate the establishment of county or regional property taxing districts for schools, where these do not currently exist.[5]

The ACIR proposal contemplates that most of any local taxation for schools would be provided on a regional or countywide basis. Wider school taxing districts are not unprecedented, of course; in some states, notably in the South, public schools are already administered by countywide systems. Another precedent for this action exists in states that allow countywide taxes to be imposed for school purposes, allocable to contained districts on a formula basis. These programs generally finance only a small part of local education however.[6]

The advantage of wider taxation districts is that dollars raised by property taxes can be shifted from localities having the greatest resources to those having the greatest educational needs—factors usually inversely related. In metropolitan areas, needs usually concentrate in central-city schools. And therein lies an important obstacle to this change. The residents of wealthier suburbs are not happy over the prospect of outsiders using revenue produced by their property to finance someone else's schools. Nor are they happy that state aid for school and nonschool purposes has been changed in many states so as to allocate fewer dollars to their better-off communities, thus forcing them to raise property taxes.

Suburbanites can be expected to resist regional taxing districts for education and all other proposals that take away dollars or authority over dollars from themselves, their friends, and neighbors. In doing so they can be expected to invoke faithfully the symbolism of the "grass-roots" tradition, which emphasizes "government close to the people."

The issue of fiscal disparities among taxing jurisdictions is central to the debate about financing the schools. If the disparity in property valuation per pupil between a state's wealthiest and poorest district is, say, 10 to 1, property owners in the poor district have to pay ten times the tax rate of property owners in the wealthy district to raise the same amount of revenue. This example may seem extreme, but the ratio between the richest and poorest district in California has been reported as 25 to 1, in Michigan 30 to 1, and in Illinois 20 to 1.[7] Such disparities have led to historic court decisions.[8] The California supreme court, for example, has said that the property tax system of financing the schools makes the quality of a child's education depend on the resources of his school district and ultimately on the pocketbook of his parents. "We find that such financing system as presently constituted is not necessary to the attainment of any compelling state interest . . . it denies to the plaintiffs and others similarly situated the equal protection of the laws."[9]

Following this decision in 1971, the California legislature moved to make school spending more equitable, but the state supreme court ruled its remedies insufficient. The court said that district spending cannot vary by more than $100 per pupil, and it suggested alternatives to local property taxes as the principal means of financing public education. It mentioned full state funding with a statewide property tax, consolidating the more than 1,000 school districts into about 500 with boundaries drawn to equalize property value, and taxing commercial and industrial property at the state rather than local level. This latest ruling, although long expected, is likely to have a major impact, all the more so because it comes at a time when California property owners are in near revolt over spiraling taxes.[10] The California legislature is now considering a bill designed to equalize per-pupil expenditures among the state's school districts.

In 1973, Wisconsin took a controversial step to help equalize the fiscal disparities of its school taxing districts. The state goal was to guarantee each pupil in the state the same tax base, in order that each school district might have an equal ability to choose the educational services it wished to provide. The key provision of the new formula was that any district with a per-pupil tax base higher than the state-guaranteed base would pay the state property tax money for transfer to other districts. "Thus a rich district with a given level of spending planned per pupil and a valuation 150 percent above the guaranteed valuation would be required to raise 150 percent of the amount it actually wished to spend per pupil and turn one-third of its revenues over to the state for redistribution."[11] It was determined that 40 of Wisconsin's more than 400 school districts would have to share their property taxes with less wealthy districts. These included not only resort towns and some wealthy residential communities in the Milwaukee area but also a working-class suburb in the Milwaukee area whose per-pupil property valuation was high because of industrial property.[12]

Tempers flared over the proposal. It was called "the most sinister thing ever concocted by any government." And opponents charged that the main purpose of the program was to finance "high class schools with a lot of frills in Madison and Milwaukee."[13]

Inevitably, the law was challenged in court. In 1976 the Wisconsin supreme court declared that the program, which had yet to go into effect, violated the state constitution. Specifically, the program was held to contravene a requirement that taxation be uniform. The court said that a tax had to pertain to a public purpose of the district within which it was levied. The taxes to be raised under this program were local taxes, but the purpose was a state one. The state could not constitutionally compel one school district to levy a tax for the direct benefit of other school districts, or the state, rather than for its own benefit.[14]

This decision disappointed those who were most enthusiastic about equalizing per-pupil tax bases. But it did not rule out equalizing state aids of a conventional nature. Wisconsin school aids have expressly reflected the goal of equalization since 1949. Under the Wisconsin formula, districts with a higher per-pupil tax base got and still get less aid.[15] If the district's actual property valuation per pupil is less than the statutorily guaranteed valuation per pupil, the state, from general funds, provides the difference between the amount per pupil that the district actually raised by applying its mill rate to its own valuation per pupil and the amount the district would have raised had its own mill rate been applied to the state-guaranteed valuation per pupil.[16]

Recent evidence indicates that a substantial measure of equalization is indeed accomplished. Where equalization occurs, we would expect an inverse relationship between measures of local wealth and dollars of school aid, and that is, in fact, the case. Two measures of wealth/fiscal capacity not employed in the Wisconsin formula correlate negatively with dollars allocated to school districts. (The measures are full value of property per capita and adjusted gross income per capita.

The measure employed by the state has been mentioned: per-pupil property valuation.)[17]

If per-pupil property value were the best indicator of ability to pay for educational services, the Wisconsin system would be not only equalizing among taxing districts but also progressive in the sense of recognizing differences among individual taxpayers in their abilities to pay taxes. However, the property tax base is not a very good indicator of ability to pay. The pattern of industrial location and income distribution in a state may produce districts with mostly low-income residents that have per-pupil tax bases similar to those of districts containing mostly high-income residents. In the Milwaukee area, for example, there is one school district with very low per capita income but very high per-pupil property valuation.[18]

A recent study dramatizes the difference that inclusion of a personal income factor would make in the distribution of Wisconsin school aids. Researchers computed aid dollars using four different formulas: (1) the one in current use—that is, school district property valuation as the sole measure of wealth, (2) individual income taxes in the district as the sole measure of wealth, (3) the aggregate of property valuations and individual income taxes as a combined measure of wealth, and (4) a formula that would allocate 50 percent of the aid on the basis of property valuation and the other 50 percent on the basis of individual income taxes. Using the first formula, one Milwaukee suburban district got $243,000. With the second formula, it would have gotten nothing. With the third, it would have gotten $135,000, and with the fourth about $122,000.[19]

The states could opt for a program of school aid that equalizes the per-pupil tax base among districts and modifies the impact of that program on individual taxpayers by providing expanded property tax relief for those taxpayers whose tax burdens exceed a certain percent of income. Expanded property tax relief has the advantage of making the property tax more progressive, and it speaks directly to the problem of income-poor individuals in property-rich school districts. It also maintains a kind of accountability because the property tax is still paid by the individual; so he is aware of the general level of taxation for school purposes.[20] On the other hand, to expand or widen eligibility for property tax relief payments implies an increase in state taxes. Where the state income tax is already very high relative to other states, policy makers must consider the possibility of an adverse effect on the economy if a property tax relief program is funded by increases in the income tax.[21] Further, there are philosophical objections. Expanded programs of property tax relief are likely to be opposed as efforts to redistribute wealth.

Alternatively, the states could provide that where a municipality is wholly within a school district's boundaries, the municipality could finance education from whatever local revenue sources are available to the jurisdiction.[22] The option of using other revenue sources to support education could help reduce reliance on the property tax. But at a time of public concern about taxes, alternative sources may be less than readily available.

A similar problem confronts another possibility—the uniform, statewide property tax. Revenues from that tax could be distributed along with the state's general revenue commitment to schools through the school aid program. But increased property taxes are most unwelcome nowadays, whether levied by local or by state authorities.

The Pressure of State-Mandated Local Services

As noted in Chapter 2, burdens on local revenue capabilities are increased when state governments mandate a service and require that it be financed out of local revenues. A recent study by the Wisconsin Department of Revenue details the impacts of such mandated services on local governments—specifically, towns, villages, and cities in Iowa County, Wisconsin. The study found that a state can mandate local provision of services in three basic ways: (1) by "shall" requirements in state statutes (for example, "the provision of community health service shall be administered by local governmental units"); (2) by making a service optional, but subject to state program requirements if it is implemented; or (3) by offering inducements (such as state aid) to local governments to provide such services, which, if implemented, would be subject to state performance standards.

The fiscal impact of mandated services is significant, according to the Wisconsin study. In Iowa County for fiscal year 1975, mandated services accounted for almost 25 percent of total local government expenditures. Also, all forms of local government, except towns, spent over 50 percent of their state aid to cover the costs of state-mandated services (towns spent 39 percent on mandated services). Most of these expenses were involved in the construction and maintenance of highways. This, however, is due to Iowa County's rural nature; one would expect urban counties (such as Milwaukee) to spend a higher proportion of their mandated costs on services such as public health, safety, and environmental protection.

If the states decided to compensate local governments for the provision of state-mandated services, which is what many localities would like, the cost would be tremendous. In fiscal 1975, for example, total reimbursement by the state of Wisconsin to Iowa County for the provision of mandated services would have been $1.7 million. If each of Wisconsin's 72 counties had received similar reimbursements, the total reimbursement bill for the state would have been $120 million.[23] Undoubtedly, this figure is an underestimate, since it is based on a rural county's expenditures, which are surely smaller than those of Wisconsin's urban counties.

The effect of state-mandated services is further illustrated by recent events in the city of Milwaukee. In 1975, Milwaukee taxpayers faced a substantial property tax increase due to increased costs of operation. The public schools alone sought a 15.8 percent increase.

A major portion of the school increase was due to a new state law requiring local school districts to identify and educate all children with mental, physical, emotional, and learning disabilities (12,800 of them in the Milwaukee system). This requirement produced a new staff of 272 for exceptional education and 122 additional teachers and aides for reading programs. This increase more than offset the loss of 149 regular teacher and staff positions from enrollment declines.[24]

As commendable as such action is from the perspective of educational opportunity, the failure of the state to assume the cost placed a considerable strain on Milwaukee. Milwaukee taxpayers revolted, led by the members of the Milwaukee Common Council, who were using the school budget to divert attention from the city's 1974 reassessment (which increased the proportional tax burden on residential property) and who were trying to build a political base for legislation to get more school costs financed by means other than the property tax.[25]

Wisconsin law charges the Milwaukee Common Council with the responsibility to levy and collect whatever taxes are deemed necessary by the Milwaukee school board to run the schools. During the fall of 1974, the council twice flouted state law and refused to levy the taxes that the board requested. The aldermen simply said that taxes were too high. The school board finally was forced to file suit against the council to get it to collect the taxes.[26]

This was not the end of the issue, however. Stirred by the actions of the council, a group of citizens organized a drive to recall the 15 members of the Milwaukee school board. The petitions against each member of the board required 6,800 signatures (25 percent of the 1974 city vote for governor divided by five, the number of school board candidates in a regular election).[27] The recall petition for each board member stated that:

This member of the Milwaukee School Board has voted for the approval of a budget resulting in a $26.3 million tax levy increase, which is an increase of 26% over last year. At the same time the City of

Milwaukee and Milwaukee County have actually cut their tax levy by over $1.5 million. The school board of which this elected official is a member has also requested an additional $25 million in bonding for construction purposes at a time when enrollment decline has been over 13,000 students the past three years; and according to all projections decreases are expected to continue in following years. . . . Due to inflation, layoffs and other considerations, the citizens of Milwaukee are unable to support such tax increases which will raise the Milwaukee property tax rate to over $10 per $1,000 of assessed evaluation, causing the owner of a $25,000 home to pay over $500 in school taxes alone.[28]

The next move was the school board's. One board member indicated that he would introduce a resolution supporting a citizens' group suit challenging the constitutionality of the property tax to support schools. The school board president indicated that he would go along with the resolution, adding that he has consistently opposed the property tax as the way to finance schools.[29]

The recall petition succeeded. Within a month after the drive began, leaders of the Wisconsin Citizens for Legal Recall announced that they had more than 12,000 signatures on each petition—almost twice the required number.[30] By the time of the petition deadline, between 33,000 and 34,000 signatures had been obtained.

However, the petition drive itself was challenged in court, and there the entire enterprise died. Circuit Judge George A. Burns, Jr., ruled that under Wisconsin law, school board members, who were not officers of the city, were not subject to popular recall by petition, but only by the courts.[31] Ultimately the school district budget, with its state-mandated costs, was passed by the Common Council; and the resultant tax burden was placed on the shoulders of city of Milwaukee property taxpayers.

Wisconsin is among the heavy mandating states, but the problem of state mandating is widespread. While there is little or no controversy over some mandates, particularly those relating to the organization and procedures of local government, "it would be difficult to find an issue that sparks more resentment among local officials than that caused by state-mandated expenditures."[32] Full or partial reimbursement may assuage local bitterness, but the cost of reimbursement may put that solution out of reach.

A general principle to guide mandated services might be that a state should mandate only essential levels of state priority services that realize state goals. When mutual state-local goals are involved, there should be a sharing of financial responsibility between the state and local units.[33] In any case, the question of mandated services and their fiscal impacts on states and localities is a complex issue that needs more research. It threatens to become a serious strain upon state-local fiscal and political relations.

Relief from Property Taxes

Local reliance on the property tax, whether for school or nonschool purposes, is rooted in state constitutional provisions. It is also strongly influenced by the state's delegation to local governments of specific functional responsibilities and by the fact that property tax valuations often enter into state grant formulas.[34] These features make it difficult to change.

As already indicated, however, proposals have been put forward to provide relief from property taxes.

State-financed relief for taxpayers whose property tax burdens are greatest relative to income include circuit-breaker programs that have been pioneered in Minnesota, Wisconsin, and Vermont. They are called this because they operate as a circuit breaker in stopping the outflow of property tax funds to the tax collector when the property tax burden reaches a certain percentage of personal income.[35] Commonly, the circuit-breaker program is part of the state income tax system. When the taxpayer files his income tax return, the state revenue agency examines the total reported income and the property tax liability and then computes the amount of property tax deemed to be excessive. The agency either credits the amount of relief against the state income tax or issues a refund check.

New Mexico has gone beyond the usual circuit-breaker program in attempting to relieve tax overload. The "low-income comprehensive tax rebate" is designed to lessen the overall regressivity of New Mexico's state-local tax system for those at the lower end of the income scale. Although it is a partial reimbursement for taxes of all types, including sales taxes, property taxes, and others, the program is treated as an income tax rebate for administrative convenience. The rebate is obtained by completing a section of the personal income tax form. New Mexico officials believe that their approach is a good one for reducing the regressive effect of state and local tax systems. They therefore feel a responsibility to inform members of the public about the program and convince them that it is not just another "giveaway."[36] An alternative method of lessening the regressivity of state taxes—exempting food and medicine from the sales tax—is criticized because all families, high and low income, would have their tax burden reduced.[37] Also such programs reduce the tax revenues that would otherwise be available from the general sales tax. Money would therefore have to be drawn from other sources or a lower level of services would have to be accepted. Increases in the income tax are one source of such funding, but resistance to this is likely in states that already have high income taxes.

Any change in tax instruments has disadvantages that have to be offset or accepted. A variety of alternative trade-offs are possible. For example, a study commission in Wisconsin has recommended increased relief from personal property taxes on farmers' livestock and merchants' and manufacturers' inventories. Funds for this "personal property tax relief" would be obtained from taxes on the income of the types of enterprises receiving such tax relief. But one member of the commission objects to the funding suggestion on the grounds that Wisconsin's individual income tax is already third highest in the country. His preference is to put a sales tax on food (currently exempt) and offset the regressive effect of that action by a credit under the circuit-breaker program.[38] Of course, that credit would also have to be made up or reduced revenue would have to be accepted.

Local income taxes may also be used to relieve the property tax burden. Imposition of such taxes was closely coupled with property tax reduction in Flint and Saginaw, Michigan. When Indiana and Ohio decided to permit localities to levy an income tax, they required that it be used for property tax relief. There is some evidence also that cities with income taxes have lower property and total taxes per capita. In addition, upper-income flight is not much in evidence as a result of local income taxes, despite the fact that upper-income persons are most capable of fleeing their imposition.[39]

Reducing Disparities in Local Fiscal Resources by Tax Base Sharing

Another reform relating to property taxes is Minnesota's Fiscal Disparities Law.[40] It addresses the fact that wealthier communities (in terms of property values) can support a given level of municipal services with a tax rate that is lower than less wealthy communities. This is of course a disparities problem. The Minnesota law applies to the Twin Cities metropolitan area and is administered by a unique regional unit of government, the Twin Cities Metropolitan Council. The system that is set up shares tax base, not tax revenue, and is therefore an alternative to equalizing state aid. It establishes an areawide tax base pool to which is assigned 40 percent of the increase of commercial and industrial property values above the 1971 base year. In determining the amount of each municipality's annual contribution to this areawide tax base pool, consideration is given to the effects of new construction, inflation, depreciation, and other factors on the value of lands zoned for commercial and industrial uses. The portion of the valuation of each municipality that goes to the areawide tax base is not subject to the municipality's own tax rate. Allocations are made from the areawide tax base pool to 300 jurisdictions in the area by a formula that reflects population and per capita property values. The formula works to the advantage of municipalities with increasing populations and lower-than-average property values.

The community's own tax base, minus its contribution to the area-wide base, plus its distribution from the areawide base, make up the effective tax base upon which it may levy taxes.

Proponents of the Fiscal Disparities Law argue that it provides some equalization of tax base among municipalities in the metropolitan area, reduces competition among municipalities for new commercial and industrial development, and reduces incentives to zone out residential property that may not pay its way. The physical location of a key type of taxable property is no longer the determining factor in a juris-diction's property tax return. Some critics argue that the law tries to do too much. They say that equalization of wealth could be accomplished more effectively by establishing a new source of revenue, such as a metropolitan-wide sales tax, which would then be distributed to the area's municipalities on an equalization formula.

LOCAL GOVERNMENT REVENUE DIVERSIFICATION

Diversification is an alternative strategy that the states may employ to assist their localities financially. It refers to the state authorizing alternative local revenue sources, and it may be contrasted with increased reliance on state revenue sources and correspondingly increased state aid distributions.[41] Revenue diversification programs focus principally on a local income tax, sales tax, motor vehicle fee, and user fees. Commonly justified as a way to reduce property taxes as the major source of local revenue, the adoption of such alternatives is potentially controversial. If one locality adopts a tax, it may be to the disadvantage of local businesses and also stimulate the flight of relatively well-off citizens. For this reason, revenue diversification is often proposed for larger units of government, such as counties, or on a regional scale.

For example, a commission of the state of Wisconsin recommends that counties be authorized to enact a 1 percent sales tax for the purpose of decreasing their dependence on the property tax as the major source of revenue. The county sales tax would be piggybacked on the state's sales tax structure; the state would retain a small percentage of county sales tax collections for administrative costs; and at least 50 percent of county sales tax revenues (less state administrative costs) would be distributed to the municipalities within the county, based on population and applied as a credit against property taxes levied by each municipality.[42] Like the state sales tax, the county sales tax would be deductable from federal income tax liabilities. Therefore, the federal government would pay part of any county sales tax.

It can be argued, moreover, that adding the sales tax would provide for a more balanced county revenue system. The property tax is a stable yielder but is regressive in impact. The sales tax is more subject to fluctuations, but with food and medicine exempt it is more progressive. This puts the two in the position of balancing each other. It is also argued that, by itself, the county sales tax would not be a strong factor in the decision of individuals and businesses to flee urban counties (thus encouraging urban sprawl). Presumably, water and sewer lines, highway and bus lines, and such public facilities as schools have a greater bearing on locational choices.[43]

Even if the base of local and state sales taxes is the same, if the tax is collected and administered by the state and the jurisdiction levying the tax is geographically extensive, there are still arguments against the sales tax. For example, the sales tax is condemned as not much different from the property tax in terms of the distribution of its burden. Therefore some people oppose it with equity arguments. Also, a property-tax/sales-tax revenue system for counties does not overcome differences in the fiscal capacities of counties. "Disparities" will exist in their property values and retail sales. In addition, high-income persons, who are more mobile than low-income persons, can still migrate to counties with low sales and property taxes. If that happens, the poorer counties will have to raise their rates to yield higher revenues.[44]

The Wisconsin commission further recommends that towns, villages, and cities be permitted to levy a motor vehicle tax equal to 50 percent of the state motor vehicle fee on all passenger vehicles garaged within the jurisdiction. The commission also recommends that the Wisconsin statutes be amended to permit complete local option to establish user fees sufficient to cover the actual cost of any service provided.[45]

If one looks at all the Wisconsin recommendations together, it is clear that what is contemplated is a new system of local revenue. Counties would be able to finance their activities from a local sales tax and user fees as well as the established property tax. Cities, towns, and villages would be able to employ user fees to reduce property taxes, and impose a wheel tax as well.[46] (The commission also considered, but did not recommend, a local income tax for each city, town, and village, to be imposed on both residents and commuters.) It can be argued that such a diversified system both provides adequate revenue raising tools and permits a reduction in local reliance on the property tax.

However, there is a general objection to the whole concept of local revenue diversification. In a sense, it is contradictory. As some see it, the financial problem of local governments in the United States

> is that those general local governments with little ability to pay are by their very nature the same units of local governments with great financial need. Therefore, allowing this type of local government more power to tax its citizens is in reality no solution at all, since these are the very same type of citizens who lack financial ability, whether the tax is a property tax or an income tax."[47]

BIAS, BENEFIT, AND CONFLICT IN STATE INTERGOVERNMENTAL AID

Analysis by the ACIR indicates that state aid is not generally allocated in a manner that equalizes local fiscal capacities. This important generalization is reached in the following way. Allocations are deemed partly equalizing if allocation formulas include at least one of the following components: population, tax capacity, tax effort, fiscal needs, and property tax rates. Of course, the mere presence of such factors in a formula does not indicate the degree of equalization, but the inference is made by the ACIR that formulas employing these factors achieve some equalization of fiscal capacities.[48] Education aids are an exception to the generalization that state aid is not equalizing.[49]

Nonequalizing aids have definite implications in terms of benefiting localities. They mean that localities with larger populations, with lower-income persons, with lower property values, and/or that make greater tax efforts are not benefited by state aid relative to those localities with smaller populations, more wealth, and a smaller tax effort.

Correlation analysis reveals diverse patterns of equalization and nonequalization among and within states. The New York State aid system, for example, displays a significant and negative relationship between total per capita state aid and per capita income (when the New York City area is excluded).[50] Similarly, state grants in Kentucky are equalizing, as indicated by the same kind of negative or inverse relationship between state aid and income. In Oregon, this relationship appears for counties but not for cities or school districts. On the other hand, state aid in Illinois does not serve to equalize the fiscal capacities of counties, but, among municipalities, there is a significant negative correlation with income. Yet, in Virginia, the relationship is not equalizing for municipalities.[51]

Correlation analysis of 1973 Wisconsin data indicates that total state aid does not clearly benefit cities having less fiscal capacity, making a greater property tax effort, or exhibiting more fiscal need. Therefore total aid in Wisconsin does not adhere to the equalization principle. The same is true of the categorical forms of aid, except education. Consistent with the ACIR evidence, education aid in Wisconsin is equalizing. There is a negative correlation between education payments and both income and property valuation (all per capita).[52]

The diversity of findings in different states, the lack of consistency within states, and the realization that many programs of state aid were adopted on a piecemeal basis with little regard for the effect of one part on another have prompted some observers to suggest that state aid is a patchwork of inconsistent and conflicting goals or principles.[53]

State revenue sharing merits special attention because of the current interest in unrestricted forms of aid. State revenue sharing may yet achieve some of the prominence that federal revenue sharing has gained in recent years. At present, only about 10 percent of state aid payments nationally are in the form of shared taxes,[54] but some states rely on this device much more. Wisconsin is among these states. Twenty-four percent of the revenue received by Wisconsin cities is in the form of state-shared taxes. For towns, the figure is 31 percent and for villages, 37 percent (1973 figures).

Tax sharing can be accomplished so as to serve equalization goals.[55] Wisconsin's shared tax program has moved in this direction. Up to 1971, shared taxes were intentionally returned to localities based on point of origin. It was argued that local jurisdictions raising large amounts of revenue had large needs.

In that year, a decision was made to distribute shared taxes according to three separate formulas. Some money was distributed on a per capita basis, some on the basis of tax effort, and some on the basis of certain utility properties in the jurisdiction. This three-part program has had some equalizing effect. Analysis reveals that it benefits cities paying higher taxes per capita to the state—that is, it generally returns revenue to its point of origin. Wisconsin's shared tax formula also contains one component intended to produce some equalization of local fiscal capacities. When this component's allocations are examined separately, they are indeed equalizing, but the total of shared aid is not. Beginning in 1976, the equalization component was changed and strengthened. Property valuation per capita is now part of the formula. For any given tax rate, payments diminish as per capita property valuation increases between $15,000 and $30,000. Above $30,000 per capita valuation, payments are zero.[56] The effect of this new policy has been to reduce state aid payments to some better-off localities and force them to increase their property taxes, cut services, achieve efficiencies, or work out some combination of the three.[57]

Of course, virtually any change in state-local financial arrangements can produce controversy, but changes that redistribute wealth or reduce state aid revenues for some recipients are particularly volatile. Complex interrelationships exist, not just between state and local units, but also among local units—and between state policies regarding aid and local policies regarding own-source revenue. Recent events in Wisconsin illustrate these complexities.

The kick-off of the controversy came with the release of a study commissioned by the village of Brown Deer concerning the impact of the new revenue-sharing policy. The study, released in May 1976, stated that if Brown Deer were to attract a $10 million nonresidential development, the village would lose money from state-shared tax funds and be forced to raise its property tax rate by 33 cents per $1,000 of assessed valuation. This, the study claimed, was a result of changes in state aid formulas that served to decrease aid to a municipality if its tax base increased faster than those of other municipalities. Also at fault, according to the Brown Deer study, was the state's policy of exempting industrial equipment and machinery from the property tax rolls, which left municipalities unable to tax a substantial portion of their industrial development and unwilling to encourage new, largely nontaxable industrial development. Thus, recently changed state aid and tax policies were described as deterrents, rather than incentives, for municipalities to attract industry.[58]

The state administration in Madison was so concerned over the Brown Deer study and the antiadministration feelings it was generating that it commissioned a University of Wisconsin professor to perform a similar study. In his report, the professor claimed to have found a calculation error in the Brown Deer study, which, he stated, invalidated that study's findings. Instead of meaning a tax increase of 33 cents per $1,000, a $10 million commercial development would lower Brown Deer's property tax by 26 cents per $1,000. Brown Deer officials were embittered by this finding and also by the language of a former revenue secretary who labeled Brown Deer's study "erroneous and careless." Brown Deer officials now criticized the professor, saying that he had inconsistently applied state, county, and vocational taxes in his calculations, which invalidated his study.[59]

In the wake of this haggling over a few pennies of tax increase or decrease, some state officials agreed that a community's financial incentives to encourage industrial development had been removed and that Wisconsin policies were "essentially neutral with regard to industrial development."[60] That such financial policies were adopted by a state that was, and still is, in the midst of a national advertising campaign designed to lure industry was called a contradiction of ends and means.

However, a Milwaukee *Journal* editorial from September 7, 1976, stated that the new policies had indeed improved Wisconsin's overall tax climate and had curbed the problem of one community "stealing" industry from another within the state. State officials began to push the idea that the new state policies force local governments to look beyond the tax and revenue aspects of development to such other aspects as the effect of each prospective development on jobs and the environment.[61]

The most recent battle in the Wisconsin shared revenue/property tax controversy was over the content of the 1977–79 state budget. Both the city of Milwaukee and its suburbs voiced fierce opposition to various sections of the proposed budget, leading to several media altercations between representatives of those interests and the secretary of the Wisconsin Department of Revenue and others.

In September 1976, the revenue secretary was quoted in the Milwaukee *Journal* as saying that he would recommend to the governor a policy of no tax increase for the 1977–79 budget, which would thus be the third straight no-tax-increase budget produced by the Democratic administration of Patrick Lucey.[62] The secretary also remarked that the administration was emphasizing new redistribution and tax equalization themes, meaning that rural residents of, for example, Wood County, would have to contribute tax dollars toward alleviating the social ills of Milwaukee, while Milwaukeeans' tax dollars would help aid the elderly residents of Wood County. A state senator issued a press release stating that what the secretary really meant was that administration "taxation policies were going to make all state residents pay for Milwaukee's problems."[63]

The Milwaukee suburbs, using the village of Shorewood as an example, opposed the governor's proposed 1977–79 budget, saying that although the state income tax rates had not increased for the past four years, local property taxes had been forced upward to keep pace with inflation and because of state politics. The December 1976 and April 1977 issues of the Shorewood *Official Bulletin* claimed that, between 1971 and 1977, local property taxpayers' share of local government expenses had risen from 43 percent to 62 percent, while the state's share had fallen from 57 percent to 38 percent. The December *Official Bulletin* stated that "it can be fairly said that State taxes are being held level at the expense of the property taxpayers."

The city of Milwaukee also opposed the budget proposal. Mayor Henry Maier, who has often blamed Milwaukee's woes on its suburbs, said that all Wisconsin cities, villages, and towns must unite against Lucey's budget, or their interests would be destroyed.[64] The Milwaukee Common Council organized a massive lobby effort in Madison against the proposed budget and sent mailings to city residents that encouraged opposition to the budget. This caused a tremendous furor, with media confrontations between state and city officials concerning the effects of the proposed budget. The state claimed that Milwaukee property taxes on a $30,000 home would be reduced by $103 by 1979 under current administration policies, while the city claimed that those same policies would result in a tax increase of $137 on a $30,000 home![65]

The proposed budget passed the state legislature virtually unaltered.

One may ask why the administration would back revenue policies that arouse so much municipal opposition. A possible answer is that, while alienating municipal officials, Wisconsin's recent policies have the support of the voters because they have received tremendously increased property tax relief from the state. From 1970 to 1977, the state payout of property tax relief increased by 87.8 percent. Wisconsin has also distributed an additional $333 million and $248 million in school aids and county welfare support respectively since 1971.

While the cities complain that their portion of the shared tax fund has not kept pace with that fund's growth, the administration skims money from that fund and sends it directly to individuals to pay for the circuit-breaker program and for personal property tax relief, thus winning the support of low- and middle-income property owners. While municipalities complain about the removal of manufacturing machinery and equipment from the property tax rolls, the administration skims more money from the shared tax fund to pay for this loss, winning the support of business and industry. Milwaukee *Sentinel* reporter Neil Shively has summarized the administration's tax policy, saying, "its emphasis is on sending the money to the taxpayer, not the tax collector's purse. It is a populist, share the wealth doctrine that has appeal. . . ."[66]

Some consideration has been given to a completely different basis for sharing Wisconsin's revenues with local governments. The idea would be to eliminate both the per capita payment and the payment based on property valuation in order to finance a greatly expanded tax relief program aimed at equalizing not the financial capacity of jurisdictions but the ability of individuals to pay taxes. This idea addresses the distinction between two kinds of equalization: equalization of the fiscal capacity of jurisdictions to finance services, and equalization of the ability of individuals to bear the local tax burden.[67] Indeed, that is not the only change contemplated by the proposal. It provides for three things: (1) elimination of state shared taxes (except for the sharing of utility taxes), (2) revenue diversification for counties to include a sales tax, and for cities, villages, and towns to include an income tax on residents and commuters, and (3) tax relief expanded in scope to provide relief for both property and sales taxes and paid directly to individuals based on ability to pay. Tax relief would also be expanded in terms of the total dollar commitment.[68]

While such a system is probably not politically feasible in its entirety, it is a comprehensive solution to problems that beset many local governments. The overall goal is the financing of local government based on ability to pay. Such a system would also reduce overall reliance on the property tax for local purposes.[69]

NOTES

1. Advisory Commission on Intergovernmental Relations, *Improving Urban America: A Challenge to Fiscal Federalism* (Washington, D.C.: ACIR, 1976), p. 39.

2. Ibid., p. 41. For a general discussion of school finance see also a special section on "School Finance Reform," by Cynthia Parsons, *Christian Science Monitor*, November 7, 1977.

3. Ibid., p. 45.

4. Ibid., p. 46.

5. Ibid., pp. 41–43.

6. Ibid., p. 44.

7. David L. Kirp, "Judicial Policy-Making: Inequitable Public School Financing and the Serrano Case (1971)," in *Policy and Politics in America*, ed. Allan P. Sindler (Boston: Little, Brown and Company, 1973), p. 88. The difference in expenditure per pupil between the lowest and highest spending district is not as dramatic as the difference in property valuation. Evidently, the reason is intergovernmental revenue. A recent survey of the states by the *Christian Science Monitor* puts the Michigan ratio at 4 to 1, the California ratio at 7 to 1, and the Illinois ratio at about 6 to 1. *Christian Science Monitor*, October 31, 1977.

8. *Serrano* v. *Priest*, 5 California 3d. 584, 487p. 2d. 1214 (1971); and *Rodriguez* v. *San Antonio Ind. School District*, 377F. Supp. 280 (W.D. Tex., 1971).

9. Quoted in Kirp, op. cit., p. 103. It should be noted that the reasoning here is subject to challenge on the grounds that "quality of education" may not correlate in any direct or significant way with more dollars. Indeed, there is evidence that it does not. For a typical summation of the evidence, see Fred M. Hechinger (New York *Times* Service), "School Daze: Even the Experts Don't Seem to Know What Makes a Good One," Milwaukee *Journal*, November 20, 1977.

10. Brad Knickerbocker, "California Ponders State Ban on School Tax," *Christian Science Monitor*, January 3, 1977.

11. David W. Schodt et al., *An Evaluation of Selected State-Local Fiscal Relationships in Wisconsin* (Madison: Prepared for the Commission on State-Local Relations and Financing Policy, 1976), pp. 22–25.

12. Charles E. Friederich, "40 of 400 Districts Would Pay Negative Aid," Milwaukee *Journal,* October 29, 1975.

13. Steve Hannah, "Negative Aid Stirs Negative Response," Milwaukee *Journal,* April 11, 1976.

14. *Buse et al.* v. *Smith et al.,* no. 75–552, August Term, 1976.

15. Schodt et al., op. cit., pp. 33–34.

16. *Buse* v. *Smith,* op. cit., p. 7 of the majority decision.

17. Brett W. Hawkins, Gary Portenier, and Linda Hawkins, "A Study of the Distributive Consequences of State Aid to Cities" (Milwaukee: Milwaukee Urban Observatory, 1977).

18. Schodt et al., op. cit., p. 33.

19. Wisconsin Legislative Council Staff, "Reprint of Alternative Computations of State Aid in 1975–76 Using Income as a Measure of School District Wealth," Information Memorandum 76–27 (Madison: the Council, September 22, 1976).

20. Wisconsin Commission on State-Local Relations and Financing Policy, "K-12 School Aids," Alternative Paper no. 11, part 2 (Madison: the Commission, November 1976), p. 5.

21. Wisconsin Commission on State-Local Relations and Financing Policy, *The Final Report of the Commission on State-Local Relations and Financing Policy* (Madison: the Commission, January 1977), pp. MR (minority reports) 12–13.

22. Ibid., p. 2.

23. Catherine McLaughlin and Marilee Wertlake, draft of a study of state-mandated service costs in Iowa County, Wis. (Madison: Bureau of Local Fiscal Information and Analysis, Wisconsin Department of Revenue, June 1977).

24. Citizens' Governmental Research Bureau, *Bulletin* 62 (Milwaukee: the Bureau, December 28, 1974).

25. "Could School Board Ease Heat?" Milwaukee *Journal,* November 27, 1974.

26. "OK School Tax, Court Tells City," Milwaukee *Journal,* December 2, 1974.

27. "Board Recall Sought," Milwaukee *Journal,* December 4, 1974.

28. "Leader in Recall Hails Signups," Milwaukee *Journal,* December 9, 1974.

29. "School Board Urged to Aid Tax Fight," Milwaukee *Journal,* December 13, 1974.

30. "Recall Vote Drive Far over the Top," Milwaukee *Journal,* January 7, 1975.

31. David Bednarek, "Board Recall Thrown Out," Milwaukee *Journal,* February 21, 1975 and telephone interview with Bednarek, August 10, 1977.

32. John Shannon and L. Richard Gabler, "Tax Lids and Expenditure Mandates: The Case for Fiscal Fair Play," *Intergovernmental Perspective* 3 (Summer 1977): 9.

33. Wisconsin Commission, *Final Report,* op. cit., p. 19.

34. ACIR, op. cit., p. 55.

35. Ibid., p. 57.

36. Charles D. Turpen, "The Low-Income Comprehensive Tax Rebate: New Mexico's Broad-Based Tax Relief Program," *Revenue Review* (Santa Fe: New Mexico Bureau of Revenue, March 1977).

37. Ibid., p. 2.

38. Wisconsin Commission, *Final Report,* op. cit., p. MR-12.

39. Charles J. Sykes, "Tax for City Possible Here," Milwaukee *Journal,* August 16, 1977.

40. This section draws extensively on Wisconsin Commission on State-Local Relations and Financing Policy, "Local Government Revenue Sources: Alternative Revenue Sources," Issue Paper no. 15, Part B (Madison: the Commission, July 1976), pp. 13–15.

41. Wisconsin Commission, *Final Report,* op. cit., p. MR-1.

42. Ibid., p. 18.

43. Wisconsin Commission on State-Local Relations and Financing Policy, "State and Local Sources of Funds," Alternative Paper no. 10, part 2 (Madison: the Commission, November 1976), pp. 4–5.

44. Ibid. Additional arguments are covered here.

45. Wisconsin Commission, *Final Report*, op. cit., p. 18.

46. Wisconsin Commission, Alternative Paper no. 10, Part 2, op. cit., p. 20.

47. Wisconsin Commission, *Final Report*, op. cit., p. MR-2.

48. Advisory Commission on Intergovernmental Relations, *The States and Intergovernmental Aids* (Washington, D.C.: ACIR, 1977), pp. 23–25; and Advisory Commission on Intergovernmental Relations, *Information Bulletin*, September 1975, p. 3.

49. ACIR, *States and Intergovernmental Aids*, op. cit., p. 25; and ACIR, *Information Bulletin*, op. cit., p. 3.

50. ACIR, *States and Intergovernmental Aids*, op. cit., p. 45.

51. Ibid., pp. 47–55.

52. Hawkins, Portenier, and Hawkins, op. cit.

53. Ibid.; and John C. Bollens and Henry J. Schmandt, *The Metropolis* (New York: Harper and Row, 1975), p. 226.

54. ACIR, *Information Bulletin*, op. cit., p. 4.

55. A memo from Wisconsin State Senator P. Offner, April 29, 1975, makes this case.

56. Hawkins, Portenier, and Hawkins, op. cit.; and Schodt et al., op. cit., p. 87.

57. Village of Shorewood (Wisconsin), *Official Bulletin*, December 1976 and April 1977.

58. Charles J. Sykes, "City-Industry Honeymoon Seems Over," Milwaukee *Journal*, August 1, 1976.

59. Charles J. Sykes, "Study of State Tax Policies Stirs a Tempest," Milwaukee *Journal*, September 15, 1976.

60. Ibid.

61. Ibid.

62. Eugene C. Harrington, "Conta Will Seek Tax Lid," Milwaukee *Journal*, September 12, 1976.

63. "Revenue Chief, Senator Spar over Tax Points," Milwaukee *Journal*, September 3, 1976.

64. "Maier Says Budget Would Ruin Cities," Milwaukee *Journal*, April 22, 1977.

65. "State Office's Tax Projection Contradicts City's," Milwaukee *Journal*, May 26, 1977.

66. Neil H. Shively, "Lucey's Tax Policies Win Voters," Milwaukee *Sentinel*, March 28, 1977.

67. Wisconsin Commission, *Final Report*, op. cit., Policy Themes of Commission Recommendations.

68. Wisconsin Commission on State-Local Relations and Financing Policy, "State Aid to Municipalities," Alternative Paper no. 11, part 1 (Madison: the Commission, November 1976), pp. 2–3.

69. Ibid.

7

The Impact of the
Socioeconomic Environment
upon Revenue Policy

Richard D. Bingham, Brett W. Hawkins,
F. Ted Hebert, Roby Robertson, T. R. Carr,
and Robert M. Stein

Explaining the choice of policy X over policy Y has been a goal of political scientists for the last two decades. Just why does city A build public housing and does city B not? Just why does state C fund public education at a level much higher than that of state D? Earlier research focused principally upon the structure and functioning of the political system, but now the content of the policies that flow from that system receives equal emphasis. In fact, this book, devoted as it is to a particular policy area, reflects that trend—a desire to know more about the policies themselves and to explain them.

The effort to explain policy outcomes has typically utilized a model that portrays relationships between the outcomes and the forces that shape them. The outcomes are visualized as results of forces bearing on a system that produces responses or policies. Analyses of many state and local policies have followed this systems approach.[1] They have shown that socioeconomic characteristics of states or cities partially determine the nature of the political systems and that both socioeconomic characteristics and the structures and processes of these systems shape value commitments or policy outcomes.[2]

In applying this systems approach, statistical techniques have been used to examine the relationships between variables in the model. Before such techniques can be applied, however, means must be devised for measuring the variables, beginning with the policies themselves. For example, just what is the education policy of state C? Most commonly, such a question is answered by indicating state C's expenditures for education and, as was suggested above, comparing those with expenditures of other states. Scores of studies have been published on correlations of socioeconomic characteristics of states and localities with public expenditures in particular policy areas.[3] In this chapter we will be applying the same basic approach and methodology, but looking at state and local revenue policy. A major difficulty we face is the inability to use expenditures as an operational measure.

In a later portion of this chapter, we return to policies measured by expenditures. There we contend that certain revenue policies may themselves affect expenditure patterns.

SOCIOECONOMIC AND POLITICAL CORRELATES OF REVENUE POLICY

In the previous chapters, important differences in state and local revenue policies were noted, but there was little consideration of how these policies are related to the various jurisdictions' environments. One problem confronted in an attempt to do so is that of selecting the appropriate revenue system to be analyzed. The dependent variable might be state taxes only, or a combination of state and local taxes, local taxes only, or any of these three, but including nontax revenue. The few studies that have viewed tax or revenue policy as a dependent variable have not been uniform in their concentrations. Dye, for example, concentrated on state and local taxes,[4] Campbell and Sacks on local taxes,[5] and Sharkansky on state taxes.[6] While findings of these and other studies are reviewed below, our primary emphasis is on state tax systems. As Penniman suggests,

> . . . more and more political scientists believe that confining our attention to the state political system and its tax policy decisions in current years is the most profitable area of research. Local property taxes are those that remain after the state political system has determined general levels of taxes, types of taxes, and locally shared tax and grant-in-aid policies.[7]

STATE PLUS LOCAL REVENUE POLICY

The 1952 work of Solomon Fabricant, examining the relationships that three principal variables (per capita income, population density, and percent urban) had with per capita expenditures of state and local governments set the trend for many later studies of public policy.[8] With these variables Fabricant was able to account for 72 percent of the variation in per capita state spending for all functions. Although the variance that could be explained was not the same in all cases, these variables were found also to be correlated highly with spending in selected functional categories. Fabricant, as well as a later investigator,

Fisher,[9] found that per capita income was the variable of greatest importance.

Expanding on this effort, Dye, in *Politics, Economics, and the Public,* used a lengthy list of economic and political variables and found them strongly correlated with many measures of state policy. For example, his independent variables accounted for 74 percent of interstate variation in expenditures per pupil for education, 27 percent of the variation in per capita welfare expenditures, and 66 percent of the variance in per capita highway expenditures.[10] Of more direct interest, however, was Dye's analysis of the relationship between socioeconomic characteristics and state-local tax policy. He found several significant relationships between socioeconomic characteristics and measures of tax policy.[11] State wealth, urbanization, and industrialization were positively related to high per capita tax collections and negatively related to tax burdens and levels of federal and state aid. Wealthier, more urbanized, and industrialized states tended to rely heavily on local governments for the collection of revenues and provision of services and thus depended heavily on the property tax.

Although 79 percent of per capita tax collections were explained by his combination of economic and political variables, these variables were far less powerful in explaining the use of specific taxes. They accounted for only 18 percent of the variance in the use of income taxes, 20 percent of the variance in sales taxes, 16 percent of the variance in alcohol and tobacco taxes, and 28 percent of the variance in motor fuel taxes. Only for the property tax were the socioeconomic and political variables powerful predictors—accounting for 64 percent of the variance. Thus, the socioeconomic variables in Dye's study had far more impact upon expenditure policy than upon tax policy.

LOCAL REVENUE POLICY

Surprisingly, there has been little concern with the impact of the environment upon revenue policies of cities. One of the more extensive explorations of both local and state-local fiscal behavior was accomplished over ten years ago by Campbell and Sacks.[12] Their study, like the others mentioned, emphasized variation in expenditures; nevertheless, they did examine the impact of five independent variables on local taxes: density, percent urban, per capita, per capita state aid, and per capita federal aid.[13] These five variables explained 58.7 percent of interstate variation in per capita local taxes. This figure was not much more than the 52.1 percent found to be dependent on the income level of the population.

In examining an additional aspect of local revenue policy, Murphy and Rehfuss note that there are substantial differences both between central cities and suburbs and between different types of suburbs in the amounts of taxes raised.[14] Central cities tax residents at a higher rate than suburbs—suburbs exert only two-thirds of the tax éffort of central cities. Property tax rates in central cities and in low-income residential suburbs tend to be substantially higher than in other classes of suburbs. The low tax rate in wealthy residential suburbs is explained by the high residential assessments in these communities. Industrial suburbs owe their low tax rates to heavy industrial assessment, while balanced suburbs are also in a relatively strong fiscal position, with much of their taxable income derived from industry and business. (Industrial suburbs are defined as those in which over 60 percent of the property tax is derived from business real estate. Residential suburbs obtain more than 60 percent of revenues from residential properties while balanced suburbs collect 40 to 50 percent of their property taxes from residences.)

The Suburbs

In one of the most comprehensive examinations of local tax policy to date Susan MacManus described and contrasted patterns of change in the revenue levels and reliance patterns of 340 suburban municipalities over a ten-year period (1962–72).[15] Such research is difficult to accomplish. The restrictions placed on local government taxing powers by the states provide almost insurmountable obstacles to any study of the determinants of local revenues. However, even with the existence of these legal constraints, it is important to examine the demographic, socioeconomic, and political determinants of change in local revenue policy. "This is possible because changes in such environmental conditions have, in the past, worked to effect changes in legal restrictions on usage of certain revenues."[16]

MacManus found that increases in property tax levels were greatest among suburbs located in the Northeast, those with diversified-manufacturing economic bases, those with unreformed governments, and those responsible for performing all of the "least common" functional responsibilities (education, welfare, hospitals, housing, and urban renewal). On the other hand, suburbs located in the western states, those with industrial economic bases, those with reformed governments, and those with none of the responsibilities for performing the least common functions showed the greatest increases in nonproperty tax levels. Strangely, cities with populations between 25,000 and 50,000 showed large increases in tax levels in both categories—that is, in both property and nonproperty tax levels. Changes in nontax revenue levels (charges, miscellaneous general revenues) were greatest in southern suburbs, those with industrial economic bases, in reformed suburbs, and in smaller suburbs—those with populations below 25,000.

The changes in revenue level cited above are important; yet they present only a partial picture. Changes in the patterns of reliance on specific revenue sources are equally important. During the period 1961–72, the proportional reliance of suburbs on intergovernmental revenues and tax revenues increased while reliance on nontax revenues decreased. Increased reliance on the property tax was greatest among northeastern suburbs, those with diversified-manufacturing and industrial economic bases, and those with none of the responsibilities for the least common functions. Suburbs without responsibilities for the least common functions also showed increased reliance on nonproperty taxes as did suburbs located in the South, the largest suburbs, and those with diversified-manufacturing economic bases.

But what caused these changes? MacManus found that changes in local demographic and socioeconomic conditions could best explain changes in locally raised revenue levels. Changes in property tax levels are best explained by changes in density, various measures of social pathology (such as crime rates), changes in functional responsibility, income, racial balance, and crowding. These same factors were also found to be important determinants of changes in nonproperty tax levels.

The patterns of reliance upon given revenue sources are not consistently explained by socioeconomic character, however. Community indicators explained much of the variance in changes in nonproperty tax reliance and nontax revenue reliance but were not very successful in explaining changes in property tax reliance. The factors most affecting property tax reliance appear to be state restrictions on property tax use and political constraints on property tax increases. Increases in home ownership, income, and education, coupled with decreases in residential crowding, poverty, and the number of black and aged residents in a community, accounted for most of the variance in changes in nonproperty tax reliance. Nontax revenue reliance, on the other hand, was best explained by increases in density and crime, and decreases in income, the birth rate, and education.

Thus MacManus identified the changes in demographic and socioeconomic characteristics generally associated with changing local revenue policies—at least among suburbs. Changes in certain of these characteristics were good predictors of changes in both revenue levels and reliance patterns—with the exception of property tax reliance, which was better explained by political variables.

Intergovernmental Revenue

Political variables were also more closely related to intergovernmental revenue from Washington, according to our recent study of grant recipients over a six-year period among 144 municipalities (excluding the city of Milwaukee) in the seven-county Milwaukee metropolitan region. The study addresses local government capabilities to secure federally supplied revenue and thus reflects the growing interest among localities in "improving [their] capabilities to raise money and utilize current resources."[17]

Of course, the provisions of grant formulas are not the only factors that determine who gets federal dollars. As we have seen, about four-fifths of all federal grants are in the form of project categoricals. These are not distributed automatically by formula. They require application and are competitive. They therefore place a premium on grantsmanship abilities that are not distributed equally among localities that are potential grant seekers.

Also unequally distributed is another factor that is relevant to getting project grants—financial capability. Project grants typically require local matching funds; and even if matching requirements are varied inversely with local fiscal capacity, localities may be deterred from applying by financial considerations. Overhead costs must often be absorbed locally; and an effect may be feared whereby the grant leads to pressures to spend local money on complementary activities that would otherwise not be funded. We therefore hypothesized a positive relationship between local fiscal capacity and the securing of federal project grants. We assumed that communities with greater fiscal capacity could more easily afford whatever dollar costs were imposed by aid seeking and that such communities would tend to seek outside aid in order to shift at least some costs of local development onto others.

Financial capability was measured by the following: (1) median value of owner-occupied dwellings, (2) percent of labor force employed in white-collar jobs, (3) state-estimated full value of all classes of local property, (4) adjusted gross income per capita (after business expenses but before deductions), and (5) percent of persons classified by the Office of Economic Opportunity as below the poverty line (a negative indicator).

Income, occupation, and real property are the aspects of local financial capability represented by these indicators. They reflect a fairly typical approach among political scientists to measuring financial abilities or potential.

Measuring grantsmanship potential is trickier. Here it was measured in surrogate fashion with indicators of the capability of the local jurisdiction's planning organization. The rationale for this approach was that planners claim an ability to generate grants, that project grants are subject to planning requirements, that planning capacity generally means more information concerning grant programs, more skills and experience in proposal writing, higher standards of providing public services (which may stimulate a search for outside help), and a greater willingness to pay the psychological costs of making demands against "experts" in Washington. Planning capacity is (among other things) a kind of technical or intellectual ability to get outside help in advancing the quality of local life, thus shifting some of the cost onto others. Three aspects of planning capacity are represented by our indicators: organizational development of the local agency (nos. 1, 2, 3), professional output (nos. 5, 6), and extralocal planning and technical assistance (nos. 6, 7, 8, 9). The latter sometimes takes the form of direct help in writing grant proposals.

A community may be expected to have a greater aid-seeking capability if its planning organization has more (1) total members, (2) full-time planning staff, (3) part-time planning staff, (4) plans and technical studies completed or under way, (5) enacted plan implementation devices proposed by the local planning organization, (6) regional council assistance in preparing plans, (7) regional council assistance for planning implementation devices, (8) county and privately retained assistance in planning and study activities, and (9) county and privately retained assistance in producing planning implementation devices. We shall refer to these statistics as measures of planning capability, which in turn indicates grantsmanship.

The main research question was whether financial and planning capability factors both correlate with success in getting grants and, if so, which one to the greater degree.

It is important to note that among Milwaukee-area localities, every application for a grant resulted in at least some money being received, although not necessarily all that was asked for. Thus the number of applications is a valid measure of the number of times aid was received (but not of dollar amounts). A note of caution is in order, however. Milwaukee area localities applied only for land development, sewerage, and water pollution grants in the six years that we studied. The findings may not hold for a wider range of grant programs.

The data revealed that planning capability was strongly related to getting grants, but financial capability was not related. This was indicated by two types of evidence. We first reasoned that if success in getting grants is a function of financial and planning capabilities, then communities that received three or more grants should be higher in measured capability than those that received one or more grants, which in turn should be higher than those that received no grants at all. In fact, this pattern occurred only for planning capability. Regression analysis confirmed that financial capability was unrelated to success in grant getting. (Neither was another financial phenomenon—fiscal effort.)

We considered the possibility that particular grant programs account for our findings. Securing project grants may be a function of the type of grants available as much as local capabilities. Clearly, different types of grant programs are not equally attractive to all communities. However, separate analyses within grant programs—land development, sewerage, and water pollution—do not produce results that deviate from the findings reported above. Nevertheless, the narrow range of grant programs on which this analysis must rest makes it reasonable to hypothesize that an investigation into a wider range of grants would show success in grant getting to vary both with planning capabilities and type of grant program.

We also considered the possibility that the findings are due to degree of urbanization, with applications coming disproportionately from the more highly urbanized segments of the seven-county metropolitan region. We therefore divided recipients into those located in the two densest central counties (containing 75 percent of the region's population) and those located in the remaining counties. In fact, recipients come about equally from the two types (52 percent from the central counties).

In sum, the capabilities of a jurisdiction's planning organization are more predictive of success in grant getting than are the jurisdiction's financial capabilities. This finding not only reveals that a political factor is more closely associated with the receipt of intergovernmental revenue than a socioeconomic factor but also points to a strategy that local jurisdictions may employ to improve their ability to raise money—that is, build their planning capacity. In pursuing this strategy, they may wish to seek the help of regional planning agencies, as indeed many Milwaukee-area localities have.

STATE REVENUE POLICY

The most comprehensive efforts to examine revenue policy have concerned the state level. Penniman and Sharkansky, for example, examined the relationships between industrialization and affluence of the state and their tax policies. Although they hypothesized that highly industrialized and affluent states would emphasize income and sales taxes, they found that neither industrialization nor affluence was systematically related to either policy choice. States using income taxes extensively and those using sales taxes extensively were found both in high and low per capita income groups and in both rural and urban-industrial groups.[18]

One interesting conclusion that Penniman reached, which is in accord with that of investigators examining other policy areas,[19] is that "the best predictor of types of taxes, tax emphases, and tax levels for a given state is its own past."[20] She bases this conclusion primarily upon a case study of Oregon and upon the demonstrated tendency for changes in policy to be incremental, with only marginal change from the previous year under ordinary circumstances.

An interesting view of the states, and one that is related to state revenue policy, is presented by Sharkansky.[21] He sees the United States as both a developed and a developing country. He notes that the less-developed states resemble developing nations in many political respects. Centralization of government, strong chief executives, and limited party competition are among these characteristics. Furthermore, he notes that the taxes of poor countries and poor states place their heaviest burdens on the lowest-income classes—that tax structures in these nations and states tend to be regressive. Further, low-income states and nations tend to promote economic growth while higher-income ones are more concerned with conservation.

Sharkansky views California as being at the height of American development—close to the criteria that define a postindustrial society. California has a model system of higher education, ranks near the top on measures for total population and income, and has a highly developed service sector. The key features of a postindustrial society as defined by Sharkansky are an economy dominated by a service sector, a dependence on sophisticated technology, rapidly changing institutions, and a major role for government in providing social benefits.

At the other end of the spectrum are such states as Arkansas, Mississippi, and West Virginia. Their economies are industrial and preindustrial. Industries are labor intensive, much of the agricultural economy is at a subsistence level, and indicators of social conditions are low.[22] Sharkansky suggests that these and other poor states are poor not only in an economic sense; they also exhibit political, structural, and policy traits that resemble those found in the developing countries of Africa, Asia, and Latin America. He indicates a number of parallels between the poor states of the United States and the developing nations.

First, developing states and nations receive significant financial and techical assistance from other governments and outside private capital. Thus, Canada, Sweden, the Soviet Union, the United States, and West Germany are major sources of aid to the developing nations. In the

United States, the federal government provides more aid to the developing states than to wealthier ones, if aid is measured on a per capita basis. During 1971-72, for example, the ten least developed states received an average of $160.51 in per capita federal aid compared to $148.62 for the remaining 40 states. In addition, federal aid in the least developed states accounted for 33.2 percent of state and local revenues compared to 22.1 percent in the other states.

Developing nations and states are also heavily reliant on outside jurisdictions to supply models for institutions, procedures, and policies that may be adapted to their own circumstances. Institution building has long been a major form of aid supplied by developed nations.* Within the United States, the less developed states appear to take their policy cues from the more developed.[24]

Developing states and nations undertake similar efforts to induce economic growth. Both pursue industrialization with tax subsidies and/or with the promise of publicly constructed plants. Both have problems with marginal industries attracted by such schemes, and both rely heavily on low-skilled and low-paid workers.

The least developed jurisdictions also tend toward governmental centralization and political concentration. In the American states, centralization is most clearly shown in the location of the revenue-raising function. Between 1958 and 1972, the ten states with the least developed economies raised 69.1 percent of state and local revenues at the state level while the most developed states raised only 54.7 percent of revenues at the state level. This is particularly apparent in the area of public school finance. In the least developed states, local sources accounted for only 28 percent of revenues for schools during 1972–73. Most of the revenue came from the state (55.4 percent) and federal (16.7 percent) governments. The other states, however, raised 57 percent of school revenues from local sources with only 37.4 percent coming from the states and 5.5 percent from the federal government.

As noted above, regressive taxing and spending policies are also characteristic of developing states and nations. Regressive taxes and expenditures take a disproportionate share of wealth from low-income groups and/or provide a disproportionate share of services to the upper-income population. In developing countries, regressive taxes are typically levied on imported consumer goods, fuel, cloth, and processed foods. In the United States, the sales tax exemplifies regressive taxation, while the income tax is an example of progressive taxation. From 1958 through 1972 the ten least developed states drew 30.5 percent of reve-

---

*Institution building is the creation of organizations in developing countries to protect and promote new social functions, values, and physical or social technologies.[23]

nues from sales taxes and only 17.6 percent from income taxes. On the other hand, the ten most highly developed states relied on sales taxes for only 21.3 percent of income while income taxes were much more important—accounting for 24.3 percent of revenues.[25]

In summary, developed nations and American states thus have a number of characteristics of their revenue systems in common—characteristics significantly different from more developed countries and states. The less developed rely heavily upon outside sources of funds and tend to centralize the revenue-raising function. In addition, they rely heavily upon regressive taxes that place heavy burdens on lower-income populations.

SOCIOECONOMIC AND POLITICAL CORRELATES OF STATE TAX RELIANCE

If Sharkansky and others are correct that "development" or some other socioeconomic condition has marked impact upon the revenue policies states follow, it should be possible, through statistical analysis, to see just how strong that impact is. To focus this effort, we will here limit ourselves to state-level taxes. This is done in order to examine a single decision process. Although local revenue sources are partially determined by state-level decisions, they are determined also by local decisions. Similarly, intergovernmental revenue and "charges and miscellaneous revenue" contribute importantly to state funding, but the decision processes that lead to a grant application or to a hike in college tuition are different from those that set tax rates. So, taxes are the focus.

The difficulty of measuring revenue policy was described in Chapter 1. For the analysis here we will use two such measures. The first is tax reliance—the degree to which particular states rely upon a particular tax. In other words, what role does a particular tax play in the state's total tax system? Table 7.1 presents a summary of the development of state general revenue sources in the last 50 year.

Table 7.2 presents, for each major tax, the range of reliance upon that tax and notes those states at the extremes. Additionally, the mean level of reliance is shown, together with the standard deviation. For most of the taxes, the lower end is defined by those states that make no use of the tax. From this level, reliance ranges upward to more than 50 percent for three taxes—general sales, selective sales, and individual income. In some cases, however, the upper level is defined by a state that is truly extreme. The severance tax is an example. The mean reliance is only 2.15 percent, but Louisiana receives 29.6 percent of its tax revenue from this source.

TABLE 7.1: State General Revenue, Selected Years Including Intergovernmental Revenue (percent)

	1974	1970	1965	1960	1950	1940	1932	1922
Individual income tax	14.0	11.8	8.9	8.1	6.4	4.6	3.1	3.4
Corporate income tax	4.9	4.8	4.7	4.3	5.2	3.5	3.3	4.6
Sales and gross receipts tax	33.2	35.1	36.8	38.4	41.5	41.4	30.0	10.7
Property tax	1.1	1.4	1.9	2.2	2.7	5.8	13.5	27.8
Other taxes	7.5	8.6	11.5	12.9	14.6	20.8	28.2	29.0
Intergovernmental revenue	27.1	26.0	25.2	24.7	21.5	16.2	11.0	10.0
Charges and miscellaneous	12.2	12.3	11.0	9.4	8.1	7.7	11.0	14.4
Total	100.0	100.0	100.0	100.0	100.0	100.0	100.0	100.0

Source: Compiled by the authors.

TABLE 7.2: Percentage Use of Tax Sources, 1974

Tax	Low Use	High Use	Mean	Standard Deviation
General sales	0 Alaska Delaware Montana New Hampshire Oregon	57.7 Washington	30.17	13.77
Selective sales	14.2 Hawaii	57.1 New Hampshire	26.64	7.66
Individual income	0 Florida Nevada South Dakota Texas Washington Wyoming	50.2 Oregon	20.77	13.27
Corporate income	0 Nevada Texas Washington Wyoming	14.5 New Hampshire	6.75	3.68
License	1.4 Hawaii	30.2 Delaware	9.56	4.84
Death and gift	0 Nevada	5.0 Connecticut	1.69	1.10
Property	0 Alaska Connecticut Hawaii Iowa Louisiana Massachusetts Oklahoma Oregon South Dakota Tennessee	10.2 Montara	1.79	2.37
Severance	0 (24 states)	29.6 Louisiana	2.15	5.41
Other	0 (20 states)	4.7 Florida	.48	.85

Source: Compiled by the authors.

145

Table 7.2 confirms the heavy reliance of states upon the sales tax, divided into its two major categories: general sales and selective sales. The means of these are very similar, 30 percent and 27 percent, respectively; but the standard deviations indicate a greater variation in reliance upon general sales than upon selective sales. Individual income and corporate income taxes comprise a smaller proportion of state tax revenue than the sales taxes. Notice, however, that variation in the use of the individual income tax is as great as variation in use of the general sales tax. Notice, also, that property taxes comprise only 1.8 percent of average state tax revenue, with little variation among states. The process of withdrawal by states from the property tax field is nearly complete.

Data shown in Table 7.2 are drawn from a complete listing of each tax and the degree to which each state relies upon that tax. It is this listing that can be treated as a measure of state tax policy, focusing upon the utilization of each particular tax in comparison with other tax sources. Measuring tax policy in this way, we examined state political, economic, and social characteristics that might lead decision makers to rely upon one tax (or group of taxes) over others. Additionally, we used as a measure of tax policy a variable called tax effort developed by the ACIR.

Correlates of Tax Reliance

Table 7.3 provides a list of our independent variables, divided into three general classes: socioeconomic, political, and tax related. For conconceptual clarity and to avoid statistical problems with multicollinearity, no two independent variables that are highly correlated were included in the same equation. Thus, when percent metropolitan was used in the analysis, percent urban was excluded, since these two correlate at .909. (All correlations were Pearson product moment correlations.) The same was true for the political variables, especially in the case of percent Democratic in the upper and lower houses of the state legislatures, which correlate at .960.

Most of the variables in Table 7.3 are self-explanatory and were derived from data available in Bureau of the Census publications. The exceptions are the two innovation variables, which have been constructed. Modeled on the technique developed by Walker, the method identifies patterns of adoption by states of the two major tax innovations of the twentieth century: general sales tax and individual income tax. Each state's score was determined by finding the length of time from the first adoption to the point at which the particular state adopted the tax and dividing that result by the total amount of time since the first

TABLE 7.3: Independent Variables for Taxation Analysis

Socioeconomic	Political	Tax-Related
% metro	% Democratic vote for president (1960–72)	Federal aid to state/local per capita
% urban	% Democratic vote for U.S. Senate (1968–72)	Innovation scale, general sales
Per capita income	% Democratic vote for U.S. House (1968–72)	Innovation scale, individual income
Population change	% Democratic vote for governor (1968–72)	Per capita tax, 1974
Population net migration	% Democratic vote for lower house of legislature (1968–72)	
% black	% Democratic vote for upper house of legislature (1968–72)	
% high school graduates	% population voting for president (1960–72)	
Industrialization index	% population voting for U.S. House, off-year (1962–70)	
Mineral production		
Value-added manufacturing (per capita)		

Note: All data are 1970 figures unless otherwise noted.
Source: Compiled by the authors.

adoption. The resulting score was then subtracted from 100 so that high scores signify early adoption

The equation is:

$$I = 100 - \frac{A-F}{T}$$

Where

I = Innovation score
A = Year of adoption by the state
F = First year the innovation was adopted by any state
T = Total number of years since first adoption.

Tax Reliance

As a first step in seeking explanations for the various levels of tax reliance, zero-order correlation coefficients were calculated between each of the selected independent variables and the percentage use figures. These two-variable relationships are presented in the first column of Tables 7.4 through 7.8. For the general sales tax, the model included the sales tax innovation score, since it was hypothesized that the early adopting states would be most dependent upon the sales tax. Per capita income was used as a general measure of affluence. Additionally, the percent black and the percent living in metropolitan areas were employed. These are commonly used measures of general social characteristics. Also included was another social variable—net migration. Finally, two aggregate political variables were introduced, percent voting Democratic for governor and percent Democratic in the lower house of the state legislature. These final two variables are the political measures used with all of the tax reliance items.

All of the variables were entered into a stepwise regression procedure that permitted determination of the relationship each variable had with general sales tax reliance, with all other variables controlled. Table 7.4 indicates that all of the independent variables combined explained 46 percent of the variation among the states in sales tax reliance, but most of this was explained by one variable—sales tax innovation score. Notice that the weak relationships that existed at the zero-order level largely disappear when other variables are controlled. As in earlier studies, socioeconomic and political variables are of little help in explaining sales tax reliance.

Table 7.5 presents the relationships between the independent variables and individual income tax reliance. As with the general sales tax, the innovation score is the major explanatory variable. Others that were thought to have some explanatory power and showed weak zero-order correlations contribute little to the total explained variance of 47 percent. With other variables controlled, the Democratic vote for governor does explain 5 percent of the variance. Surprisingly, the relationship is negative; that is, with other variables controlled, those states that had higher Democratic votes for governor in the 1968–72 period are slightly less dependent upon the income tax. As with so many findings with regard to party, this may result from peculiarities in the southern states.

The correlates of reliance upon selective sales taxes are presented in Table 7.6. Independent variables included in the model explained only 6 percent of the variance, possibly because this dependent variable is an amalgam of a diverse set of taxes. If the independent variables impact differently upon various tax policies, it is not surprising that explaining variance in a conglomerate category would prove difficult.

There was slightly more success in explaining variance in reliance upon property taxes, with 17 percent explained as is shown in Table 7.7.

TABLE 7.4: Stepwise Regression of General Sales Tax Reliance

Independent Variable	r	Partial r^2	Beta
Innovation score—general sales tax	.653	.370	.608
Population net migration	.105	.010	.076
Per capita income	−.188	.040	−.298
% metropolitan population	−.006	.032	.240
% Democratic in lower house	.030	.018	−.160
% black population	.103	.002	.046
% Democratic vote for governor	.210	.000	−.010

Note: $R^2 = .457$.
Source: Compiled by the authors.

TABLE 7.5: Stepwise Regression of Individual Income Tax Reliance

Independent Variable	r	Partial r^2	Beta
Innovation score—income tax	.538	.385	.654
Per capita income	.217	.035	.247
% Democratic vote for governor	−.260	.050	−.193
% metropolitan population	.153	.006	.093
Industrialization index	.070	.000	−.005
% Democratic in lower house	−.008	.000	.003

Note: $R^2 = .470$.
Source: Compiled by the authors.

TABLE 7.6: Stepwise Regression of Selective Sales Tax Reliance

Independent Variable	r	Partial r^2	Beta
Per capita income	−.205	.007	−.131
% Democratic vote for governor	.017	.006	−.100
% high school graduates	−.178	.012	−.220
Value-added manufacturing per capita	−.056	.004	−.087
% Democratic in lower house	.073	.002	−.064
% black	.068	.000	−.100

Note: R^2 = .064.
Source: Compiled by the authors.

As Table 7.2 revealed, actual reliance upon the property tax by states is quite low and, more important, there is little variance in that reliance. Dye, using his many variables, succeeded in accounting for 64 percent of property tax variation. However, Dye was examining state and local property tax reliance, a fact that both increased the level of reliance and resulted in greater variance.

The last tax considered is the corporate income tax, and findings with regard to it are presented in Table 7.8. While the total variance explained is 31 percent, most of this is accounted for by the explanatory power of the industrialization index. Industrialized states rely more heavily upon the corporate income tax than do less industrialized ones. Interestingly, with other variables controlled, there is virtually no relationship between party strength and use of the corporate income tax.

Finally, Table 7.9 presents the results of an attempt to find correlates of total per capita state taxes. The independent variables explain only 27 percent of total variance. Even though two variables (per capita income and percent metro) reflect strong zero-order correlations, their ability to explain variation in per capita tax disappears in our model. No single socioeconomic or political variable demonstrates any particular strength in contributing to explained variance.

Correlates of State and Local Tax Effort

In order to see how sensitive our findings might be to our particular choice of dependent variable, we next explored revenue policy as measured by an index developed by the ACIR and presented in its publication *Measuring the Fiscal Capacity and Effort of State and Local Areas.*[26]

In Chapter 1 we noted the difficulty of comparing tax rates that results from wide state-to-state variation in the bases to which those rates are applied. Our use of tax reliance, while avoiding that difficulty, does fail to take account of differences in states' capacities to use certain taxes—for example, only states with mineral wealth can rely upon severance taxes.

The ACIR measures of fiscal capacity and tax effort represent attempts to overcome both difficulties. First, there is devised what might be termed a representative base, which is fairly typical of those bases used by the states employing the tax under study. Next, an "average rate" is determined by dividing the nationwide yield of the tax by the sum of the state representative base amounts. This average rate is applied to the representative base in each state to obtain the fiscal capacity of the state for that particular tax. The state's effort for the tax is calculated by dividing the amount actually collected with the tax by the capacity.

The measure of policy that interests us is tax effort. We do, though, face one difficulty. The ACIR figures are for state and local effort, combined. So, we are forced to depart from our path of using only state tax

TABLE 7.7:   Stepwise Regression of Property Tax Reliance

Independent Variable	r	Partial r^2	Beta
Industrialization index	−.327	.039	−.265
Population change	.263	.032	.222
% Democratic in lower house	−.216	.016	−.177
% Democratic vote for governor	−.139	.006	−.089
% black	−.209	.003	.093
Per capita income	.466	.001	−.050

Note: $R^2 = .171$.
Source: Compiled by the authors.

TABLE 7.8:   Stepwise Regression of Corporate Income Tax Reliance

Independent Variable	r	Partial r^2	Beta
Industrialization index	.437	.224	.715
% black population	.021	.048	−.351
Per capita income	.259	.050	.372
% metropolitan population	.167	.061	−.424
Population change	−.028	.018	.166
% Democratic in lower house	−.058	.004	.081
% Democratic vote for governor	−.128	.003	.054

Note: $R^2 = .314$.
Source: Compiled by the authors.

TABLE 7.9: Stepwise Regression of Per Capita Tax Reliance

Independent Variable	r	Partial r^2	Beta
Per capita income	.466	.045	.402
% Democratic in lower house	−.027	.011	.119
Federal aid to state and local	.13	.016	.139
% metropolitan population	.414	.012	.187
Industrialization index	−.010	.009	−.099
% Democratic vote for governor	−.123	.003	.051

Note: R^2 = .274.
Source: Compiled by the authors.

measures.* The data presented below are correlations of various socio-economic, political, and tax-related variables with state/local tax effort. The "per capita income" independent variable has been eliminated, since this might be interpreted as a rough measure of tax capacity; capacity is a part of the ACIR calculation and should not be duplicated. We have substituted "per capita tax," a possible indicator of tax pressure on individuals. We want to know if those states that collect higher taxes per resident are the same as those that make greater effort relative to tax capacity.

Tables 7.10 through 7.14 present the zero-order and partial correlations of the independent variables with each of the tax effort measures as well as the total explained variance. With regard to the general sales tax, the zero-order coefficients suggest that the strongest variable is, again, the general sales tax innovation score. With other variables controlled, this remains the most powerful variable, and the direction of the relationship reveals that earlier adopters make greater tax effort. Per capita tax is fairly strongly associated with sales tax effort, even with controls. States with higher per capita taxes make a greater sales tax effort. Of the remaining variables, only the percentage of Democrats in the lower house seems to have any impact. The total explained variance is 67 percent. This is considerably above the level obtained when reliance was employed rather than effort.

As with general sales tax effort, individual income tax effort is explained primarily by the innovation score, the tax per capita, and the percentage of Democrats in the lower house. Notice, however, that the direction of relationship with the latter variable is the reverse of the

*Many of the independent variables are for 1970 or later although the tax effort was computed for 1966. The 1970 variables were not changed, as evidence does not suggest that tax decisions are so responsive to changes in these variables that differences that may have developed over a few years would have a substantial impact.

TABLE 7.10:   Stepwise Regression of General Sales Tax Effort

Independent Variable	r	Partial r^2	Beta
Innovation score—general sales tax	.724	.612	.773
Per capita tax	.194	.197	.324
% Democratic in lower house	.245	.067	.228
Population net migration	.000	.007	−.050
% black population	.207	.001	−.029
% Democratic vote for governor	.253	.001	−.020
% metropolitan population	.073	.000	−.004

Note: $R^2 = .667$.
Source: Compiled by the authors.

TABLE 7.11:   Stepwise Regression of Individual Income Tax Effort

Independent Variable	r	Partial r^2	Beta
Innovation score—income tax	.660	.523	.674
Per capita tax	.489	.274	.411
% Democratic in lower house	−.041	.050	−.158
% Democratic vote for governor	−.123	.013	−.075
% metropolitan population	.027	.001	.016
Industrialization index	.000	.000	.000

Note: $R^2 = .662$.
Source: Compiled by the authors.

relationship with sales tax effort. That is, although higher percentages of Democrats are associated with higher sales tax efforts, it is higher percentages of Republicans that are associated with increased income tax effort. However, because the partial r² in each equation is relatively low, conclusions must be considerably tempered.

Table 7.12 presents the model for selective sales tax effort. As with tax reliance, little variance is explained. Unlike general sales tax and individual income tax effort, per capita tax shows only a slight relationship to selective sales tax effort. Thus, those states that collect higher taxes per capita clearly make a greater effort in using general sales and personal income taxes, but there exists no particular pattern in their use of selective sales taxes.

The regression model for property tax effort is notably more successful in accounting for variance than was the model for property tax reliance. It is impossible to determine whether this results simply from the difference in the two measures or from the inclusion of local property tax data in the effort figures. In the present case, the strongest single explanatory variable for property tax effort is percentage black

TABLE 7.12: Stepwise Regression of Selective Sales Tax Effort

Independent Variable	r	Partial r^2	Beta
% Democratic in lower house	.313	.057	.367
Per capita tax	.183	.047	.217
% black population	.137	.021	−.238
% high school graduates	−.174	.013	−.173
Value-added manufacturing per capita	−.064	.002	−.045
% Democratic vote for governor	.110	.001	.033

Note: $R^2 = .159$.
Source: Compiled by the authors.

in the population. Those states with a high percentage black make a lesser effort to use property taxes. Further, states with a greater percentage of Republicans in the lower house and those that are more industrialized make a greater property tax effort.

Finally, Table 7.14 explores corporate income tax effort. Only two variables contribute markedly to explaining the variance, per capita tax and industrialization. In both cases the relationships are positive. A total of 38 percent of the variance is explained.

Summary

Explaining tax systems as being, in part, the result of socioeconomic and political factors is relatively rare among students of taxation. Research in public finance, economics, and public administration has been concerned primarily with normative aspects of taxation—that is, emphasis has centered upon what the tax structure ought to be and upon how the tax burden should be shifted to different income classes. When

TABLE 7.13: Stepwise Regression of Property Tax Effort

Independent Variable	r	Partial r^2	Beta
% Democratic in lower house	−.616	.097	−.351
% black population	−.587	.127	−.500
Industrialization index	−.112	.077	.2691
Per capita tax	−.048	.021	−.112
Population change	−.053	.001	.022
% Democratic vote for governor	−.321	.001	.020

Note: $R^2 = .476$.
Source: Compiled by the authors.

TABLE 7.14: Stepwise Regression of Corporate Income Tax Effort

Independent Variable	r	Partial r^2	Beta
Per capita tax	.445	.277	.542
% black population	.320	.007	.128
Industrialization index	.315	.062	.324
% metropolitan population	.126	.034	−.239
Population change	.049	.008	.104
% Democratic vote for governor	.146	.006	.071
% Democratic in lower house	.265	.002	.058

Note: R^2 = .385.
Source: Compiled by the authors.

explanation has been the goal of the researcher, it has usually been subservient to macro-level theory on the linkage of government and the economy.

Undoubtedly, these normative concerns play a major role in determining taxation policy, whether at the federal or state level, but they alone do not explain the differences in taxes among governmental units, since a fundamental element in the process, the policy maker, is often ignored. The fact remains that political leaders, both executive and legislative, determine and change state taxation policy. Ignoring this fundamental political process can only lead to misconceptions and general failure to explain tax policy. Normative economic theorists, engaged in making prescriptive statements and in forecasting the needs for taxation, have carried a great deal of prestige and weight in taxation research. Science, however, has twin goals: explanation and prediction. The latter area has been the prime emphasis of taxation research to date. The failure to define and explain taxation policy cannot be ignored. Thus, greater research attention must be directed toward explaining tax policy differences.

Taking cues from earlier studies of state expenditures, we have both described state tax structure and attempted to explain differences among the states by using socioeconomic, political, and tax-related variables. The greatest success centered on the two principal tax structures of the states: general sales taxes and individual income taxes. Yet the prime explanatory variables are not those that describe current social, economic, or political divisions within a state. The strongest single variable is the time of adoption of the tax: the earlier a state's adoption of the tax, the greater the reliance on that tax. This proposition remains true for both percentage use of general sales and individual income taxes and for the tax efforts of the states.

Earlier work noted the strong relationship between current-year state tax policy and that of the previous year, because changes from year to year are usually slight. This incremental model, while obviously correct, is only a first step. The question remains as to how each succeeding year's tax structure adapted as it did. Our innovation score variable aids in answering this. The original adoption of the tax becomes the crucial variable in explaining tax usage, so that the preceding year as well as the length of time that the tax has been in use constitute the prime explanatory variable.

The success of the innovation score variable is offset somewhat by the weak contributions of socioeconomic and political variables. There are three possible reasons for these weaknesses. First, the adequacy of the independent variables as indicators of political and socioeconomic conditions in the states can be called into question. Rough aggregate measures of party voting for various state and national offices may give little indication of the true political patterns in the states. Second, there is the possibility that state political and socioeconomic patterns have no effect on the tax structure. The third possibility, however, is that measures of current taxation policy will never be completely explained by current political and socioeconomic conditions, because most tax policies were set in previous years and are reviewed with less frequency than are spending decisions.

Future analyses of taxation patterns in the states must measure those crucial time points when policy makers made key tax policy changes. Doing this form of analysis would require the gathering of tax information for the past 40 to 50 years and then finding those key time periods when new taxes were begun or tax bases were drastically changed. For example, did states that shifted to greater reliance on general sales taxes do so during Democratic administrations? Asking this implies not that tax policy should be analyzed by case studies of each individual state's shifts in tax structure but instead that it requires a more sophisticated exploration of shifts through use of time-series analysis.

Finally, research on tax policy requires a better method for comparative study of state tax rates. A scheme must be created that allows for quantitative differentiation of the various exemptions and credits on these taxes. The ACIR effort was an important step. Hopefully, it can be brought up to date and can be constructed to separate state and local effort.

The present attempt to explain differences among the states has been only partially successful. As steps to acquire improved data are taken, it is likely that the explanatory power of socioeconomic and political variables will increase.

THE LOCATION OF THE REVENUE FUNCTION

Thus far this chapter has been concerned largely with the impact of socioeconomic conditions. Now we explore the location of revenue raising and emphasis on expenditures. More precisely, we examine a major political dimension of policy determination in the states—the relationship between decisions affecting the proportion of state and local revenues raised at the state level and public expenditures made by state and local governments. This issue was raised earlier by Bingham and McLemore in a preliminary analysis of the impact of the location of state and local revenue function on expenditure priorities.[27] They found, when comparing states with their neighboring states, that the political decision to centralize the revenue-gathering function at the state level was associated with an increased emphasis on expenditures traditionally associated with state, as opposed to local, government.

Other research examining the relationship between the location of the revenue function and expenditures has produced mixed results. Campbell and Sacks believe that the higher the assignment of tax responsibility to the local level, the greater are state and local taxes. "If the policy goal . . . is to devote greater resources to the public sector, thereby generally raising service levels, it follows that high local tax assignment will help in accomplishing this end."[28] Others argue that locating revenue responsibility at the state level is associated with higher levels of expenditures. Mushkin and Cotton argue that the bias against a new program increases the closer the program is to its citizens.[29] Sharkansky found a significant relationship between the percentage of state and local revenue originating at nonlocal sources and total state per capita expenditures.[30]

We hypothesized that the location of the revenue function at either the state or local level would have an impact on expenditures, but the nature of contemporary American federalism and the relationships among the states made devising a method to assess this impact more difficult. States are not independent units relying upon internally generated demands and resources in the creation of policy.[31] As we have seen, federal grant programs have had a clear impact on state and local expenditures as have political cultures[32] and emulation and competition among the states.[33]

It was important, therefore, to control for the effects of regionalism and emulation when examining the impact of the location of revenue functions upon expenditure priorities. Census data show, for example, that southern states raise a larger percentage of state and local revenue at the state level than do the New England states. We also know that per-pupil expenditures for public education are higher in Maine than in Mississippi, yet the relationships between the revenue location and expenditures of Maine and Mississippi may be confounded by influences of political culture and regionalism. That is, differences between Maine and Mississippi may partially result from their being located in different regions rather than from their varied political or socioeconomic characteristics. Controlling for regionalism is quite difficult, however—there are probably as many conceptions of regionalism floating around as there are states.[34] We return to this problem below.

In the remainder of this chapter, we are interested in the fiscal and regional influences on spending emphasis in the American states. Spending emphasis is defined as the percent of total state and local expenditures allotted to a given function. Our major questions are: Can the fiscally significant antecedents of differences in the proportional assignment of revenue responsibility to state and local governments be identified? Do differences in the proportional assignment of revenue responsibility to state government, as opposed to local, make a difference in state and local expenditure emphasis? Does regionalism play a systematic role in these relationships?

We hypothesized that the poorer states would have a high revenue effort to provide adequate funding for public services and this need for

FIGURE 7.1: Hypothesized Relationships Between State Fiscal Capacity, Revenue Effort, Revenue Assignment, and Spending Emphasis

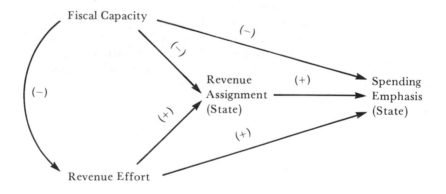

Source: Compiled by the authors.

high effort would lead to consolidation of the revenue function at the state level of government. We expected, in turn, that total state/local expenditure policies would be affected by increasing the emphasis given expenditures that normally occur at the state level. Figure 7.1 presents a diagrammatic representation of the hypothesized relationships between fiscal capacity (state per capita income), revenue effort (state and local per capita revenue from own sources), revenue assignment (the percent of state and local revenue from own sources raised at the state level), and spending emphasis. Spending emphasis was examined across six functions. Two of the functions are traditionally accomplished at the state level (higher education and highways), and four are usually assigned to local governments (local schools, health and hospitals, police protection, and fire protection). Expenditure emphasis for public welfare was not examined, as the location of this function is not assigned predominantly to any one level of government.[35] All data are for 1972–73.[36]

We used two data sets for this analysis. The first set of data consisted of simply the appropriate figures for each state. In the description below we refer to this as the aggregate analysis; it represents the traditional type of analysis of state fiscal variables found in many of the works of Dye, Sharkansky, and others.

Our second set of data represents an attempt to control for regionalism by considering states only in relation to neighboring (contiguous) states. We developed a set of "difference" data for each state by comparing the value of each variable for a given state with the values of that variable for all contiguous states. Consider the following hypothetical example. Vermont is bordered by three states—Massachusetts, New Hampshire, and New York. Assume that the percentages of all state and local expenditures devoted to local schools were the following:

Vermont	33%	
Massachusetts	26%	(+7)
New Hampshire	34%	(−1)
New York	28%	(+5)

It is clear that of total spending in Vermont, 7 percent more went for local schools than was true in Massachusetts, 5 percent more went for schools than in New York, and 1 point less than in New Hampshire. To develop a compositional score for Vermont on this variable, we took the total difference between the percent spent on local schools in Vermont and the percent spent in the three contiguous states (+11) and divided by the number of contiguous states (3). Thus Vermont, on the average, spent 3.7 percent more of its total state and local expenditures on local schools than did its neighbors and was assigned a difference score of +3.7 on this variable.

In the analysis shown in the following paragraphs, we developed six pairs of path models. Each pair portrays the differences between aggregate and compositional analysis.

Our purpose was, first, to discover the independent effect of each phenomenon on state and local expenditure priorities after statistically removing the effect of the others. Such net effects are called direct effects. We also determined if there were sequences of influence running from fiscal capacity to revenue assignment to each expenditure priority and from fiscal capacity to revenue effort to revenue assignment. Path analysis, a multivariate statistical technique that enables one to investigate both independent and sequential associations, was selected for this portion of the analysis.

It was also necessary to test the various models to determine which of our independent variables was most "important" in explaining the variation in state and local expenditure priorities. We hypothesized, for example, that revenue assignment would be the most important explanatory variable in accounting for variations in state and local expenditure priorities. Stepwise multiple regression and correlation was used in this portion of the analysis.

Finally, we attempted to determine whether aggregate variables or compositional variables were more significant in the analysis. Partial correlation coefficients were used for this purpose. For example, a partial was computed between aggregate revenue assignment and aggregate fiscal capacity controlling for compositional fiscal capacity. Then a partial was computed between aggregate revenue assignment and compositional fiscal capacity controlling for aggregate fiscal capacity. Compositional revenue assignment was then correlated with compositional fiscal capacity controlling for aggregate fiscal capacity, and so on until all of the partial relationships between the independent variables and two types of intervening variables (aggregate and compositional revenue assignment) were computed.

Findings

Figure 7.2 presents the differences in the aggregate and compositional analyses in explaining emphasis on expenditures for higher education. The solid lines represent paths for which the independent variable accounts for 10 percent or more of variation in the dependent variable. The broken lines represent paths for which the independent variable accounts for 5 percent or more variation in the dependent variable. Fiscal capacity shows no significant relationship with revenue

FIGURE 7.2: Direct Effects Between Fiscal Capacity, Revenue Effort, Revenue Assignment, and Emphasis on Higher Education

Aggregate Analysis

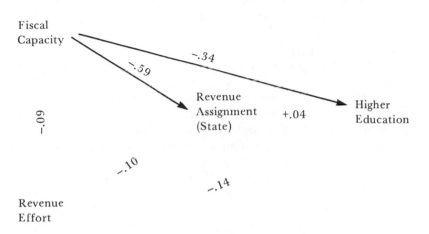

Compositional Analysis

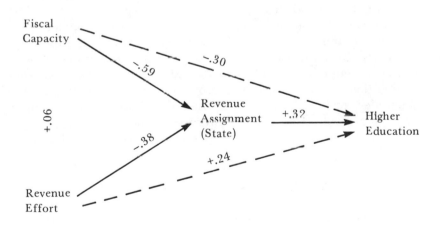

Source: Compiled by the authors.

effort—no matter which analysis is used. Revenue effort, therefore, seems to be unrelated to fiscal capacity, with or without controls for regional variations.

Fiscal capacity was strongly related to revenue assignment under both modes of analysis—and in the negative direction. States with low levels of fiscal capacity are likely to raise a higher percentage of total state and local revenues at the state level than are their counterparts. Again, this relationship holds regardless of the effects of regionalism.

The direct path between revenue effort and revenue assignment is not so easily explained, however. There was virtually no relationship between the two variables using aggregate data, and the relationship between the variables using compositional data was not in the expected direction! Under controls for regionalism, the direct path coefficient between revenue effort and revenue assignment was negative. Thus, when controlling for regionalism, states with a lower revenue effort than their neighbors tend to raise a greater portion of total state and local revenue at the state level than do the higher effort neighbors. While the relationship was not in the expected direction, there is little need for concern. Since fiscal capacity was not related to revenue effort, there is really no longer any reason to hypothesize a positive relationship between revenue effort and revenue assignment.

The superior explanatory power of the compositional data is clearly shown by the direct paths between the independent variables and the percent of state and local revenue spent for higher education. Each of the direct paths using compositional data explained 5 percent or more of the variation in the percent spent for higher education—and the relationships are in the expected directions. The path coefficient between revenue assignment and the dependent variable was slightly higher than the other two coefficients, suggesting that revenue emphasis, under our unique control for regionalism, was indeed an important determinant of expenditure priorities.

The model tested using aggregate data, however, did not make much sense. The only path of significance was the negative path between fiscal capacity and the percent spent for higher education. It thus appears that regionalism masks the hypothesized relationships and may lead to erroneous conclusions relative to the importance of revenue assignment. Analysis of the compositional data suggests that where states raise their money (state versus local level) may indeed influence expenditure patterns.

Furthermore, the compositional variables explain more of the variation in the compositional dependent variable ($R = .55$) than did the aggregate independent variables in the aggregate dependent variable ($R = .38$). To further weigh the relative importance of the aggregate and compositional independent variables, a second set of multiple correlation coefficients was computed. A stepwise regression and correlation was computed between all of the aggregate and compositional independent variables and the aggregate dependent variable. The computed coefficient was $R = .49$. The addition of the compositional independent variables to the aggregate model increased the R from .38 to .49. On the other hand, when the aggregate independent variables were added to the compositional model, the R was only increased from .55 to .59. Thus the addition of the compositional independent variables to the aggregate model contributes more than the addition of the aggregate independent variables to the compositional model. In both stepwise routines, however, fiscal capacity (and not revenue assignment) was the first variable to enter. The aggregate fiscal capacity variable was the first variable entered in the model explaining variation in the aggregate dependent variable, while the compositional fiscal capacity variable was first in the model explaining variation in the compositional dependent variables.

Figure 7.3 presents the differences in the aggregate and compositional analyses in explaining emphasis on expenditures for highways. Again, the solid lines represent paths for which the independent variable accounts for 10 percent or more of the variation in the dependent variable while the broken line represents 5 percent or more variation. Since only direct paths are shown, the relationships between fiscal capacity, revenue effort, and revenue assignment remain unchanged from those in the higher education model. Further discussion of these relationships would therefore be redundant.

There was little difference in the explanatory power of the two models—in both cases, the independent variables explained approximately 30 percent of the variance in the dependent variables. Revenue assignment was again important in the compositional model, explaining approximately 6 percent of the variance in state and local highway emphasis, with controls for regionalism.

As in the case of higher education, compositional independent variables were added to the aggregate model and aggregate independent variables were added to the compositional model. Again, stepwise regressions were performed. The compositional variables increased the R in the aggregate model from .55 to .61, while the addition of the aggregate independent variables to the compositional model did not increase the value of R at all—it remained .55. In both cases, the fiscal capacity variable was the first variable added. The aggregate fiscal ca-

FIGURE 7.3: Direct Effects Between Fiscal Capacity, Revenue Effort, Revenue Assignment, and Emphasis on Highways

Aggregate Analysis

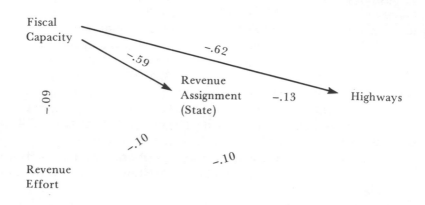

Compositional Analysis

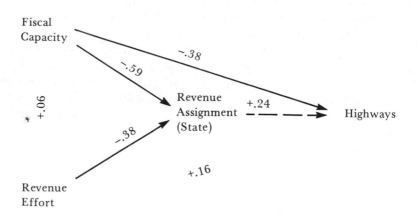

Source: Compiled by the authors.

pacity variable was the first variable entered in the aggregate model, and compositional fiscal capacity was the first entered in the compositional model.

Figure 7.4 presents the direct paths explaining variations in the percent of state and local revenues spent for health and hospitals. As is shown, the aggregate model was not operative. None of the independent variables produced path coefficients large enough to explain even 5 percent of the variation in health and hospital expenditures. The multiple correlation coefficient was only $R = .21$.

Once our control for regionalism was introduced, however, the performance of the model improved dramatically. The use of compositional data produced an R of .53 and emphasized the importance of both revenue effort and revenue assignment. Path coefficients were $-.50$ in both cases. Health and hospitals was the first dependent variable that we expected to find negatively related to revenue assignment, as health and hospital expenditures are predominantly local. This was indeed the case. Strong direct negative paths existed between revenue emphasis and health and hospitals and revenue effort and health and hospitals. Thus, once regionalism is controlled, a tendency to raise revenue at the state level is associated with a decreased emphasis on expenditures for health and hospitals.

Addition of the compositional variables to the aggregate model resulted in a rather dramatic increase in R. R increased from the .21 of the aggregate model to .65. The addition of the compositional variables thus increased the explanatory power of the independent variables from less than 5 percent to 30 percent. Aggregate fiscal capacity was again the first variable entered.

Addition of the aggregate independent variables to the compositional model, however, only increased R from .53 to .55. Thus the addition of the compositional variables contributed much more to the aggregate model than the aggregate variables contributed to the compositional model.

Figure 7.5 presents the models explaining expenditure emphasis for local schools. Differences in the explanatory power of the independent variable are negligible. In both models, fiscal capacity and revenue effort were positively related to emphasis on local schools, while revenue assignment was not. Addition of the compositional independent variables to the aggregate model and the aggregate independent variables to the compositional model did not markedly affect the explanatory power of either model. The multiple correlation coefficient produced in the aggregate model increased only from .41 to .42 with the addition of the compositional independent variables (although the compositional measure of fiscal capacity was the first variable entered

FIGURE 7.4: Direct Effects Between Fiscal Capacity, Revenue Effort, Revenue Assignment, and Emphasis on Health and Hospitals

Aggregate Analysis

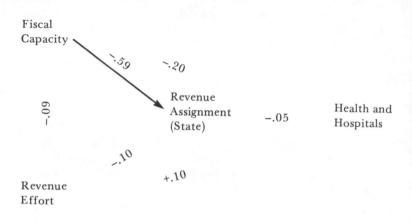

Compositional Analysis

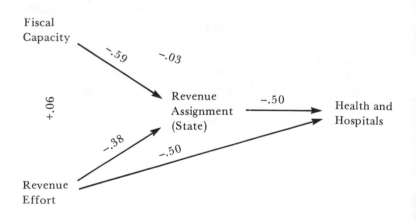

Source: Compiled by the authors.

FIGURE 7.5: Direct Effects Between Fiscal Capacity, Revenue Effort, Revenue Assignment, and Emphasis on Local Schools

Compositional Analysis

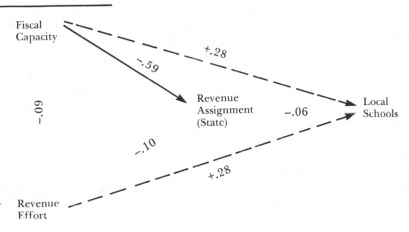

Aggregate Analysis

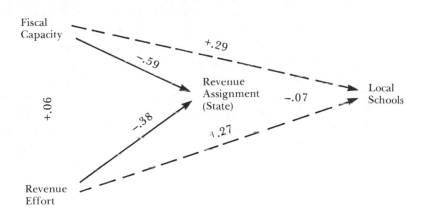

Source: compiled by the authors.

in the stepwise routine and explained 9.6 percent of the variance in the percent of state and local revenue spent for public schools). Similarly, the addition of the aggregate independent variables to the compositional model increased the R only from .46 to .47.

The significance of the use of the compositional data is probably best illustrated by the analysis of expenditure priorities for the last two local emphasis variables—the percent of state and local revenue spent for police protection and for fire protection. Figure 7.6 presents the police expenditure models while Figure 7.7 presents the fire expenditure models. The findings are very similar. Analysis of the models using aggregate data indicates that fiscal capacity is the most important direct determinant of expenditure emphasis while the compositional data illustrate the dominance of revenue assignment as a determinant of expenditure priorities. The negative coefficients between revenue assignment and expenditures again substantiate our original expectations —that is, states raising a high percentage of state and local revenues at the state level will not emphasize expenditures for functions that are largely local. As was the case with local schools, the addition of the compositional independent variables to the aggregate models and vice versa did not appreciably increase the R in any of the four situations tested. The R of the aggregate police model increased only from .45 to .49, and the fire model increased only from .61 to .63. The situation was not improved when the aggregate independent variables were added to the compositional model. Compositional explanation of emphasis on expenditures for police increased only from .42 to .43, and explanation of emphasis on fire increased only by the same amount—from .74 to .75.

We now turn our attention to an examination of the relative "importance" of the aggregate and compositional independent variables. In an attempt to make such a determination, we treated revenue assignment, both aggregate and compositional, as our dependent variables and used partial correlation coefficients to weigh the relative impact of both aggregate and compositional values of fiscal capacity and revenue effort on these dependent variables. The results of these computations are shown in Table 7.15. The first relationships shown in Table 7.15 are the partials between aggregate fiscal capacity and both aggregate and compositional revenue assignment, controlling for compositional fiscal capacity. The second set of partials merely reverses the relationships between the independent and control variables. Thus the second set of partials reflects the relationships between the compositional measure of fiscal capacity and the dependent variables controlling for aggregate fiscal capacity.

FIGURE 7.6: Direct Effects Between Fiscal Capacity, Revenue Effort, Revenue Assignment, and Emphasis on Police Protection

Aggregate Analysis

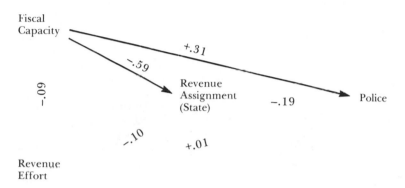

Compositional Analysis

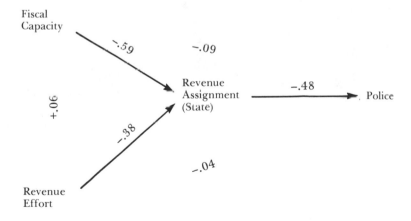

Source: compiled by the authors.

FIGURE 7.7: Direct Effects Between Fiscal Capacity, Revenue Effort, Revenue Assignment, and Emphasis on Fire Protection

Aggregate Analysis

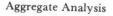

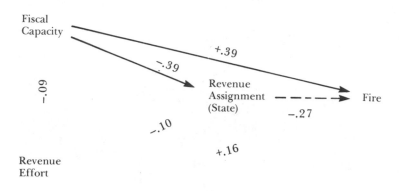

Compositional Analysis

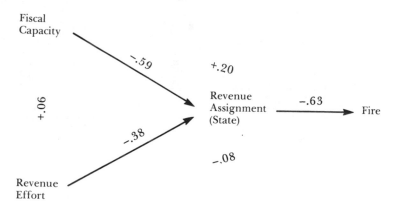

Source: compiled by the authors.

The results of all of the computations in Table 7.15 clearly show the importance of the compositional variables relative to the aggregate. When the relationship between the aggregate independent variables and the aggregate dependent variables is controlled for the compositional variables, barely 10 percent of the variance is explained. Their correlations with the compositional dependent variable were not significant at even the .05 level. The compositional independent variables, on the other hand, showed important independent relationships with both aggregate and compositional revenue assignment. Only one partial, that between compositional fiscal capacity and aggregate revenue emphasis, was not substantial. The partials thus clearly show the substantial significance of the compositional analysis relative to the aggregate.

Summary

While this brief examination of the impact of the location of the revenue function is clearly exploratory, we believe that the results presented in the preceding paragraphs have important policy implications. The comparison between the aggregate and compositional analyses indicates the importance of examining revenue decisions within a regional context. Aggregate analysis hides many significant and important relationships. In the aggregate analysis, the fiscal capacity of the state was clearly the dominant variable in determining state and local expenditure priorities. For all six expenditure priorities studied, the direct path coefficients between fiscal capacity and spending emphasis were .20 or greater.

TABLE 7.15: Partial Correlation Coefficients Between Fiscal Capacity and Revenue Effort Measures and Revenue Assignment

	Aggregate Revenue Assignment	Compositional Revenue Assignment
Aggregate fiscal capacity	−.32[a]	.02
Compositional fiscal capacity	−.23	−.48[c]
Aggregate revenue effort	.32[a]	.11
Compositional revenue effort	−.44[c]	−.35[b]

[a]Significant at the .05 level
[b]Significant at the .01 level
[c]Significant at the .001 level
Source: Compiled by the authors.

When compositional analysis was used, however, the findings changed rather dramatically. Revenue assignment then became dominant, with direct path coefficients of .20 or greater between assignment and spending emphasis in five of the six models. Thus, with regionalism controlled, we found important relationships between revenue assignment, or where revenue is raised, and expenditure emphasis. When states raise large portions of state and local revenues at the state level, functions traditionally handled by the state are emphasized. Conversely, states raising levels of their total revenue locally emphasize those functions usually accomplished by local governments.

Within the compositional models, we also noted direct relationships between fiscal capacity and revenue assignment and revenue effort and revenue assignment. Within a regional context, poorer states and those with lower revenue efforts were most likely to raise revenues at the state level. These states then emphasized traditional state expenditure functions over local.

While the socioeconomic conditions of the state (as measured by fiscal capacity and revenue effort) seem to determine where revenues are raised, state policy makers should be aware of the potential impact of the location of revenue raising on expenditure priorities. Within a regional context, heavy reliance upon centralization of revenue-raising activities means that traditional state functions will be emphasized over traditional local functions. In the aggregate, other factors are obviously important (Texas would be more likely to emphasize highway expenditures than Rhode Island). If, however, states are much like their neighbors in terms of socioeconomic and demographic characteristics, the compositional findings have significant policy implications within a regional context.

NOTES

1. David Easton, *A Framework for Political Analysis* (New York: Prentice-Hall, 1965).

2. Thomas R. Dye, *Politics, Economics, and the Public: Policy Outcomes in the American State* (Chicago: Rand McNally, 1966), pp. 3–4.

3. See, for example, Robert H. Haveman and Julius Margolis, eds., *Public Expenditures and Policy Analysis* (Chicago: Markham, 1970); Richard H. Leach and Timothy G. O'Rourke, eds., *Dimensions of State and Urban Policy Making* (New York: Macmillan, 1975); Ira Sharkansky, ed., *Policy Analysis in Political Science* (Chicago: Markham, 1970); David R. Morgan and Samuel A. Kirkpatrick, eds., *Urban Political Analysis: A Systems Approach* (New York: Free Press, 1972).

4. Dye, op. cit.

5. Alan K. Campbell and Seymour Sacks, *Metropolitan America: Fiscal Patterns and Governmental Systems* (New York: Free Press, 1967).

6. Ira Sharkansky, *The United States: A Study of a Developing Country* (New York: David McKay, 1975).

7. Clara Penniman, "The Politics of Taxation," in *Politics in the American States: A Comparative Analysis*, ed. Herbert Jacob and Kenneth N. Vines, 2d ed. (Boston: Little, Brown and Co., 1971), p. 541.

8. Solomon Fabricant, *The Trend of Governmental Activity in the United States Since 1900* (New York: National Bureau of Economic Research, 1952).

9. Glenn W. Fisher, "Interstate Variation in State and Local Expenditures," *National Tax Journal* 17 (March 1964): 57–74.

10. Dye, op. cit., pp. 74–177.

11. Ibid., pp. 178–209.

12. Campbell and Sacks, op. cit.

13. Ibid., pp. 53–66.

14. Thomas P. Murphy and John Rehfuss, *Urban Politics in the Suburban Era* (Homewood, Ill.: Dorsey, 1976), pp. 92–119.

15. Susan A. MacManus, "Changing Revenue Patterns in American Suburbs: A Potential Fiscal Crisis?" paper presented at the 1977 Annual Meeting of the Southwestern Political Science Association, Dallas, March 30–April 2, 1977.

16. Ibid., p. 6.

17. Carol S. Weissert, "Restraint and Reappraisal: Federalism in 1976," *Intergovernmental Perspective* 3 (Winter 1977): 10.

18. Penniman, op. cit., p. 543.

19. Ira Sharkansky, *Spending in the American States* (Chicago: Rand McNally, 1968), pp. 35–54.

20. Penniman, op. cit., p. 553.

21. Ira Sharkansky, *The United States: A Study of a Developing Country* (New York: David McKay, 1975).

22. Ibid., pp. 9–24.

23. For a discussion see Thomas M. Hill and Howard Bumgartel, *Institution Building in India: A Study of International Collaboration in Management Education* (Boston: Harvard University, Graduate School of Business, 1973); Joseph W. Eaton, ed., *Institution Building and Development from Concepts to Application* (Beverly Hills, Calif.: Sage Publications, 1972).

24. Jack L. Walker, "The Diffusion of Innovations Among the American States," *American Political Science Review* 63 (September 1969): 880–99.

25. Sharkansky, *United States*, op. cit. pp. 38–70.

26. Advisory Commission on Intergovernmental Relations, *Measuring the Fiscal Capacity and Effort of State and Local Areas* (Washington, D.C.: ACIR, 1971).

27. Richard D. Bingham and Lelan McLemore, "Regionalism in American State Politics: A New Approach to State Fiscal Measures," a paper presented at the 1975 Annual Meeting of the Southwestern Political Science Association, San Antonio, Texas, March 27–29, 1975.

28. Alan K. Campbell and Seymour Sacks, *Metropolitan America* (New York: Free Press, 1967), p. 182.

29. Selma J. Mushkin and John F. Cotton, *Sharing Federal Funds for State and Local Needs* (New York: Praeger Publishers, 1969), p. 30.

30. Ira Sharkansky, "Regional Patterns in the Expenditures of American States," *Western Political Quarterly* 20 (December 1967): 955–71.

31. Douglas D. Rose, "National and Local Forces in State Politics: The Implications of Multilevel Policy Analysis," *American Political Science Review* 62 (December 1973): 1162–73.

32. Daniel J. Elazar, *American Federalism: A View from the States*, 2d ed. (New York: Thomas Y. Crowell, 1972); Ira Sharkansky, *Regionalism in American Politics* (Indianapolis: Bobbs-Merrill, 1970).

33. Robert L. Crain, "Fluoridation: The Diffusion of Innovation Among Cities," *Social Forces* 44 (June 1966): 467–76; Thomas M. Scott, "The Diffusion of Urban Governmental Forms as a Case of Social Learning," *Journal of Politics* 30 (November 1968): 1091–1108; Jack L. Walker, "The Diffusion of Innovations Among the American States," *American Political Science Review* 63 (September 1969): 880–99.

34. See, for example, Ira Sharkansky, "Regionalism, Economic Status, and the Public Policies of American States," *Social Science Quarterly* 49 (June 1968): 9–26; Norman R. Luttbeg, "Classifying the American States: An Empirical Attempt to Identify Internal Variations," *Midwest Journal of Political Science* 15 (November 1971): 703–21.

35. Timothy J. Sampson, *Welfare: A Handbook for Friend and Foe* (Philadelphia: United Church Press, 1972), pp. 30–31.

36. U.S. Department of Commerce/Bureau of the Census, *Governmental Finances in 1972–73* (Washington, D.C.: Government Printing Office, 1974).

8
Economic Impacts on
State and Local Revenues

At a recent conference held at New York University, Burkhead and Campbell stated: "The supply of taxable resources available to a jurisdiction is most evidently a function of the economic activity that occurs within its boundaries and when that activity declines, fiscal problems will increase in intensity."[1] One purpose of this chapter is to examine the impacts of economic activity on state and local revenues and to see how economic activity (or lack of it) contributes to fiscal problems. We also examine the tax burden on individuals in an attempt to answer the question "Who bears the tax burden?" We then briefly examine public attitudes about state and local taxes. Is the public willing to have taxes increased to provide additional services? If so, which taxes? We then consider the impact of inflation on state and local revenues—specifically examining the impact of inflation on state income taxes and local property taxes. We examine also the more general impacts of inflation and employment on state and local fiscal health. Finally, the chapter concludes with a discussion of the Frostbelt-Sunbelt issue. Some authorities claim that federal expenditure policies are biased in favor of the high-growth southern and western states and are contributing to the decay of northern cities. Others maintain that the northern states are quite well-off and that federal expenditures should be increasingly directed toward the South and Southwest. Federal expenditures, constituting 32.4 percent of the GNP in 1976, have an obvious impact on state and local employment and thus a significant impact upon state and local revenues. Consequently the distribution of federal expenditures among the states is an important policy issue.

THE TAX BURDEN

Economists have long been concerned with the question "Who bears the tax burden?"[2] That is, is our total tax system progressive, proportional, or regressive? A tax is considered to be progressive if the ratio of tax to income is higher for upper-income classes than for lower. It is regressive if the ratio of tax to income is lower for upper-income classes, and it is proportional if the ratio of tax to income is the same for all income classes. Thus, under a progressive tax system, high-income individuals or families pay a larger percentage of their incomes in taxes than do poorer individuals or families. Under a regressive system the opposite is true—low-income families pay a higher percentage of their incomes in taxes than do the wealthy. Under a proportional system, all families, regardless of income, devote the same percentage of their income to taxes.

Unfortunately, there seems to be no clear-cut answer to the question "Who bears the tax burden?" To some degree the answer depends on assumptions about the incidence of major taxes. Traditionally, the income tax was assumed to be borne by those who paid it, the sales tax by the consumer, and the property tax on residences by those who lived in the residences, including renters to whom it was shifted by property owners. Payroll taxes on employers, on the other hand, have often been considered to be shifted partly to employees and partly to consumers.[3]

Under the traditional assumptions concerning the incidence of the residential property tax, the property tax has generally been considered to be one of the most regressive taxes in the state and local tax system. The ACIR, for example, states, "No other major tax in our public finance system bears down so harshly on low-income households, or is so capriciously related to the ability to pay taxes."[4] On the other hand, Aaron, by assuming that the property tax is not shifted to the consumers of the goods and services produced by the taxed property but is borne by the owners of capital, suggests that the property tax is a progressive, not a regressive, tax.[5] Thus, to a large degree, views concerning that tax burden are shaped by the assumptions regarding tax incidence.

In a refreshing examination of the tax system, Pechman and Okner examine the question of the tax burden under eight different tax-incidence assumptions. Under their most progressive assumption, payroll taxes are borne by employees, the corporate income tax is divided between dividends and property income, and the property tax on both land and improvements is borne by property income. In the least progressive assumption, on the other hand, payroll taxes on employers are borne by both employees and consumers, the corporate income tax is assigned to both property income and consumption, the property tax on land is borne by landowners, and the tax on improvements is assigned to shelter and consumption.[6] Using a 1966 sample of 72,000 families, Pechman and Okner calculated tax rates under each of the eight assumptions throughout a scale of family incomes. The relationship between the effective tax rate and adjusted family income for the most progressive and least progressive assumptions are shown in Figure 8.1. The tax-burden on low-income families is high under both assumptions. The tax burden is unquestionably regressive until the $3,000 income level is reached. Under both sets of assumptions the tax rates stabilize at 20 to 25 percent of income until an income level of $20,000 is reached. The tax burdens under the two assumptions diverge at $25,000 and are substantially different for higher-income families. Under the least progressive set of assumptions, the tax burden reaches a maximum of only 30 percent of income for families with incomes of $100,000 or more. Under the most progressive assumptions, on the other hand, the tax rate rises to almost 50 percent of income for families with incomes of $1 million.

Figure 8.1 taken by itself does not give a true picture of the tax burden on the total population, however. Figure 8.2 shows the effective rates of federal, state, and local taxes under the most and least progressive sets of incidence assumptions by population percentile. The figure clearly shows that there is very little difference in the effective rates of taxation for families between the tenth and ninety-seventh percentiles. Thus, for that 87 percent of all families whose incomes in 1966 fell between $2,000 and $30,000, the tax system is proportional under the least progressive set of assumptions, or slightly progressive under the most progressive set of assumptions.[7]

Pechman and Okner also calculated tax burdens by type of tax. They found that the individual income tax is progressive over virtually the entire income scale, although it becomes regressive near the very top. The regressive nature of the tax for very high-income families was found to be a result of the fact that very high-income families are not subject to income tax at either the federal or state levels of government. Apparently very high-income families have learned to avoid the income tax.

Sales and excise taxes, on the other hand, were found to be regressive throughout the scale. The effective rate for these types of taxes begins at over 9 percent of income for the lowest-income families and declines to 1 percent of income for families at the high end of the income continuum.

This finding reflects the fact that the proportion of family income spent on goods and services subject to taxation falls as income rises. Payroll taxes were found to be progressive for families with incomes up to about $10,000. At $10,000 they reach a maximum of about 6 percent; at this point the tax becomes regressive. Personal property taxes were found to be regressive at the lower end of the income scale but proportional or slightly progressive for higher-income groups (depending upon the incidence assumptions).

FIGURE 8.1: Effective Rates of Federal, State, and Local Taxes Under Most and Least Progressive Incidence Variants, by Adjusted Family Income Class, 1966

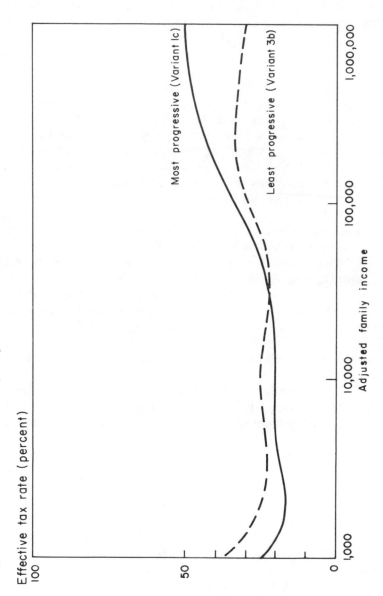

Source: Joseph A. Pechman and Benjamin A. Okner, *Who Bears the Tax Burden?* (Washington, D.C.: Brookings Institution, 1974), p. 4.

FIGURE 8.2: Effective Rates of Federal, State, and Local Taxes Under Most and Least Progressive Incidence Variants, by Population Percentile, 1966

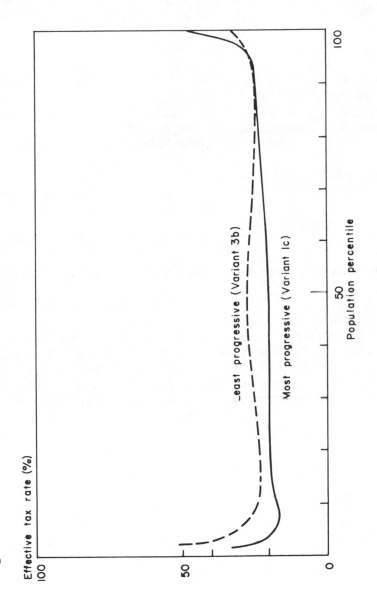

Source: Joseph A. Pechman and Benjamin A. Okner, *Who Bears the Tax Burden?* (Washington, D.C.: Brookings Institution, 1974), p. 5.

Pechman and Okner also conclude that state and local taxes are generally regressive (depending on the assumed incidence of the property tax) while federal taxes, largely due to the influence of income taxes, are progressive throughout the income scale. Regardless of incidence assumptions, however, "the total tax system is virtually proportional for the vast majority of families in the United States." Under the most progressive set of assumptions, taxes reduce income inequality by less than 5 percent; under the least progressive assumptions, income inequality is reduced by only about 0.5 percent.[8]

While, in general, state and local tax systems are regressive, not all state systems are. In an excellent analysis of the state and local tax burden, Phares found that 11 states have proportional state and local tax systems (39 regressive). Delaware, Kentucky, North Carolina, and Wisconsin, in general, have proportional tax systems, while the tax systems of Wyoming, South Dakota, and Illinois are among the most regressive. The generally regressive nature of the state and local tax system, in Phares' view, is the product of a heavy reliance on the property tax (Phares views the property tax as regressive). When the property tax was netted out of the analysis, Phares found two states with progressive systems and 20 with proportional ones, leaving 28 with regressive systems.[9]

PUBLIC ATTITUDES TOWARD TAXING AND SPENDING

If taxes, especially state and local taxes, can be classified as progressive, proportional, or regressive, we might then ask the question: Does the American public favor a progressive tax structure for state and local governments? Apparently not. Each year since 1972 the ACIR has contracted with the Opinion Research Corporation to gauge public opinion concerning tax instruments, federal aid, and the effectiveness of federal, state, and local governments. The 1976 report contains interesting findings about state and local revenues.[10] In response to a question regarding an increase in state taxes, most respondents (45 percent) favored an increase in the state sales tax over increases in either the state income tax (25 percent) or property tax (10 percent). Thus taxpayers favor the regressive sales tax over the progressive, or proportional, income tax.

The ACIR also probed attitudes on taxes and services. Only 5 percent of the respondents saw a need for an increase in the services provided by government and thus a need to raise taxes. On the other hand, 30 percent of those surveyed indicated a preference for decreased services and taxes; and 51 percent wanted to keep taxes and services at their present levels. It is easy to see why some scholars of public finance believe that the prevailing political mood in the nation is as "anti-government" as at any time in the last 40 years.[11]

Clearly, the public wants to hold the line on taxes and spending. But when a state or local tax increase is needed, why does the public favor an increase in the sales tax over one in the income tax? Perhaps, during periods of serious inflation, the public recognizes that state income taxes claim an increasing share of a constant real income.

INFLATION AND TAXES

The United States is currently experiencing the most prolonged severe inflation of the century. Since 1972 the consumer price index has risen by an average of 9.6 percent annually—a serious departure from the mild 2 to 3 percent rate that the United States normally had experienced since 1950. Moreover, these high rates of inflation are predicted by some to extend into the 1980s.[12] One consequence of this sustained high rate of inflation, and one that is gaining an increasing amount of attention from policy makers, is the distorting effect on the personal tax burden that results from the interplay of inflation with the progressive income tax. Since most income tax code provisions are specified in dollar amounts (for example, tax bracket boundaries, exemptions, standard deductions, low-income allowances), inflation decreases the real value of exemptions and deductions, causing taxable income to rise more rapidly than total income. As the ACIR reports:

> Inflation interacts with a progressive individual income tax to distort real tax burdens in two ways. First, if a taxpayer's nominal (money) income increases, the share of income paid as tax rises even though there may be no increase—or even a decline—in real income or purchasing power. Second, the response of the tax structure to changing real income is asymmetric: if nominal income is constant so that real income falls by the inflation rate, income taxes do not fall to reflect this taxpayer's decline in purchasing power. In short, inflation causes individual income tax burdens for any given real income to increase.[13]

Thus, if a family's income in the past year has increased only to the point where it offsets the increase in prices (for example, cost-of-living increase), income taxes will claim a larger share of that constant real income. Standard deductions and exemptions will decrease as a percent of taxable income, while, in all probability, the taxpayer will move into a higher-income tax bracket. In this manner, inflation interacts with the progressive individual income tax to generate increases in tax revenues more than proportionate to the rate of inflation.

It is the states that have benefited most from inflation-induced increases in taxing power. The federal government has enacted four major tax cuts since 1960—cuts more than offsetting the revenue benefits of inflation. A federal taxpayer in the $25,000 bracket, for example, generally paid income taxes at a lower effective tax rate in 1975 than would have been the case under the 1960 law.

States, however, have not cut their income tax rates. "From 1966 to 1973, state discretionary action in the aggregate served to increase income taxes beyond the impact of income growth and inflation. Since 1973, most states have not raised their rates but have relied on inflation's impact on their revenue to maintain their public service levels."[14] From 1971 to 1975, actual state individual income tax revenue increased at an average annual rate of 15.5 percent (compared to a 9.6 percent annual increase in the consumer price index). Furthermore, the Congressional Budget Office predicts that the average annual increase in aggregate state income tax revenue will be about 16.5 percent from 1977 to 1980.

The income tax is highly elastic* —that is, a change in taxable income produces a greater change in the revenue generated by the individual income tax. The property tax, on the other hand, is traditionally viewed as inelastic. Assessed valuation seldom keeps up with the market values of taxable property during periods of inflation. Netzer points out, however, that the concept of elasticity is more ambiguous for the property tax than for most other taxes. For one thing, the legal base of the property tax, assessed values, and the economic base of the tax, the market value of the property, do not necessarily vary proportionally with one another. Local governments do not need to be overly concerned, however, as they typically can adjust the assessment and/or the nominal tax rate. These options are not present for other taxes. Property tax elasticity is ambiguous for another reason: Property tax revenues are usually residually determined— that is, the total tax levy equals previously budgeted expenditures minus revenues from other sources. Thus, "elasticity of property tax revenue is really a reflection of the income elasticity of the demand for local government expenditures (or of residual revenue needs)."[16] Property tax revenues may thus be stabilized during periods of inflation or recession by adjusting both the assessed valuation of the property and the nominal tax rate.

---

*Elasticity is defined as the ratio of the percentage change in tax yield to the percentage change in income.[15]

INFLATION, EMPLOYMENT, AND FISCAL STRAIN

Many economists and social scientists would agree with Burkhead and Campbell's assessment that the state and local fiscal crisis started with the lack of a national stabilization policy and "the resulting unholy combination of inflation and unemployment that accentuated and in many cases precipitated the budget difficulties that so many states and cities are now experiencing."[17] No doubt, many states and cities—particularly cities—are facing an extreme fiscal crisis.[18] Part of the problems results from the relationship among inflation, revenues, and expenditures. In general, inflation has a greater impact on state and local expenditures than on state and local revenues. Thus, for example, a city may experience an increase in revenues due to inflation of 9 percent during a given year but may find that its costs have risen by 16 percent. Burkhead and Campbell estimate that during the period 1972 to 1974 the states alone lost $6.6 billion in purchasing power due to inflationary cost increases—an amount that exceeded their general revenue sharing entitlements. Thus, while inflation works on both the demand and the supply sides of the equation, adding to both revenues and expenditures, state and local governments feel the effects of inflation to a much greater degree on the expenditure side of the equation.[19] Inflation, however, is not the only cause of fiscal strain. Unemployment and population movements are at least as important in contributing to the fiscal crisis of cities. The high unemployment rate in New York City has cost millions of dollars in revenues. Had employment there grown at the national rate between 1965 and 1974, for example, the city would have had $800 million in additional revenue in 1974.[20]

Part of the inflation/revenue/expenditure problem facing state and local governments is the serious impact of shifting populations on property tax revenues. Property value differences between growing and declining central cities are widening more rapidly than income differences. Property values magnify differences in local economic trends—population loss and low growth exert multiplier effects on the value of a city's fixed stock of property. Cities such as Buffalo, Cleveland, and Pittsburgh have suffered enormous population losses in recent years—many cities have lost more than 20 percent of their population in a 13-year period. These losses are then reflected in lower housing prices. Cities experiencing such losses have had only marginal increases in housing prices while most of the country has been experiencing a period of rampant inflation in housing prices. Fast-growing cities, on the other hand, have not only benefited from the housing price inflation but also from a vigorous demand for housing that has tended to drive housing prices up.[21] This situation, of course, has an only-too-clear impact on property tax assessments and income.

THE FROSTBELT-SUNBELT ISSUE

High rates of inflation and unemployment are not the only reasons that certain state and local governments are experiencing a fiscal crisis. It is no accident that the cities identified by Clark et al. as facing heavy fiscal pressures are all located in the Northeast. As we have seen, state and local governments, even those relying heavily upon a progressive tax structure, have little control over economic conditions. Further, there is evidence that patterns of federal spending are giving certain states, notably those in the Southeast and Southwest, a major economic advantage over the rest of the nation. Articles appearing in both *Business Week*[22] and the *National Journal*[23] during 1976 are responsible for stimulating extensive debate over federal expenditure policies. According to the *National Journal:* "Federal tax and spending policies are causing a massive flow of wealth from the Northeast and Midwest to fastgrowing Southern and Western regions of the nation...."[24] This distribution policy only serves to exacerbate the negative impact of the deteriorating socioeconomic conditions of the Northeast and Midwest upon state and local revenues among the states in those regions.[25]

The Great Lakes and mid-Atlantic states have been the biggest losers. The five Great Lakes states paid $62.2 billion in federal taxes in fiscal year 1975, but they received only $43.6 billion in federal outlays. Thus they had a "balance-of-payments" deficit of $18.6 billion. The mid-Atlantic states were not much better off—their balance-of-payments deficit was $10.6 billion. On the other hand, southern and western states were in a favored position. The 16 southern states had a balance-of-payments surplus of $11.5 billion, and the states in the Pacific and Mountain regions had a surplus of $10.6 billion.

Because of these largely accidental inequities—Florida, for example, receives the largest amount per capita of federal spending for retirement programs because of its many elderly residents receiving social security benefits—a heavy flow of federal funds is moving away from states and regions under the heaviest economic strain. In general, the balance-of-payments situation is adverse where population is stagnant or declining, where the unemployment rate is highest and personal income is falling, and where state and local tax burdens are most severe. The southern and western states, those benefiting most from the imbalance, are showing heavy population gains. They also have the lowest unemployment rates, exhibit the strongest gains in per capita income, and have a low tax burden. Although the Northeast and Midwest still have some advantage in per capita income, this is rapidly becoming less sizable.

Jobs, population, and economic investment have been shifting from the Northeast to the South and West for a number of years—a shift that has accelerated since 1970. This shift has serious intergovernmental implications in that the flow of jobs, people, and money away from the East and Midwest has eroded the tax base of many of the state and local governments in these regions. This erosion may eventually force governments in these areas to raise taxes to prohibitive levels and/or drastically reduce services.

There are basically four ways in which the federal government spends money in the states. It pays salaries to its own workers in the state in which the work is performed, it makes benefit payments such as social security to individuals, it contracts with private industry for items such as submarines and airplanes, and it provides federal grants to state and local governments. Obviously, federal grants are the easiest of the four spending modes to manipulate in an attempt to correct the fiscal imbalance. Federal intergovernmental grants amounted to approximately 15 percent of the federal budget in FY 1975. The 1,030 grant programs involved in distributing this $50 billion were subject to a variety of distribution formulas. Many distribution formulas were based on population, although some were based on other factors such as poverty and unemployment.

The distribution of the federal tax burden also contributes to the inequities among the various states and regions. Federal taxes reflect income; and despite the fact that the Northeast and Midwest states have shown serious relative deterioration, per capita federal tax collection in these areas remains high. Yet the income differences between the higher-income northeastern states and their low-income southern counterparts may be illusory as the cost of living is clearly higher in the North. Thus individuals in higher-income states may not enjoy any higher standard of living but pay higher federal taxes than lower-income individuals in poorer states. New Mexico provides the most aberrant example: "Federal spending there is 50 percent greater than the national average, but New Mexico's share of the federal tax burden is 27 percent below the national average. . . . Thus, for every dollar sent to Washington in the form of taxes, New Mexico . . . received the benefit of $1.93 in federal spending—no matter how much a dollar was worth in New Mexico."[26]

Thus, according to the *National Journal,* federal policy is contributing to the financial squeeze on state and local governments in the Northeast and Midwest. Obviously, federal policy is not solely responsible for the decline in the older industrialized states, nor for the boom in the Sunbelt states; however, it may be an important contributor.

The publicity given the federal expenditure issue has heightened the consciousness of both the general public[27] and federal officials[28] concerning the apparent imbalance in federal expenditures. Ross and Shannon, staff members of the ACIR, are among those concerned with fiscal imbalance. In their estimate, the fiscal pressure on the slow- or no-growth states may be more severe than is normally believed.[29] Ross and Shannon note that the traditional measure of state-local fiscal pressure is the ratio of state-local tax collections to resident personal income for a given year. They believe that this measure suffers from two important weaknesses: First, it lacks any time-based direction component; and, second, the use of resident personal income overstates the tax effort of states that export taxes and understates the effort of those that do not.

Ross and Shannon developed a two-dimensional fiscal pressure index based on a ratio of an index of taxes from own sources as a percent of income (1975) to an index based on the average annual rate of change in fiscal pressure (1964–75). Using this single measure of "fiscal blood pressure" they divided the states into four categories: those with high and rising fiscal pressure, those with high and falling, those with low and rising, and those with low and falling. Of the 14 states in the high and rising category, all except three were located in the Northeast or Midwest. On the other hand, only one of the 17 states in the low and falling category was located outside of the Southeast, Southwest, or Plains states. Of equal importance, however, was the movement of the states away from a position of equalization. Their data show that interstate diversity has increased. Only 20 states are moving toward the median while 31 are moving away from it—that is, 31 states were either in the high and rising or low and falling categories. In general, the states of the Northeast and Midwest are moving toward positions of increased fiscal pressure, while the southern and western states are moving to positions of reduced pressure.

Ross and Shannon qualify their findings—they believe that their method understates the taxable base of mineral-rich states such as Louisiana and Texas and of tourist states like Nevada. To overcome these deficiencies, the ACIR calculated fiscal capacity indexes by state for 1966–67, estimating what the state-local revenues would have been had it made average use of all taxable resources. Using these data in their method of computing fiscal pressure, they found that 35 states are moving away from the median while only 16 are moving toward it.

It seems clear from the Ross and Shannon study that the Northeast and Midwest states are experiencing increasing tax pressure while the "Sunbelt" states are in the falling pressure category. It therefore appears likely that interregional fiscal tension will increase and that there will be growing pressure for a readjustment in federal aid.

Ross and Shannon suggest several alternatives. One alternative is that the federal government take a "wait-and-see" approach. After all, the South and Southwest are not as well off as the Northeast. There is also evidence that the heavy-spending states are placing a lid on the growth of public expenditures. Thus those supporting the wait-and-see approach might conclude that while continuous monitoring is required, no federal action should be taken at this time.

Another alternative is immediate federal action. Those favoring this approach argue that disparities in economic conditions are increasing rather than decreasing and there is little hope that corrective action can be taken by the individual states. Also, the fiscal position of high-pressure states is not a matter of their own choice. Many high-pressure states, for example, carry a disproportionate share of the welfare burden.[30]

In spite of the publicity given the issue in 1976, there apparently has been little change in the trend publicized by the *National Journal.* During 1976, the flow of federal funds from the Northeast and Midwest followed a pattern almost identical to 1975. If anything, the imbalance increased. The Northeast sent $12.6 billion more to Washington (as compared to $10.8 billion in 1975) than it received in federal spending, and the imbalance in the Great Lakes states increased from $18.6 billion to $20.1 billion.[31] Yet in one year the political ramifications of the issue have been great.[32] Northeast and Midwest congressmen are beginning to score small but important victories in the writing of federal aid formulas. In the year since fiscal disparity emerged as a major national political issue, the Northeast and Midwest "Frostbelt" forces have organized a major bipartisan machine to aid in the fight to change federal expenditure policies. The Frostbelt forces, spanning 16 states from New England and the Middle Atlantic to the Midwest, include members of Congress, state and local officials, academics, and businessmen.

The organization in the House of Representatives is highly structured and very political. The Northeast-Midwest Economic Advancement Coalition, formed on September 1, 1976 under the leadership of Rep. Michael Harrington (D—Mass.), has 204 representatives as members and is under the direction of a 31-member steering committee. The coalition has its own staff and office on Capitol Hill.

The coalition in the Senate was organized on June 9, 1977 with Senator Howard Metzenbaum (D—Ohio) serving as temporary chairman. Metzenbaum sees the coalition as "a means of sharing information and a kind of mutuality of concern."[33]

The Coalition of Northeast Governors and the Midwestern Governors Conference provide state support for the congressional groups. Private interests have also joined the fray. The economics department of the First National Bank of Boston, for example, has a program of ongoing research on the Frostbelt-Sunbelt issue. The thrust of their efforts can be noted in the titles of some of their articles: "Son of Fort Sumter: Another View," "Renewal of General Revenue Sharing: A Private Sector Proposal for the Economically Mature Industrialized States," and "The Relative Importance of Federal Grant-in-Aid Formulas in an Overall 'Agenda for the Northeast.' "[34]

The Frostbelt forces see their campaign as a necessary ingredient of self-preservation. They are seeking to revise federal aid formulas that discriminate against the region and to stimulate investment in the region through military procurement and risk-capital programs. The lobby wants a regional development bank to provide risk capital to stimulate and attract new firms to the area.

Sunbelt forces are also organized, although their organizational structure has changed little in recent years. The Southern Growth Policies Board, established in 1971, is the major research and policy arm of the South. A new organization, the Western Policy Office, was recently created by the Western Governors' Conference. In Congress the Sunbelt forces do not have the formal organization of the Frostbelt but remain a strong informal force.[35]

The furor over the *National Journal* report was not confined to the political arena. The *Wall Street Journal* called the flow-of-funds issue "the most overblown political issue of 1976,"[36] while *Fortune* questioned the quality of data used in the *National Journal* analysis.[37] Perhaps the strongest criticism of the *National Journal* study is found in a report prepared for the U.S. Department of Commerce.[38] Here Jusenius and Ledebur conclude "that the recent arguments regarding the relative economic positions of the Northeast and the South are, at best, tenuous; at worst, they are severe distortions of reality."[39]

The Department of Commerce report differed from the *National Journal* study in several important respects. First, the southwestern and western states, usually considered part of the Sunbelt, were excluded from the Department of Commerce analysis—presumably so that differences among the Sunbelt states would not be highlighted. The study initially takes issue with the *National Journal* contention that migration is a major factor in differing growth rates among regions, a contention that suggests that the net immigration into the South from the northeastern and north central states is a reversal of the dominant trend prevailing in the century. The authors believe that evidence regarding the degree to which immigration to the southern states represents a new long-term trend is inconclusive. They also suggest that, due to differences in fertility rates, the population would increase more rapidly in the South than in the Northeast-North Central regions even if no migration occurred.

In examining measures of comparative regional well-being, Jusenius and Ledebur recognize that there are greater federal expenditures in the South than in the North but point out that per capita incomes in the southern states are generally lower than those in the North. The per capita income levels of the two regions have been converging over the past 45 years, although in 1975 the trend toward convergence was reversed. The report maintains, however, that the impact of federal taxes has not significantly decreased the regional per capita income gap, as was implied by the *National Journal.* The authors further suggest that even the relatively low per capita income of the southern states overstates the economic welfare of the population in the region. In 1970, for example, 31.1 percent of the poverty population resided in the northern industrial tier but 43.7 percent were located in the South. Even with adjustment of per capita incomes to reflect cost-of-living differentials, per capita income in the North remains above that of the South.

The authors recognize, however, that the South has experienced a relatively high rate of growth in public-sector employment. In the North, government employment increased 11.8 percent while in the South public-sector employment grew at twice the rate, 23.5 percent (1970 through 1975). But the study takes issue with the suggestion of many economists that jobs and populations have been shifting from the Northeast to the West and South. While it is true that the northern tier's share of U.S. employment declined between 1970 and 1974 (3.1 percent) and the South's share increased (2 percent), the authors take issue with the contention that migration of firms has played a major role in changing employment situations. Their data indicate that over 50 percent of the employment losses that occurred in the Northeast between 1969 and 1972 was the result of the death of firms; only 1.5 percent was due to out-migration of firms. In the South, on the other hand, 64.3 percent of the employment growth was caused by the expansion of existing firms, while only 1.2 percent resulted from the immigration of firms to the region. The authors also point out that the federal government spent less per capita in both regions than in the nation as a whole. Thus while the southern states are among the poorest in the nation, they nevertheless receive less than the national average in federal government expenditures.

In conclusion the Department of Commerce study suggests that "policy decisions based on the assumption that experience of 1970 through 1975 represents a new trend may be ill considered and counter-productive in the longer run."[40]

The arguments of Jusenius and Ledebur, refuting the *National Journal* study, taken on face value, make sense. After all, if the South has a higher incidence of poverty and lower per capita income than the states of the northeastern and north central regions, should not federal expenditure policy help correct this inequity? A more recent study, however, takes issue with the Department of Commerce per capita income comparisons.[41] An analysis done by an economist with the First National Bank of Chicago compared states on the basis of adjusted per capita income—adjusting for differences in the cost of living and state and local tax loads. Suddenly, the apparent differences between the Sunbelt-Frostbelt states disappeared. Wisconsin, for example, ranked 13th among the 30 Sunbelt-Frostbelt states in terms of unadjusted per capita income with a figure of $5,669 in 1975. When adjustments were made to account for the cost of living and taxes, Wisconsin fell to 20th place with $3,670. Arkansas, Kentucky, Oklahoma, Tennessee, and West Virginia all passed Wisconsin when the adjustments were made.

On the basis of adjusted per capita income, six of the ten most affluent states are in the Sunbelt while six of the ten poorest are in the Frostbelt. New York, for example, led Alabama in terms of per capita income, $6,564 to $4,643, until adjustments were made. With adjustments, Alabama edged ahead of New York, $3,566 to $3,493.

Thus the Sunbelt-Frostbelt issue is far from settled. While both sides agree that the Sunbelt states are receiving more federal money that the Frostbelt states, it is not clear what the policy implications of this fact are. It seems to be another case of the blind men and the elephant; policy implications depend upon the perspective of the policy makers. Political and business leaders in both sections of the country will undoubtedly continue to do what they have been doing in the past —that is, to intepret the data in a manner that will bring the greatest possible benefit to their particular area of the country.

NOTES

1. Jesse Burkhead and Alan K. Campbell, "The Macroeconomics of State and Local Governments," Occasional Paper no. 28, Maxwell School of Citizenship and Public Affairs, Syracuse University, June 1976, p. 9.

2. See, for example, Richard A. Musgrave and Peggy B. Musgrave, *Public Finance in Theory and Practice* (New York: McGraw-Hill, 1973); Earl R. Rolph, *The Theory of*

Fiscal Economics (Berkeley: University of California Press, 1954); Donald Phares, *State-Local Tax Equity: An Empirical Analysis of the Fifty States* (Lexington, Mass.: D. C. Heath, 1973).

3. See Joseph A. Pechman and Benjamin A. Okner, *Who Bears the Tax Burden?* (Washington, D.C.: Brookings Institution, 1974), pp. 25–26; and Henry J. Aaron, *Who Pays the Property Tax?* (Washington, D.C.: Brookings Institution, 1975), pp. 18–20.

4. Advisory Commission on Intergovernmental Relations, *Financing Schools and Property Tax Relief: A State Responsibility* (Washington, D.C.: Government Printing Office, 1973), p. 30

5. Aaron, op. cit.

6. Pechman and Okner, op. cit., p. 38.

7. Ibid., pp. 4–8.

8. Ibid., p. 64.

9. Phares, op. cit., pp. 76–80.

10. Advisory Commission on Intergovernmental Relations, *Changing Public Attitudes on Governments and Taxes* (Washington, D.C.: Government Printing Office, 1976).

11. Burkhead and Campbell, op. cit., p. 6.

12. Advisory Commission on Intergovernmental Relations, *Inflation and Federal and State Income Taxes* (Washington, D.C.: Government Printing Office, 1976), p. 1.

13. Ibid., p. 2.

14. Ibid., p. 7.

15. Taken from Richard Goode, *The Individual Income Tax* (Washington, D.C.: Brookings Institution, 1964), p. 287.

16. Dick Netzer, *Economics of the Property Tax* (Washington, D.C.: Brookings Institution, 1966), p. 185.

17. Burkhead and Campbell, op. cit., p. 1.

18. Terry Nichols Clark et al., "How Many New Yorks?" Report no. 72 of the Comparative Study of Community Decision-Making, University of Chicago, April 22, 1976, revised June 7, 1976.

19. Burkhead and Campbell, op. cit., pp. 15–16.

20. Ibid., p. 9.

21. William Gorham and Nathan Glazer, *The Urban Predicament* (Washington, D.C.: Urban Institute, 1976), p. 53–55.

22. "The Second War Between the States," *Business Week*, May 17, 1976, pp. 92, 95.

23. "Federal Spending: The North's Loss Is the Sunbelt's Gain," *National Journal* 8 (June 26, 1976): 878–91.

24. Ibid., p. 878.

25. Ibid., p. 883.

26. Ibid., pp. 890–91.

27. See, for example, Chris Kenrick and Gary Thatcher, "Northeast, 'Sunbelt' Fight for U.S. Funds," *Christian Science Monitor*, December 9, 1976, p. 3; Richard J. Cattani, "Federal Spending Formulas Irk North," *Christian Science Monitor*, November 2, 1976, p. 6; W. W. Rostow, "Saving the North—and Other Regions," *Christian Science Monitor*, April 27, 1977.

28. Advisory Commission on Intergovernmental Relations, *Measuring the Fiscal "Bloodpressure" of the States* (Washington, D.C.: Government Printing Office, March 1977). A summary version of this report is found in John Ross and John Shannon, "Growing Diversity in State Tax Pressures: Some Implications for Fiscal Federalism," a paper presented at the University of Oklahoma, Norman, Oklahoma, October 15, 1976.

29. Ibid.

30. Ibid.

31. "Another Round to the Sunbelt," *National Journal* 9 (July 2, 1977): 1033–37.

32. Joel Havemann and Rochelle L. Stanfield, "A Year Later, the Frostbelt Strikes Back," *National Journal* 9 (July 2, 1977): 1028–32.

33. "A Look at the Frostbelt Forces," *National Journal* 9 (July 2, 1977): 1031.

34. These and other similar articles are contained in the First National Bank of Boston, *Federal/State Economic Relations* (Boston: First National Bank of Boston, August 1976).

35. "A Look at the Frostbelt Forces," op. cit., p. 1030.

36. *Wall Street Journal* (December 27, 1976) quoted in "Another Round to the Sunbelt," op. cit., p. 1037.

37. "Another Round to the Sunbelt," op. cit., p. 1037.

38. C. L. Jusenius and L. C. Ledebur, *A Myth in the Making: The Southern Economic Challenge and Northern Economic Decline* (Washington, D. C.: Office of Economic Research, Economic Development Administration, U.S. Department of Commerce, November 1976).

39. Ibid., p. 1.

40. Ibid., p. 34.

41. David L. Beal, "Study Suggests State is Poorer Than Thought," Milwaukee *Journal* (October 2, 1977), p. 18.

9
The Revenue
Decision Process

The proliferation of revenue issues can overwhelm the citizen and policy maker alike. Coping with such complexity requires concentrating on a few alternatives and the issues they generate, pushing aside other possibilities that might be superior.

For the political scientist or economist seeking to understand the total revenue policy process, such arbitrary selection is dangerous. There is the risk that the important core of the process may be excluded. The researcher could elect to study interest group activity, small-group decision making, public attitudes toward taxes, or some other aspect of revenue politics and overlook crucial information. Even if all of these aspects of the revenue process were studied, the investigator might still fail to link them together in a way that contributes to knowledge of the total process, and he or she might fail to consider the effect on that process of forces from the environment.

Research efforts have been somewhat hindered by a peculiar division of labor between political science and economics, a division that has led the former discipline to concentrate on government spending while the latter emphasized government revenue. Each discipline has its own research perspective that is tied closely to modes of analysis prevalent in the discipline. These perspectives have influenced both research techniques and ways of viewing "real-world" phenomena. Further, they have provided researchers with guides for selecting phenomena worthy of examination. For the most part, state and local revenue matters have been of interest to economists.

THE ECONOMIST'S VANTAGE POINT

Public Finance

As would be true in any discipline, the research perspective of economics has led investigators to concentrate on certain aspects of revenue raising. Unfortunately, there has been a dearth of attention devoted to others. To show this, it is helpful to subdivide the revenue policy process into four "segments": (1) environmental influences upon revenue policy, (2) revenue decision processes, (3) revenue policy outputs, and (4) revenue policy impacts.

Economists, both theorists and empirical investigators, have explored all four segments, but not in equal depth. They have been especially interested in segments 3 and 4. Major textooks in the public finance subfield of economics include a number of chapters describing the nature of various taxes, their development, rates, and methods of collection. Thanks to these careful and detailed descriptions, we are in a better position to describe revenue policies than we are to describe policies in many other areas.

Why are economists so interested in describing policy outputs? Because such description is requisite for an understanding of segment 4, revenue policy impacts. At the heart of public finance is a concern for the impact revenue policies have on functioning of the market economy. A critical question is, "How will imposition of a particular tax affect behavior of individuals or firms?" Some economists—those concerned with macroeconomics—seek an answer in order better to understand and predict major economic movements, economic stability, and economic growth. Others—those exploring microeconomics— want an answer so that behavior of firms and individuals can be better understood and so that knowledge can be used by managers.

It is probably accurate to state that American economists have "backed into" the study of public finance. Their major concern was (and is) the investigation of the market economy, even though they recognize the impact public-sector activities (taxing, borrowing, and spending) have on the private sector. Much economic research and theorizing, then, has focused upon revenue policies and their impacts.

Public Choice Theory

In the 1960s, economists began to show greater interest in segment 2, the decision process. This interest was expressed in expanded attention given to formal models of the public sector. Although they recognize the extreme complexity of the public-sector decision process, public choice theorists have built models with which they attempt to predict the outcomes of that process. Assumptions are made that simplify variables and the interactions among them.

Development of these models requires constant checking against actual decisions. Where the fit is not satisfactory, there is need for changes in either the assumptions or the linkages the models posit.

THE POLITICAL SCIENTIST'S VANTAGE POINT

The Institutions

Political science was, for many decades, concerned principally with institutions for making public policy. These concerns were for segment 2 and were limited largely to the formal aspects of that segment. That federal revenue measures were required to originate in the House of Representatives was considered a fact of great importance, as were the legal and constitutional restrictions that controlled state and local revenue policies. These restrictions were described in great detail, and their implications for the functioning of a democracy were debated. That they had large impact on policies was assumed, but not tested; that there were environmental forces at work molding policy was largely ignored, except for periodic references to interest groups. Outputs were noted principally to cite examples of "good" or "bad" administration—and property tax administration was usually cited as bad.

In the last few decades, the study of what goes on within decisional institutions has received greater attention. The tracking of legislative voting on tax matters[1] and the examination of legislative committee power are two examples.[2]

Policy Analysis

The expression "policy analysis" has been widely employed since the late 1960s. Thomas Dye, in commenting upon the shifting focus of political science toward the study of public policy, refers to this type of study as "the description and explanation of the causes and consequences of government activity."

> This involves a description of the content of public policy; an assessment of the impact of environmental forces on the content of public policy; an analysis of the effect of various institutional arrangements and political processes on public policy; an inquiry into the consequences of various public policies for the political system; and an evaluation of the impact of public policies on society, both in terms of expected and unexpected consequences."[3]

Much (perhaps most) political science research carrying the "public policy" label has consisted of statistical analyses testing the link of environmental characteristics to policy outputs—research of the type we presented in Chapter 7.

Decision Making

More recently, political scientists have become interested in the process whereby environmental influences are translated into policy outputs and even impacts. They have sought better to describe and understand the actual functioning of the institutions and mechanisms through which environmental forces effect policy. This particular approach can take several paths, ranging from study of small-group decision making to examination of hundreds of decisions made in an equally large number of government units.

A FRAMEWORK

Regardless of one's particular vantage point, whether it be that of the economist or the political scientist, it is useful (if not essential) that the systemic character of the revenue policy process be recognized. In previous chapters we have mentioned many issues and many policy process participants. But none of these issues is settled in isolation from others, nor do participants function in isolation.

Figure 9.1 presents the four segments of the process and some of the components of each, in a way that emphasizes the interconnectedness of them all. Beginning on the left (although feedback inherent to the process leaves no obvious starting point), there is a partial list of environmental influences. Resolution of each of the issues discussed previously will probably be influenced by several of these, in any particular jurisdiction.

The left portion of the diagram presents a categorization of environmental influences acting upon revenue policy. The broken line around the decision process segment represents permeability. Not only do these environmental influences have potential for impact upon public attitudes, leader attitudes, and leader perceptions, they have potential for influencing the nature of relationships among these and between each of these and revenue policy output. A couple of examples are in order.

1. The constitutional-legal provisions that were probably established years prior to consideration of a particular policy may critically influence the importance of public attitudes. These provisions may provide that all local taxation matters must be submitted to popular vote, a requirement that increases the importance of the public-attitudes/policy-output link. Also, it is most likely that both leader attitudes and leader perceptions would be affected by such a provision. If

FIGURE 9.1: State and Local Revenue Policy System

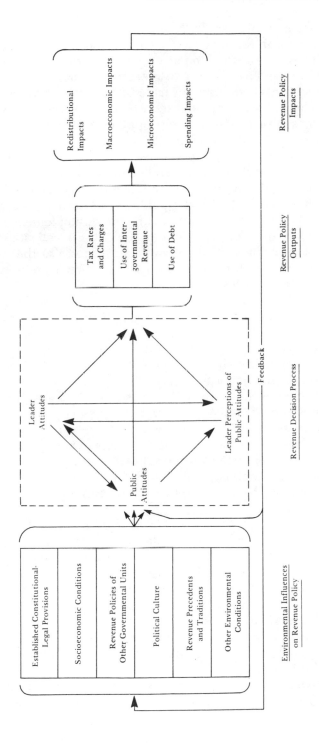

Source: Compiled by the authors.

the provision is of long standing, most of the leaders probably have been influenced by it in forming their own attitudes relevant to revenues, and they may have learned to pay greater attention to public attitudes and hence to perceive them with greater accuracy.

2. Precedents and traditions have been shown to be good predictors of public policy in a number of instances. Ira Sharkansky discusses the "routines of politics"—the development of decision rules that are widely employed, focus attention on a limited number of considerations, and thus simplify the decisions to be made.[4] In describing the revenue decision system of Oakland, California, Arnold Meltsner reports a well-established practice of the revenue leadership's assiduously avoiding direct conflict with the public. One means of doing so is to allow other cities (perhaps nearby) to be first in implementing innovative taxes. Only after the precedent for such a tax is well established will Oakland take the plunge.[5] This example illustrates, also, the impact that revenue policies in other governmental jurisdictions may have upon the local decision process.

Reflection upon previous chapters will provide other examples, including the impact of federal aid availability, the impact of per capita income, and so on.

We conceptualize the decision process, segment 2, as involving both the public and political leaders. Public attitudes refer here to the diffuse attitudes of the public at large and also to the aggregated attitudes represented by interest groups and political parties. Along with numerous students of legislative behavior, we expect that decisions made by official leaders are products of their own attitudes as well as their perceptions of public attitudes. Further, it is possible for an individual leader's perceptions to be colored by his own attitudes just as his own attitudes may be influenced by the perception he holds of public views.

Since both state and local laws of many states permit direct public participation in setting revenue policies (through initiative petitions, required referendums, and referendums demanded by petition), there is an arrow directly from public attitudes to the policy outputs.

The third segment, the policy outputs, includes matters about which we have already said much. The items are three broad categories into which previously discussed issues can be classified. What we show here are, really, the three revenue sources open to governments. Within each of these, there are many specific options, and each option raises multiple issues.

The fourth segment, the impacts, also is presented in the form of broad categories. Here, too, are many issues that become central to debates over adoption of particular policy proposals. Both proponents and opponents will present their contentions regarding impacts likely to flow from acceptance of the proposals.

Finally, Figure 9.1 has a feedback loop. In the dynamic political process, it is likely that a policy output and impact at one point in time will result in alterations of public attitudes at a later point. Feedback may change any or all of the items in the environment and thus influence the decision process. Further, though, the fact that a decision has been made may quite directly influence attitudes and perceptions of the public and of leaders, in anticipation of the environmental impact.

Since much of the material in previous chapters has presented issues that face revenue policy makers today, it is appropriate that we conclude by briefly examining what is known about the processes that have been used to resolve such issues in the past, and that may be used in the future.

Environmental Influences

Chapter 7 looked at some of the environmental influences. We know from it that socioeconomic characteristics have some impact upon policy, along with an impact on the history of use of a particular revenue source.

Similarly, we know from Chapter 2 that legal structures severely restrict decision makers. Some of these limits will probably be removed in the future. The trend today is toward permitting greater latitude in choice of policies—letting local voters and leaders decide. But many restraints will remain, including those requiring due process of law and equality of treatment, restraints of constitutional origin.

In what is probably the best study of the revenue policy process, Arnold Meltsner stresses the importance of other units' revenue policies. He found that Oakland's officials simplified the search for new or improved revenue sources by seeing what other cities were doing. This effort was aided by contacts with officials of the League of California Cities through which officials could check both the administrative and political feasibility of tax sources. Of special political importance was adoption of a tax by the large cities—San Francisco and Los Angeles.[6]

A study of adoption of city sales taxes in Oklahoma revealed clusters of adopting cities in various parts of the state. Cities apparently followed the lead of their neighbors in employing the newly available source. This was especially true in the years right after the granting to the cities of authority that permitted use of the sales tax.[7]

Thus, in addition to the rather direct impact that other units can have (such as the federal government through grants and other localities by structuring taxes to attract away shoppers), there is an indirect impact they may have by breaking the political ice and testing the water. Present Oklahoma statutes can be construed in a way that would allow adoption of a municipal income tax. But each time this possibility is raised, it is countered with the argument that the first city to do so must bear extraordinary administrative and legal costs—so none wants to be first.

The final environmental influence we will mention is political culture. While we did not use that term, the discussion of regionalism in Chapter 7 can be interpreted as a consideration of political culture. Daniel Elazar defines political culture as "the particular pattern of orientation to political action in which each political system is embedded."[8] Each locality and each state has a set of traditions, regarding not just revenue but all of political action. These traditions may, for example, establish the degree of "openness" of political decision making; they may even prescribe the selection of members of certain families to leadership positions; they may, of course, proscribe the use of certain revenue sources. While not immutable, these cultural forces can exercise powerful influences on the decision process.

How can our discussion of regionalism be interpreted in this way? Political culture does not always respect political boundaries. Frequently, adjoining states will share in some components of a given culture. Consequently, our finding that regionalism is of some importance in explaining revenue policies may be a reflection of shared culture.

The Decision Process

What we know about revenue decision making is garnered from numerous investigations—mostly case studies. Meltsner's is one of these. He systematically examined decision making in Oakland and found a prime feature to be leadership efforts to avoid public conflict. One means of doing so is to rely on "old" sources—those already accepted. Small adjustments in rates or changes in bases can be made without public involvement and with the assumption that, given alternatives available, this would be preferred by the public.[9]

When the leaders finally reach the decision stage they try carefully to predict the level of public acceptance and the ease of administration. These are balanced against potential revenue yield. Most often, the method chosen is one that has both low political costs and low revenue yield,[10] a choice that usually leads to a "nickel and dime" approach to revenue decisions.

An example of a city council that chose a more direct approach to revenue raising is that of Norman, Oklahoma. Facing the need for an increase, the council approved substantial increases in utility rates. (Profits from public utilities reach the general fund.) Public reaction was swift and came in the form of two petitions—one demanding a public vote on the rate increase and the other a vote on a charter amendment to require that all future increases receive referendum approval. Both provisions received voter approval, and future council actions were thereby restrained. Some months later the council did submit to the voters a proposal to increase the sales tax from 1 percent to 2 percent, which was approved.

Judging by the adoption of taxes not previously used, state-level decision makers have faced revenue raising fairly directly in recent years. Table 9.1 shows the number of states enacting major taxes or increasing rates. Since many states passed multiple increases, the total number of enactments and increases is 627. This converts to 37 per year. On the average, there was a tax enactment or increase by each state once every sixteen months over the entire 17 year period.

Interest Groups

An important aspect of the state decision process is the role played by interest groups. While some taxes have fairly general impact, others are felt by particular classes of citizens. When the latter is the case, one can expect organized opposition.

To see just what interest groups are active on state tax issues, we sent questionnaires to "informants" in each state. These informants were of several types. If there was in the state a state-wide group

TABLE 9.1: Enactment and Increase of Selected State Taxes, 1959–76

Taxes	Number of States
Sales	41
Personal income	39
Corporation income	42
Motor fuel	46
Cigarette	50
Alcohol beverage	49

Source: Advisory Commission on Intergovernmental Relations, *Significant Features of Fiscal Federalism, 1976–77 Edition*, vol. 2 (Washington, D.C.: Government Printing Office, 1977) p. 105.

devoted to tax research and lobbying we addressed our questionnaire to its director. If there was no such group (or if we received no response), we queried the director of the state municipal association or of a university research bureau. We received usable responses from 28 states. In each case, the informant considered eight separate taxes (four broad-based, three selective sales, and the severance tax) on which a decision might have been made during the last ten years. If there had been such a decision, the informant listed interest groups that favored the increase and those that opposed the increase. Additionally, the informant indicated tactics interest groups employed.

Table 9.2 lists all of the groups named by the 28 informants, in order of frequency of mention. Business groups and individual businesses are, by far, the most frequently involved. The "general business" category shows 62 mentions, and to this may be added references to particular industrial groups—tobacco, liquor, forest, mining, petroluem, and road construction. The total is 124 mentions. As is shown below, the activities of some of these industrial groups are concentrated on particular tax issues.

Second in frequency are the associations of local governments. These organizations serve as representatives of their constituents (the governing bodies and officials) before the legislature. While many of their activities concern matters unrelated to taxes (such as open-meeting laws, civil service procedures, and charter change procedures), we have clear evidence of their important role in tax matters. A few informants mentioned individual cities (by name or just as "cities") and those are included here, but most references were to the associations of local governments.

Forty-two mentions were made of the governor or of executive branch agencies. We do not include these in our definition of interest groups, but references to these and to legislators were so frequent that they must be noted. Especially significant is that all references to the executive branch but one were in terms of support for tax increases. In many cases, informants listed no traditional interest groups that supported an increase and so named the governor as the only supporter.

Employee groups are also important, especially the teachers. With 31 mentions, teacher groups are listed fourth. Other state and local employees received eight mentions and were ranked eleventh. Taxpayer groups, operating under a variety of names, are generally supported by the business community and usually campaign for low taxes. They received 25 mentions, and of these, 20 were as opponents to tax increases. Other interest groups, some of which are traditionally influential in state politics generally, are found to be involved in tax matters

TABLE 9.2: Interest Groups Involved in State Tax Issues

Group	Number of Mentions
1. General business groups, chambers of commerce, association of manufacturers, etc.	62
2. Municipal league, cities, school board association, county association, etc.	55
3. Governor, executive branch, state agency*	42
4. Education association, teachers' union, teacher groups, etc.	31
5. Legislators*	26
6. Taxpayer groups, taxpayer association	25
7. Labor unions	18
7. Liquor industry	18
8. Tobacco industry	17
9. Farm groups, grange, farm bureau	16
10. Consumer and welfare groups	15
10. Highway users, truckers, automobile association	15
11. Mining industry	8
11. Petroleum industry	8
11. State and local employee groups (except teachers)	8
12. Booster groups, civic groups, economic development groups	6
12. Forest industry	6
12. Groups concerned about specific tax	6
12. League of Women Voters	6
13. Environmentalists	5
13. Health organizations	5
13. Road construction industry	5
Other (general)	20
Other (programmatic)	7

*Although these are not defined here as interest groups, informants mentioned them so frequently as sources of support or opposition, they are included.

Source: Compiled by the authors.

as well. Labor unions and farm, consumer, and welfare groups are of particular note. The highway-user groups might be classed as "consumers" but probably fit better with business groups, since trucking organizations are especially important constituents.

Data in Table 9.2 do not distinguish group activities as to taxes with which they are concerned nor as to positions of support or opposition to tax increases. To emphasize these features, Table 9.3 shows the major groups reported to support and oppose increases in the four broad-base taxes. Only those groups that received four or more mentions for that particular tax and position are shown.

The municipal league and related groups, as well as organizations of teachers, emerge as supporters of increases in all five taxes. The only tax that had as many as four mentions of business support for an increase was the sales tax; this was the only tax on which organized labor received as many as four mentions for either position—and these were for its opposition. In fact, though, all remaining mentions of labor groups (11 mentions) were for support of increases, but on no tax were there as many as four mentions.

The importance of property and sales taxes to local governments is shown by the leading supportive position of their organizations. Our property tax item asked informants to include groups that took positions on decisions to increase local rate limitations.

TABLE 9.3: Major Interest Groups Supporting and Opposing Increases in Broad-Base Taxes

Support Increase*		Oppose Increase	
Sales Tax			
Municipal league, etc.	12	General business groups, etc.	8
Governor, etc.	8	Labor unions	7
Education association, etc.	7	Consumer and welfare groups	6
General business groups, etc.	7	Taxpayer groups	4
Taxpayer groups	4		
Individual Income Tax			
Education association, etc.	7	General business groups, etc.	12
Municipal league, etc.	6	Taxpayer groups	4
Governor, etc.	4		
League of Women Voters	4		
Corporation Income Tax			
Education association, etc.	5	General business groups, etc.	20
Governor, etc.	5	Taxpayer groups	4
Municipal league, etc.	4		
Property Tax			
Municipal league, etc.	14	General business groups, etc.	9
Education association, etc.	5	Taxpayer groups	6
		Farm groups	4

*In a few cases, opposition to a decrease has been counted as support for an increase and support for a decrease as opposition to an increase. These instances were very few.

Source: Compiled by the authors.

Table 9.4 shows groups involved in decisions on selective sales and severance taxes. The activities of particular industries whose products will be taxed form major portions of the opposition to these. In the case of the motor fuels tax, the petroleum industry is joined by highway user groups, which, as mentioned, represent segments of the trucking industry. The effect of earmarking is shown by the support found in the road construction industry. Most states use motor fuel tax money for construction and maintenance of streets and highways—actions that benefit construction companies.

Informants identified the governor and legislators as major promoters of increases in alcohol beverage and severance taxes. In supporting the tobacco tax, governors were joined by health organizations and organizations of local governments. Opposition came from the tobacco industries.

To summarize, we find that employee groups, associations of local governments, and the state executive branch are primary proponents of tax increases. The business community and taxpayer groups are major opponents.

But how do the groups seek to exercise their influence? Our survey instument gave the informants opportunity to indicate tactics used by

TABLE 9.4: Major Interest Groups Supporting and Opposing Increases in Selective Sales and Severance Taxes

*Support Increase**		*Oppose Increase*	
Motor Fuels Tax			
Governor, etc.	7	Highway users, etc.	12
Municipal league, etc.	6	Petroleum industry	5
Road construction industry	5		
Tobacco Tax			
Municipal league, etc.	5	Tobacco industry	17
Governor, etc.	5		
Health organizations	5		
Alcohol Beverage Tax			
Governor, etc.	6	Liquor industry	18
Legislators	4		
Severance Tax			
Governor, etc.	6	Mining industry	8
Legislators	5	Forest industry	4

*In a few cases, opposition to a decrease has been counted as support for an increase and support for a decrease as opposition to an increase. The instances were very few.

Source: Compiled by the authors.

interest groups in promoting or opposing tax changes. Informants were asked, specifically, to indicate the two principal tactics of each group, designating two of the following items with a "1" for the most used and a "2" for next most: paid lobbyist, membership lobbyist, paid advertising, mass demonstrations, and mass letter writing. Many informants apparently were unable to be as precise as we hoped and simply indicated the one or more tactics used, without ranking them. Table 9.5 presents, for seven major types of groups, the percentage use of each. It shows that all groups were reported to make considerable use of both paid and membership lobbyists. Organizations of local governmental officials (municipal leagues, school board associations, and so on) and business groups led the way. Employee groups (outside education) made the least use of paid lobbyists and were sixth in use of membership lobbyists. They used demonstrations most extensively, a product, no doubt, of the proximity of their members to the legislative halls. Education groups were second in use of demonstrations. Organized labor made the least use of membership lobbyists, the most of advertising, and second most of letter writing. Taxpayer groups relied heavily on letter writing.

Not only are there a variety of groups interested in taxation matters, there are a variety of means for them to make themselves heard. Through these means, they play an important role in influencing the resolution of revenue issues.

Public Attitudes

Several volumes could be filled with descriptions and analyses of public attitudes about all aspects of state and local revenue. There are, of course, attitudes about all the issues we have described, and a variety of positions on each of them. While we cannot present them all, we can present a few paragraphs that indicate both the nature of some of the major ones and their impact on revenue decision making.

We have available two principal measures of public attitudes— public opinion surveys and votes cast in revenue referendums. Unfortunately, neither of these is the one most used by those making revenue policy; they rely on their own perceptions of public attitudes. While we have little systematic knowledge of these perceptions, we do have available conclusions about them formed by students of the decision process.

At several points in previous chapters, there have been references to the continuing effort of the ACIR to monitor public attitudes. Table 9.6 shows results of three surveys that asked a general question about the relationship between taxes and services. In each year, the largest group

TABLE 9.5: Interest Group Tactics to Influence Tax Decisions (percent)

	Paid Lobbyists	Membership Lobbyists	Paid Advertising	Mass Demonstrations	Mass Letter Writing	Total
General business groups, etc.	42.9	38.0	4.5	1.3	13.4	100.1
Municipal league, etc.	44.2	42.3	2.9	1.0	9.6	100.0
Education associations, etc.	39.1	33.3	2.9	8.7	15.9	99.9
Taxpayer groups	32.1	33.9	5.4	—	28.6	100.0
Labor unions	36.6	26.8	12.2	4.9	19.5	100.0
Farm groups	36.0	44.0	8.0	—	12.0	100.0
Employee groups	29.4	29.4	5.9	17.6	17.6	99.9

Source: Compiled by the authors.

TABLE 9.6: Attitude Toward Taxes and Services

Attitude	Percent of U.S. Public		
	1977	1976	1975
Keep taxes and services about where they are	52	51	45
Decrease services and taxes	31	30	38
Increase services and raise taxes	4	5	5
No opinion	13	14	12
Total	100	100	100

Source: Advisory Commission on Intergovernmental Relations, Changing Public Attitudes on Governments and Taxes, 1977 (Washington, D.C.: Government Printing Office, 1977), p. 7. The question was: "Considering all government services on the one hand and taxes on the other, which of the following statements comes closest to your view?"

of respondents desired to keep both taxes and services about where they are; this group was a majority in both 1976 and 1977. About one-third desired decreases in both, and only about 5 percent wanted increases.

Table 9.7 is a bit more specific, showing choices of the least fair tax. In each year, except 1974, the local property tax was most frequently chosen, with federal income tax being second (and first in 1974). It is interesting to view this finding in conjunction with that in Table 9.8. Here we see that Americans feel they get the most for their money from federal and local governments—relying heavily on the least liked taxes. Another question asked in 1972 and 1976 found that, if taxes must be raised, Americans would much prefer the state sales tax—a major source of revenue for the level from which they feel they get the least return.

Surveys like these, while instructive, are of limited use to the policy maker. Options open to him or her are usually more limited than these broad questions would indicate. (Of what use is there for a city councilman in Grambling, Louisiana, to know that citizens—even citizens of Grambling—prefer the federal income tax?) Public attitudes are one part of the decision process, but only one.

Expressions of public attitudes by referendums can be best seen by looking at school districts. Many states require voter approval of school budgets, of property tax rates, or of bond issues. Table 9.9 presents the recent history of one type of referendum—bond elections. Most notable has been the declining approval rate. Often labeled a "taxpayer revolt," this trend and a companion one in tax elections continue to frustrate school administrators and, in some communities, to result in the closing of public schools.[11] The decline continues, despite a sharp reduction in the number of bond issues submitted to the voters. Direct involvement of the public (at least the voting segment of it) in revenue decision making is less frequent among other types of local governments and among state governments. They are not free from it, however, as most of them are required, under certain circumstances, to get voter approval of revenue decisions. Additionally, as the Norman City Council learned, voters may employ petitions to compel submission of matters to the public.

Leaders have an important task in trying correctly to perceive public attitudes. Meltsner's description of Oakland stresses what he sees as leadership misperception of public attitudes.[12] His investigation led

TABLE 9.7: Choice of Least Fair Tax

Tax	Percent of U.S. Public				
	1977	1975	1974	1973	1972
Federal income tax	28	28	30	30	19
State income tax	11	11	10	10	13
State sales tax	17	23	20	20	13
Local property tax	33	29	28	31	45
Don't know	11	10	14	11	11
Total	100	101	102	102	101

Source: Advisory Commission on Intergovernmental Relations, Changing Public Attitudes on Government and Taxes, 1977 (Washington, D.C.: Government Printing Office, 1977), p. 11. The question was: "Which do you think is the worst tax—that is, the least fair?"

TABLE 9.8: Level from Which Americans "Get Most for Money"

Level	Percent of U.S. Public					
	1977	1976	1975	1974	1973	1972
Federal	36	36	38	29	35	39
State	20	20	20	24	18	18
Local	26	25	25	28	25	26
Don't know	18	19	17	19	22	17
Total	100	100	100	100	100	100

Source: Advisory Commission on Intergovernmental Relations, Changing Public Attitudes on Government and Taxes, 1977 (Washington, D.C.: Government Printing Office, 1977), p. 3. The question was: "From which level of government do you feel you get the most for your money—federal, state, or local?"

TABLE 9.9: Public School Bond Elections, 1965–75

Fiscal Year	Elections Held	Number Approved	Percent Approved
1965	2,041	1,525	74.7
1966	1,745	1,265	72.5
1967	1,625	1,082	66.6
1968	1,750	1,183	67.6
1969	1,341	762	56.8
1970	1,216	647	53.2
1971	1,086	507	46.7
1972	1,153	542	47.0
1973	1,273	719	56.5
1974	1,386	779	56.2
1975	929	430	46.3

Source: Richard H. Barr, Bond Sales For Public School Purposes, 1974–1975 (Washington, D.C.: Government Printing Office, n.d.), p. 2.

to the conclusion that Oakland's officials underestimated the level of taxes that the public would accept. But these perceptions were critical determinants of the city's revenue policy. In time, actual attitudes and leaders' perceptions might converge, due to either changed perceptions or changed attitudes.

Since state legislators are less likely to face the immediate check a referendum provides, it is probable that their perceptions of public attitudes and, even, their own attitudes are much more important than are actual public attitudes. We know that most Americans pay little attention to the votes of their state legislators; legislators have considerable freedom to act as they judge best.

CONCLUSION

A look at Figure 9.1 suggests that we should elaborate upon the link between segment 3 (policy outputs) and segment 4 (policy impacts). Since this link has been a prime interest of economists, we will not do so. We should, however, note again the dynamic character of revenue politics. The feedback loop encourages constant adjustment, as do ever changing environmental conditions.

We have presented the major state and local revenue issues of today. Some have been issues for decades; others are new. Many will remain issues for decades to come; others will fade away. But as we follow the development of state and local revenue systems, we will see the effect of today's efforts (successful or unsuccessful) to resolve present issues.

NOTES

1. E. Lee Bernick, *Legislative Decision Making and the Politics of Tax Reform: The Oklahoma Senate* (Norman: Bureau of Government Research, University of Oklahoma, 1975).

2. John F. Manley, *The Politics of Finance* (Boston: Little, Brown and Co., 1970).

3. Thomas R. Dye, *Understanding Public Policy* (Englewood Cliffs, N.J.: Prentice-Hall, 1972), p. 3.

4. Ira Sharkansky, *The Routines of Politics* (New York: Van Nostrand Reinhold, 1970).

5. Arnold J. Meltsner, *The Politics of City Revenue* (Berkeley: University of California Press, 1971), p. 103.

6. Ibid., p. 100.

7. Don K. Lange, "Patterns of Adoption of the City Sales Tax in Oklahoma" (unpublished paper).

8. Daniel J. Elazar, *American Federalism: A View from the States* (New York: Thomas Y. Crowell, 1966), p. 79.

9. Meltsner, op. cit., pp. 89–90.

10. Ibid., p. 101.

11. See Phillip K. Piele and John Stuart Hall, *Budgets, Bonds and Ballots* (Lexington, Mass.: Lexington Books, 1973) for discussion of these trends.

12. Meltsner, op. cit., Chap. 3.

Index

About the Authors

Richard D. Bingham is Associate Professor of Political Science and Chairperson of the Department of Urban Affairs at the University of Wisconsin—Milwaukee. Until 1975 he was Assistant Professor of Political Science at Marquette University, Milwaukee, Wisconsin.

Dr. Bingham is author of *Public Housing and Urban Renewal: An Analysis of Federal-Local Relations* (Praeger, 1975) and *The Adoption of Innovation by Local Government* (D.C. Heath, 1976). His articles have appeared in *Urban Affairs Quarterly, Social Service Review,* and *Policy Studies Journal.*

Dr. Bingham holds a B.S. in Business Administration from Boston University and a M.A.P.A. and Ph.D. from the University of Oklahoma.

Brett W. Hawkins is Professor of Political Science at the University of Wisconsin—Milwaukee. Until 1970 he was Associate Professor of Political Science at the University of Georgia, Athens, Georgia.

Dr. Hawkins is author of *Nashville Metro* (Vanderbilt University Press, 1966), *Politics of the Metropolis* (Bobbs-Merrill, 1971), *and Politics and Urban Policies* (Bobbs-Merrill, 1971). His articles have appeared in *Journal of Politics, American Journal of Sociology, Polity, and Social Science Quarterly.*

Dr. Hawkins holds an A.B. from the University of Rochester and an M.A. and Ph.D. from Vanderbilt University.

F. Ted Hebert is Associate Professor of Political Science and Assistant Dean of the Graduate College at the University of Oklahoma.

Dr. Hebert's articles have appeared in *Urban Affairs Quarterly, Public Administration Review, American Journal of Political Science,* and the *Midwest Review of Public Administration.*

Dr. Hebert holds a B.A. from Louisiana Tech University and an M.A. and Ph.D. from the University of Iowa.